FIGHTING ARMIES
NATO and the
Warsaw Pact

Other Greenwood Books by Richard A. Gabriel

The New Red Legions: An Attitudinal Portrait of the Soviet Soldier

To Serve with Honor: A Treatise on Military Ethics and the Way of the Soldier

Fighting Armies: Antagonists in the Middle East—A Combat Assessment

Fighting Armies: Nonaligned, Third World, and Other Ground Armies—A Combat Assessment

The Antagonists: A Comparative Assessment of the Soviet and the American Soldier

FIGHTING ARMIES

NATO and the
Warsaw Pact
A Combat Assessment

Edited by Richard A. Gabriel

FOREWORD BY COLONEL REUVEN GAL

GREENWOOD PRESS

WESTPORT, CONNECTICUT
LONDON, ENGLAND

Library of Congress Cataloging in Publication Data

Main entry under title:

NATO and the Warsaw Pact.   c͟ʟ

    (Fighting armies)
    Bibliography: p.
    Includes index.
    1. North Atlantic Treaty Organization—Armed Forces.
2. Warsaw Treaty Organization—Armed Forces.
I. Gabriel, Richard A. II. Series.
UA646.N37 1983   355'.033'0048   83-1521
ISBN 0-313-23903-7 (lib. bdg.)

Library of Congress Catalog Card Number: 83-1521
ISBN: 0-313-23903-7

First published in 1983

Greenwood Press
A division of Congressional Information Service, Inc.
88 Post Road West
Westport, Connecticut 06881

Printed in the United States of America

10 9 8 7 6 5 4 3 2 1

To my mother, Esther,
who gave me life and taught
me to love....

Contents

THE WARSAW PACT

Maps

Tables

Foreword

Assessing the combat ability of fighting armies is an extremely complicated task. Armies are ultimately required to prove their performance in one particularly testing situation—the battlefield. However, it is always valuable to analyze the combat-effectiveness of a given army *prior* to engagement on the battlefield. It is within this arena of prediction and appraisal that the ordinary student of military effectiveness often loses his way.

Whenever the strength of a given army is assessed or comparisons of different armies are made, the focus inevitably falls upon quantitative measures: numbers of troops, number of tanks, aircraft, and missiles, quantities of munitions and ordnance. More sophisticated analysts will also include figures delineating rates of mobilization and various employment techniques, but they will continue to remain on the safe ground of facts and figures. Indeed, it is easier to make quite accurate assessments based on these dimensions, which are, after all *measurable.*

Most studies fail in their attempt to analyze the qualitative aspects of military organizations. In fact, they often avoid an analysis of these aspects altogether. Concepts such as value systems, quality of combatants, morale of combat units, codes of ethics, norms of command, and leadership—these are too difficult to evaluate, too vague to measure, and hence are not included in traditional analyses of modern armies. The present work is therefore unique in its attempt to challenge the issue of those nonmeasurable qualities which are so fundamental in military assessment, and in incorporating within its categories components such as "quality of troops," "quality of officers," "cohesion," "vulnerability," and "morale."

Recently, an obscure report noted that since World War II more than 200 wars have occurred in various parts of the globe. The two most recent wars were fought in the Falkland Islands and Lebanon, but it seems quite apparent that they, like their predecessors, will shortly be forgotten. As in the past, current wars between nations are part of the political, economic, and/or cultural relations between contesting nations. As Karl von Clausewitz observed long ago, war is but one alternative for achieving political goals, and an army is the means toward applying that alternative. Hence, the employment of armies in warfare depends primarily upon the political relationships and the ongoing changes in these relationships.

In the present work, Richard A. Gabriel and the other contributors to this book have managed to produce qualitative analyses of modern armies and then to project them onto possible scenarios in which these armies could find themselves involved. These scenarios, imaginative as they may be, are the result of careful examination of past and present diplomatic and political processes taking place among the societies under analysis.

The social, cultural, and political background of each of the nations studied is well integrated in the present work into the overall analysis of military organizations. Today, more than ever, armies reflect their societies, or as Mao Tse-dong put it: "The army is to the nation as the fish is to the sea." When an army's fighting power is evaluated, one cannot ignore the social and cultural characteristics of the society which developed that army. The authors of the present study have emphasized those characteristics, thus achieving a broad and more accurate description of the "spirit" of the army as well as of its structure.

The present work, then, is based on three layers: first, a quantitative and qualitative examination of the military organization; second, a description of the interrelationships between the army and the larger society; and third, an analysis of possible scenarios in which that army might be involved. The appropriate integration of these three components into a wholistic picture guarantees the closest prediction of an army's performance on some future battlefield.

Professor Gabriel is probably the best qualified author to edit such a book and to cope with its challenges. Himself an army intelligence officer, he manages to incorporate his military experience with his widespread academic knowledge in the field of modern military organizations. In his numerous previous books and published articles, he has demonstrated his unique approach in analyzing and assessing armies such as the Soviet, American, Canadian, and Israeli. In all his analyses, he emphasizes those aspects of an army which are not measurable and yet so crucial: ethics, cohesiveness, combat-readiness, and leadership. Gabriel has retained the same emphases in the present book, thus producing a unique study in the field of modern military organizations.

Each author of the various chapters in the present book is an expert in his field and possesses extensive internal knowledge of the country he describes. Not only are these authors outstanding scholars who deal theoretically with their subjects, but also all of them, without exception, have been involved in planning, analyzing, and following up the various activities of the armies with which they deal. The result is a participant-observer's view of the inside network of each of the armies reviewed.

In sum, this is a unique book that presents a detailed, yet integrated, set of profiles, comprising quantitative, qualitative, and background variables, of more than thirty active armies all over the world.

Colonel Reuven Gal
Chief Battle Psychologist
Israeli Defense Force

Preface

As part of a three-volume study, this volume, *Fighting Armies: NATO-Warsaw Pact*, should be placed within the organizational and conceptual thrust of the larger work. Like the other volumes, this one is concerned with armies that will probably see real battle in the foreseeable future. All the military organizations examined here are designed seriously by their political establishments with a view toward actual battle. That intention is not present in relation to most armies of the world. Indeed, of the 157 entities claiming nation-state status in the United Nations, fewer than a third can be said to have serious armies that truly intend to fight other armies.

Any attempt to deal with the serious ground armies of the world forces an organization of material about the members of the NATO alliance and the Warsaw Pact. At no other point in history have two groups of adversaries possessed the masses of manpower, equipment, firepower, and territory that both alliances encompass today. Indeed, each set of adversaries possesses the power to unleash a nuclear holocaust and destruction that could forever change the face of organized social life on this planet. As a result the scholar feels that it is important to study the adversaries in essentially the same way that they have drawn the battlelines between themselves.

The omission from this volume of some members of each alliance is deliberate. Using as criteria ground armies that are seriously and genuinely designed to do battle excludes the minor members of each alliance on the grounds that their ability to contribute significant ground force components—manpower, material, logistical support, and firepower—would be marginal at best and, in times of actual conflict, even implausible. On this basis Italy, Denmark, Holland, and Belgium are excluded from this study of the NATO alliance and Romania and Bulgaria are not included in this consideration of the Warsaw Pact.

However, the inclusion of some countries is based on their manifest importance to any serious military effort that either alliance could muster.

The entire battleplan and the ability to sustain the Warsaw Pact depends heavily upon the performance of the East German and Polish armies. If either army failed to perform adequately, the ability of the Soviet Union to successfully execute a ground attack in central Europe would be brought into serious question. The same is true in NATO. The ability of the United States to influence the outcome of ground battle in central Europe depends crucially on the ability of West Germany, Britain, and France to delay and disrupt any combat thrust for several days at least. There is serious question also about the ability of the United States to add the necessary reinforcements in time.

Of course, any selection of armies for study is fundamentally arbitrary and open to criticism. Yet, in *Fighting Armies: NATO-WARSAW PACT*, one would be pressed to produce any more logical selection of ground armies worthy of study unless, of course, one were to include them all and thereby obviate the need for any selection whatsoever. Nonetheless, the selection in *Fighting Armies: NATO-Warsaw Pact* meets the most important criteria, that each army be designed seriously and genuinely to engage in battle with probable adversaries. Unfortunately, this condition exists all too clearly among the armies that stare at each other across the body of central Europe.

Acknowledgments

A work of this length and complexity would not have been possible without the cooperation and assistance of others. I am deeply indebted to each of my contributors who labored long and hard to meet the deadlines I imposed upon them. A great deal of thanks goes to Jim Sabin, my publisher at Greenwood Press, who first suggested the idea for the book. Anthony Kellet in Ottawa clearly knows the debt I owe him, as do Reuven Gal and Moishe Levin. My gratitude to St. Anselm's College in Manchester, New Hampshire, knows no bounds; my colleagues there have put up with my writings, ravings, and meanderings for some ten years now. Perhaps we are all better off for it. Finally, there are my wife, Kathie, and the two demons, Leah and Christine, who constitute the center of my life; without them nothing would be possible or worthwhile.

Introduction

Predicting how an army will perform in battle is, to say the least, a risky business. Although most nations spend millions of dollars a year on their intelligence communities to obtain just such predictions, in truth most efforts tend to fail. Consider, for example, the surprise that greeted the West when the army of the Shah rapidly disintegrated under minimal pressure from an adversary that was almost unarmed. The performance of the Chinese in their engagement with the North Vietnamese was so surprising as to raise serious questions about the ability of the West to truly understand its adversaries. More recently, the performance of the Argentines in the Falklands, the Israelis in Lebanon, the Iranians in Iraq—to say nothing of a number of terrorist organizations—all threw into sharp relief the difficulties encountered in predicting how a military force would actually perform when finally forced to take the field.

As a rule, wars are not neat affairs. Clausewitz's description of battle as the "fog of war" was echoed a century later by Helmuth von Moltke's famous dictum that most war plans could not survive twelve hours' contact with the enemy. The number of variables that affect an army's showing in battle is simply staggering.

One such variable is the performance of military equipment. For instance, almost 50 percent of the bombs that actually hit British warships during the Falklands War failed to detonate. After the war, the British task force commander asserted that he would have withdrawn the fleet rather than allow it to suffer the number of casualties that would have occurred had those bombs actually exploded. In the Israeli-Lebanon War, Soviet-made advanced ground-to-air missiles proved far less effective in battle than they were thought to be, as did the much-heralded T-72 tank with its long-range gun. Even defensive weapons often prove defective. During the Falklands War British naval defenses, heavily laden with missiles, were supplemented by the curious device of having fleet helicopters fly around target ships towing large sheets of tinfoil beneath them. The hope was that enemy missiles would home in on the foil instead of the ship. The modern American Navy also has its problems with equipment: recently, it announced that in fleet tests approximately 70 percent of conventional naval munitions tested failed to detonate or fire correctly. This says nothing about the new generation of Pershing 2 missiles that have great difficulty working or even the cruise missiles that apparently do not work very well if the ground is covered with snow. Wherever one looks, one finds military equipment that works either below standard or not at all.

Another basic failure in assessing combat performance can be traced to the fact that an army's doctrine of deployment and engagement may simply be inappropriate to the war it is fighting. It is a mistake to assume that an army successful in one type of war is likely to be successful in any other type of war. Armies commonly find themselves engaged in wars for which they have little or no doctrinal preparation. The American Army, for example, fought a war in Vietnam for ten years following a doctrine that had been developed during World War II for use in a conventional environment. Unable to develop a doctrine of unconventional war, the United States persisted in applying its traditional doctrine regardless of realities, prompting the observation that the United States had not been in Vietnam ten years; but had been there one year ten times. For their part, the Soviets, traditionally committed to the principles of mass and firepower, find themselves mired in a guerrilla war in Afghanistan, a conflict for which they have neither doctrine nor training. The successful guerrilla army of Vietnam, transformed by its victory into a conventionally configured military force, now finds itself unable to deal with insurgencies in Cambodia and Laos. Finally, judging from the failures at Song Tay and the Iran raid, we may conclude that the ability of a conventional military force to improvise successful doctrinal and practical military applications is limited.

Even if doctrinal and equipment failures could be compensated for, there would still remain the major problems of quality of manpower, leadership, and training. On balance, it does not appear that most major armies have too much difficulty meeting numerical requirements for manpower, especially in times of conflict. Yet, if the behavior of most armies in the last twenty or so years is any indication, indeed only a few correct assumptions could be made about the fighting quality of military manpower. In Vietnam, for example, American soldiers suffered consistently from a range of problems, including drug use, desertion, refusal to engage, and even the assassination of their officers. In Iran, the Shah's expensive troops surrendered without firing a shot. In the Falklands, the performance of the Argentine army officer corps and troops bordered on the dismal, while that of the air force was heroic. What we know of Soviet soldiers suggests that they generally make less than ideal combat soldiers.

The ability to predict how an army will actually perform under fire, then, is more a matter of informed guesswork than of anything approaching an exact science. A great number of variables are involved in the equation and the record of successful analysis is very slim. It is, therefore, fair to say that when two armies clash, the outcome is almost always in doubt except when the clash comes at the extreme ends of a scale of assumed capabilities. None of this uncertainty has stopped intelligence analysts or academics from speculating about the ability of an army to fight well or badly. The fact that such speculations have been as wrong as they have been right should give us pause.

Innumerable attempts have been made to assess the ability of various armies to perform in battle. While many works describe the army and list equipment, few have measured an army's ability to fight relative to specific types of wars. There is little point in measuring the combat potential of, say, the Libyan Army in terms identical to that of the British Army inasmuch as these armies would likely be called upon to fight radically different kinds of wars under very different conditions and constraints. Such analyses are essentially flat or one-dimensional and rest on the assumption that war is war and that its technical applications vary little from place to place. Anyone who watched the Shah's army disintegrate, reconstitute itself under the banner of Khomeini's Islam, and then drive the Iraqis from their territory will readily perceive the falsity of such an assumption.

This book attempts to analyze the combat ability of thirty-two ground armies relative to the type of war—combat scenarios—each army is most likely to encounter. The work contains the requisite lists of equipment and descriptions of the military structure, but tries to go beyond these, evaluating the combat ability of each army in terms of a range of additional variables such as quality of officers, NCOs, doctrine, training, and organization. Each combat scenario is evaluated in terms of the army's ability to fight under each set of circumstances. Finally, each analysis has been prepared by an individual with an extensive background—whether military, diplomatic, academic, or intelligence—in the field in which he is writing. The objective was to avoid the essentially one-dimensional analysis that seems to mark some other military reference works.

In the end, of course, the only valid test of an army's ability to fight is to commit it to battle and see what happens. And, of course, any attempt, including this one, to predict the battle-worthiness of an army is fraught with risks and shortcomings. Much would be lost, however, if we were to refuse to take those risks simply to avoid the embarrassment of being wrong. Whether we like it or not we live in an uncertain world, and war is one of its most enduring, if least endearing, characteristics. We can only obtain a semblance of intellectual order when we use our intellect to attempt to foresee how events will turn out under specified circumstances. This is no less true of war than it is of any other social phenomenon. It is hoped that this book is a small step in that direction.

NATO

The United States

Richard A. Gabriel and Paul L. Savage

For most of its 200-year life the American Army has been small and usually unobtrusive, volunteer, and almost never a ladder for social mobility. It has carried little social prestige except during major wars. Historically, it has been a civilian army relying on masses of militia for mobilization as during the Civil War, a war fought by locally raised regiments, or on masses of conscripts, the structure largely dissolving immediately after the wars. This historic and deeply rooted cultural pattern confronts the army today; the long-range historical effect has been military amateurism and institutional discontinuity.[1]

One inherent problem in the army has been its failure to develop a model of "institutionalized excellence."[2] The United States has never committed the "best and the brightest" to the business of war and must, therefore, recreate its military apparatus anew to meet each challenge on an ad hoc basis. This has been done not only for cultural reasons but also because of its remoteness from the arenas of war in both space and time.

Who Serves

Few Americans have lived within a military system with its historical values of dedication, discipline, self-sacrifice, a sense of the regimental spirit, continuity, and deep tradition—and then for only short periods. The United States is, after all, a mercantile society with a deep aversion to military service. Table 1 shows that the American military tradition is neither long nor deep. As for the tradition of sacrifice, all the wars of the nation together have cost but 575,354 battle deaths in over 200 years compared to Soviet losses of 22 million dead in World War II alone. Table 1 shows the U.S. military loss to be small, experience brief, deprivation light, and mass participation shallow. The impact of war on the United States has rarely been substantial, even considering the long Vietnam War in which battle stress was not comparable to that of World War II or Korea. The principal factor

4 RICHARD A. GABRIEL AND PAUL L. SAVAGE

has been the country's continental isolation and the fact that enemies of the United States engaged on or near the continent have been weak—the Indians, Mexicans, and Spanish. Enemies who were strong were either fellow Americans (the Confederacy) or remote, giving time for mobilization. None of these conditions applies today.

By any measure, the American military tradition and history is "thin."[3] Such "tradition" as moves the army has been carried not by the "regimental spirit," but by a small cadre of U.S. Military Academy graduates. These men are trained less for war than for management and engineering, with emphasis on careers rather than on leadership in battle. Their spirit is that of an "old boy" network, eyes set permanently on relative positions on the army promotion list. Given a society dominated by the motives of the marketplace, self-interest rather than the spirit of service, obligation, and sacrifice, this can hardly be surprising. Nor is the conduct of the country's more recent wars inconsistent with a managerial and material-oriented society. World Wars I and II, Korea, and Vietnam were supremely wars of attrition conducted from a vast resource base. None of these wars were wars motivated by military spirit. The United States buried its enemies in metal and then moved over the ruins.[4] It is extremely doubtful that "we can stand [the] degree of pain" inherent in a future war of attrition in Europe even if it is nonnuclear.[5] But this is the form of land war that the United States appears to plan.[6]

Structure

The Department of the Army (DA), organized in two top tiers, begins at the civilian level, that spread of "boxes" which contains the secretariat of political and civil appointees. In theory, the Secretary of the Army channels policy through the Chief of Staff; in practice, the two levels overlap and intermix. Both levels are in states of comparatively constant disorder on the civil and military levels. The civilians turn over at each change of administration and frequently during the presidential term. The military turn over at the usual high rates for the rest of the army. Typically, the civil functionaries have legal, commercial, or, less often, academic backgrounds. Few have any notion of the nature of war. Senior officers and juniors alike are in the permanent process of moving from one career step to another. Many exhibit amateurism and careerist motives, and few have a generalized institutional perspective characteristic of a true General Staff officer and professional.

The DA addresses a wide variety of missions and objectives—equal opportunity, race relations, base sanitation, medical support, dependent support, basic education, social problems inherent in large numbers of integrated female soldiers, extensive public relations, research and development, intelligence, supply and logistics, operations, and, finally, training and readiness for war. Obviously, without training all is hollow. How well then has the

Table 1
U.S. Army Battle Deaths and Number and Percentage of Population in Service, All Wars

Year/War	Battle Deaths	Strength	Population (Million)	Percentage of Population Serving
1775-1783 Revolutionary War	4,044	Unknown	3.8 (?)	Unknown
1789		718		
1801		5,608		
1812-1815 War of 1812	1,950	38,186		
1816-1845		Av. 8,000		
1846-1848 Mexican War	1,721	47,319 (1848)	25	
1849-1860		Av. 14,000		
1861-1865 Civil War	138,154[a]	1,000,692 (1865)	34.3[a]	2.92
1898 Spanish American War	369	280,564 (1899)		Unknown
1900-1916		Av. 85,000		
1917-1918 World War I	50,510	2,395,742 (1918)	108	2.2
1919-1940		145,000		
1941-1945 World War II	234,874	8,267,958 (1945)	136	4.5
1950-1953 Korean War	27,704	1,533,815 (1953)	150	1.0
1964-1973 Vietnam War	30,867	1,401,000 (1968)	203	0.56
1980-1981		Av. 770,000	204	0.34
Total U.S. Army battle deaths	277,257			
Total U.S. battle deaths, all services, all wars	575,354			

[a] Union forces only.
Richard A. Gabriel and Paul L. Savage, *Crisis in Command: Mismanagement in the Army*, New York: Hill and Wang, 1978, Appendix.

DA performed its last and primary task? As of 1983, the department administered a force of 774,321, of which 98,427 were officers, some 12.7 percent of strength topped by 431 general officers, one general to 1,563 enlisted men (compared to one general to 4,916 enlisted men in World War II), and 386,379 civilians of all grades. As a "War Ministry" the DA is administrative. While it will engage in war planning, it does not fight wars. It does support those who do. The DA is not limited to the Pentagon, including as it does fourteen major army commands. The department has operational control of all commands *except* the overseas armies, which, effectively, are under some form of theater command, and the Joint Chiefs of Staff.

The Department of the Army is organized along the lines of a General Staff, a form developed during the term of Secretary of War Elihu Root (1899-1904) who took the concept from that of the great German General Staff. The missing substance, and it is crucial, is that core of permanent General Staff officers who would provide the heart and soul of institutionalized military excellence.[7] While the army has long operated a schooling system arranged hierarchically much as a civil graduate school system requiring any officer aspiring to high rank to pass through this system, it has ignored, or for political reasons refused to create, a corps of true and thus permanent General Staff officers. Instead the army has pursued a debilitating career system. Beginning at the DA level, the concern for promotion has denied to army policy a permanent and stable core of military professionals. This condition, of course, infects the remainder of the force.

Order of Battle

The fighting army begins at the division level. There are sixteen regular/active divisions in the U.S. Army. Ten divisions are located in several of five Continental United States (CONUS) armies, territorial conveniences, mostly in the South and Southwest. There are two field or tactical armies: the Seventh Army in Europe and the Eighth Army in Korea. The Eighth Army is primarily one division filled out in substance with the entire Republic of Korea Army of some 600,000. The Seventh Army in Germany includes four divisions and assorted support elements. One division is in Hawaii.

There are five types of divisions.

Armored Division: Four divisions available, two in West Germany; 354 tanks, 345 armored personnel carriers, 11 battalions, 6 armor, 5 mechanized infantry, *18,000* personnel.

Mechanized Infantry Division: Five divisions available, two in West Germany; 270 tanks, 414 armored personnel carriers, 11 battalions, 6 mechanized infantry, 5 armor, *18,000* pesonnel.

Infantry Division: Five divisions available, none in Europe; predominantly foot infantry with minimum armor usually one battalion, some mechanized infantry, some with as few as six infantry battalions, mean strength *16,000*.

Air Assault Division: One division available; helicopter-borne, no armor but with one tank destroyer battalion, and one attack helicopter battalion, nine infantry battalions, *14,000* personnel.

Airborne Division: One division available; nine infantry battalions (parachute), one light armor battalion, *14,000* personnel.

All divisions follow the brigade rather than the "regimental" form of organization. Strength is maintained through individual rather than unit replacement.

Each division has three brigade headquarters with no "organic" units, and each has up to eleven maneuver battalions. Maneuver and support battalions are attached to brigades as the mission and forces available dictate. All divisions have supporting artillery. In the case of armored and mechanized divisions, forty tubes ranging from 105mm through 155mm and 8-inch howitzers, the last two with nuclear capability, are standard. In addition, there are helicopter, engineer, signal, NBC (nuclear, biological, and chemical warfare) defense company, air defense artillery battalion, and medical units. A caveat is in order here: in this work we deal with all units as if they were at 100 percent in strength; this is seldom the case, however. Of the sixteen divisions, four are missing one regular brigade, others may be missing a battalion, and all are chronically affected by personnel shortages created by schooling, transfer, and overall shortages of combat soldiers. At the center of this complex organization is the maneuver battalion, armor or infantry, on the very real expectation that future war will rest on the number and quality of basic fighting units. While the division is the single complete fighting unit, self-supporting in battle, the battalion is the fighting component that will maneuver and win, often without guidance and possibly without command contact. Maneuver battalions average some 750 in strength and have only one objective: intensive combat. Table 2 lists U.S. Army maneuver battalions, giving their strength, type, location, and manpower totals by category.

The combat personnel strength available in West Germany, which is generally considered to be the most likely area of heavy engagement, is shown in Table 3. The number of tanks and armored personnel carriers (APCs) immediately available is important. While the United States has 12,826 tanks of all types in its inventory, the important tank figures are those in the total active maneuver battalions. For the total active army, 2,916 tanks (including National Guard roundout units) are provided for, and almost all of them are in the armor and mechanized divisions. The total for armored personnel carriers in active units is 3,795 against a total inventory of 12,531.[8] In West Germany, the army has deployed 1,367 tanks and 1,518 APCs, a total of 2,885 armored vehicles. These data do not include

Table 2
Maneuver Battalions, U.S. Army

Battalion type	Strength	Total	Available	CONUS	Europe	Republic of Korea	Hawaii	Panama	Berlin	Personnel total, USA
Armor	550	48(6)[a]	54	31	21	1			0.3[b]	29,700
Mechanized infantry	891	47(8)	55	30	22	2		1		49,005
Infantry	749	39(9)	48	32		5	6	2	3	35,952
Armored cavalry	876	9		3	6					7,884
Air cavalry	963	6		6						5,778
Airborne infantry	935	10		9	1[c]					9,350
Ranger	800(?)	2		2						1,600
Tank destroyer	800(?)	1		1						800
Attack battalion	800	1		1						800
Total (Battalions)		186		115	50	8	6	3	3.3	
Total (Personnel)				94,880	37,293	6,077	4,494	2,389	2,447[d]	140,869[c]

[a] Figures in parentheses are "roundout" battalions from reserve or National guard.
[b] Tank company.
[c] One airborne battalion in Italy with "augmentation."
[d] These figures are correct only if all units are at full strength—which they frequently are not because of turbulence, difficulty in recruiting for combat arms and losses from AWOL and desertion, sickness, and military unsuitability discharge.
[e] Figures will not balance since one brigade of the 2nd Armored Division is in Germany. Battalion data are derived from James E. Dorman, Jr., consultant, *The US War Machine*, New York: Crown, 1978).

Table 3
Combat Maneuver Force Deployed in West Germany

Maneuver Troops by Type[a]	Strength
Armor/tank crewmen	11,500
Mechanized infantry	19,602
Infantry (Berlin)	2,247
Armored cavalry	5,256
Airborne (Italy)	935
	39,540

[a] All figures reflect *full* strength, which is rarely the case.

the tanks stockpiled in West Germany (three divisions) which are to be provided reinforcing units in the event of war. All armored vehicle figures assume full operability and fully skilled crews, which, of course, is unrealistic. The figures must be discounted by 10 and possibly 20 percent depending on maintenance, parts, and crews. In effect, the U.S. Army Europe (USAREUR) can immediately deploy a maneuver force of 39,540 soldiers under the best of conditions, and a total armored vehicle inventory of 2,885.

Command and Organization for Battle: Europe

Headquarters for U.S. Army Europe (USAREUR) and the U.S. Seventh Army are located in Heidelberg, Federal Republic of Germany. At the outset of war, USAREUR would dissolve into the Central Army Group, a National Atlantic Treaty Organization (NATO) organization designed to fight the ground war with a sector running roughly from the North Sea to the Bavarian Alps. The Seventh Army would become a tactical field army organized into two U.S. corps, V and VII, with an attached German Army corps, all deploying to fight a forward "Meeting Engagement." Two U.S. armored cavalry regiments would, as now, deploy to screen and delay along the eastern border with the German Democratic Republic and Czechoslovakia. If NATO retained its political and military integrity, the left flank of the Seventh Army lying just north of Frankfurt am Main would be secured by the British Army of the Rhine, two divisions, eight to twelve German divisions, one Belgian division, and two Dutch divisions. The U.S. armored brigade near Bremerhaven would reinforce northern British and German Defense with flanking attacks and delaying maneuvers against Soviet columns crossing the Elbe near Hamburg. The French Army would deploy three armored divisions in Germany, four more behind the Rhine frontier, two more armored divisions, and seven infantry divisions in the interior—a force of 16 divisions, 1,300 tanks, and 24 Pluton nuclear-armed

10   RICHARD A. GABRIEL AND PAUL L. SAVAGE

Table 4
U.S. Army
Weapons and Equipment Inventory

Weapons/Equipment	Total
M60 & M48A5	10,896
M1 tanks	371
M551 Sheridan	1,559
APCs	12,320
M2 IFV	73
M3 CFV	138
Recovery vehicles	3,294
DIVAD	0
VULCAN	260
Anti-aircraft missiles	28,327
105 artillery	1,254
155 towed	735
155 self-propelled	2,314
175 towed	—
175 tracked	—a
8" towed	126
8" self-propelled	896
Lance	54
TOW	4,999
DRAGON	9,718

a Apparently phased out of inventory. These weapons, however, are deployed by the Israeli Defense Force.

Source: DA Headquarters, Office of Public Information, May 1982.

missiles.[9] French responses to Soviet threats or actual attack cannot be known since France is not formally committed to NATO.

Under favorable political, strategic, tactical, and intelligence conditions (early and reliable warning), twenty-seven divisions could be deployed by NATO, not counting reserves marked for NATO from CONUS, Britain, or other European nations. The United States could airlift one division, airborne, in ten days and another in thirty days if there were no interdiction of transport, communications, or air-landing facilities, an unlikely prospect. No individual replacements from a reactivated draft could be expected short of 180 days. While some activated reserves would inevitably be sent, their quality and skills are in deep doubt.

The question of tactical nuclear war must necessarily be considered. The United States deploys some 7,000 nuclear weapons in Europe of varying yields and delivery ranges. The nuclear delivery systems are Lance (36), Pershing (108), Nike-Hercules (144), 8-inch howitzer (200), and 155mm howitzer (300) with yields from a fractional kiloton (155mm) to 400 kiloton (Pershing). The German Federal Army holds seventy-two Pershings and twenty Sergeant missiles, but its warheads are under U.S. control. The form, effects, and consequences of using these weapons are beyond the scope of this commentary.

Tactics and Control

The United States has found it necessary to maintain the kind of military force that would maximize maneuverability and flexibility relative to its size. This has meant the development and emphasis on infantry. Infantry units are cheap to deploy, they cost little to maintain, and, most importantly, they can be easily tailored for duty on foreign battlefields with a minimum of support and transportation facilities. Moreover, infantry forces can be easily reconfigured to fight in many types of battlefield environments. Throughout its history, American projections of military power have always been beyond its own borders to battlefields as different as Vietnam to the plains of Central Europe. For these reasons the American emphasis on infantry units remains basic doctrine.

Basic doctrine is contained in Field Manual 101-5, *Operations*. Certain propositions are key. The U.S. Army "*must above all else, prepare to win the first battle of the next war.*"[10] "...defense dispenses advantages that can be decisive (provided U.S. forces are in place first): intimate knowledge of terrain,..., cover and concealment; obstacles; and mutually supporting positions...,defenders consequently should be able to defeat attackers," as long as "they are never outnumbered or outgunned *more than 3:1* at the point and time of decision."[11]

Under very favorable circumstances, the Seventh Army would defend on a front of about 250 kilometers. If conditions were not favorable, a front of some 450 kilometers, extending from Kassel to the Austrian border, would have to be held. One of the unfavorable circumstances would occur if the American and West German forces had to stand alone. With all four American divisions and two armored cavalry regiments committed, fifty U.S. maneuver battalions would be on line or near the forward edge of the battle area (FEBA). This number of battalions permits one battalion to 5 kilometers. But with the necessity for mobile reserves, most forward edge battalions would have sectors of 7 to 10 kilometers.

The forces immediately available and committed to the Warsaw Pact are as follows: 70 divisions, armored and mechanized; 945,000 soldiers; 20,000 plus tanks; and 4,000 plus tactical aircraft.[12] With rapid Soviet mobilization, the Warsaw Pact would commit 150 divisions within ten to fifteen days. The odds against NATO, assuming NATO performs as planned, would look like this: in divisions 1:5; in armored fighting vehicles 7:1; in artillery (including multiple rocket launchers) 5:1; and in aircraft 2-3:1. The Soviets conceivably could mount these odds all along the attack front or multiply them enormously at a number of places if they so chose to concentrate. The odds would vary depending on the speed of Warsaw/Soviet mobilization.

The army knows it cannot hold a linear defensive. According to John Collins, "U.S. commanders instead are advised to concentrate winning concentrations at proper times and places, 'using reserves from the rear and forces from less threatened flanks'. . . . Success is contingent in any case on sound intelligence and 'continuous, reliable, secure comunications' because 'outnumbered forces cannot *afford* mistakes'."[13] All this implies mobility and tactical flexibility applied to forward defense—as close to the East German border as feasible. Forward defense "calls for holding critical terrain for as long as possible, and counter-attacking to reoccupy lost terrain. . . . While current doctrine envisions a lateral shifting of forces to block or destroy a massed attacking force. For the counter-attack-offensive the division commander will seek to concentrate overwhelming combat power in a ratio of at least *six to one* [emphasis mine] at the point where he wishes to conduct his penetration."[14] These tactical doctrines are basically doctrines of attrition. In brief, we intend to meet the Soviets head on and to wear them down. This is a doubtful prospect. The stupifying density of firepower on the modern European battlefield would rapidly wear *any* fighting force down. Assuming a 5-percent loss per day for the U.S. Army, in six days it would lose its combat-effectiveness since losses would exceed 30 percent. Worse, as medical facilities would be desperately short, possibly 30-percent more casualties would result. Since the American replacement system is based on the individual replacement stream, it is clear that U.S. war reserves could not cope with such a loss. First use of tactical nuclear by the United States would appear almost certain to forestall land combat defeat.

Replacements, Reserves, and Logistics

The reserve forces available to the American army are thin and ill organized. Part of the problem is related to the adoption of the "total force" concept as an adjunct to the all volunteer force (AVF). According to the total force concept, forces in being are only a "peacetime option" and in the event of war these forces must be augmented rapidly by drawing heavily upon reserves. As a consequence of this policy, emphasis is placed upon maintaining substantial reserve and National Guard units that can rapidly expand active forces to needed strength levels. Corollarily, along with transferring the main manpower function to the reserves, many of the crucial logistical and medical functions that any army needs to operate are transferred as well. The number of reserves available to the American Army is disastrously small. Under ideal circumstances, no more than 2.8 million men could be mobilized from the reserve forces, a figure that is 1 million short of the 3.8 million required.[15] These shortages would be spread by more than a half million men in the active forces, a quarter million in National Guard units, and another quarter million in reserve units. Since 1972, overall available reserve manpower forces have declined by at least 19 percent, while ready reserve forces have declined by over 50 percent of required stregth. In the last decade, ready reserve force strength has dropped from 2,494,000 to 1,222,000. The individual ready reserve is itself almost 500,000 men short of the required strength.

These shortages take on even more ominous proportions when it is realized that under the total force concept many of the vital tasks required of an effective combat army are poorly positioned in the reserve structure rather than in the active forces themselves. Thus, 54 percent of the total combat forces of the U.S. Army is located in reserves.[16] The shortages are even greater when examined in terms of specific force allocations. Accordingly, 56 percent of the army's total deployable forces are in reserve units, as are 37 percent of its aviation forces and 49 percent of its special forces groups. Also located in reserve are 52 percent of its infantry and armored battalions, 57 percent of its field artillery battalions, 65 percent of its combat engineer battalions, and 67 percent of its tactical air support units.[17] In the best of circumstances, if the U.S. Army had to go to war, more than half its combat power would be deployed in reserve units. More importantly, fully two-thirds of its logistical support and 60 percent of its combat medical support would also be deployed in reserve units.[18] The sixteen standing divisions of the American Army are not really a ready force in being, and they are not ready to fight with what they have in a "come as you are" war. Instead, they are designed to join battle only after they have been substantially augmented by reserve units. The American reliance upon reserve forces to deliver or absorb a first blow is much higher than that of the Soviet Army, and in any case it is probably much too great.

The difficulty in using reserve forces in an emergency is compounded by the fact that the United States has no real experience at rapidly mobilizing its reserve forces. Beginning in World War II and continuing through Korea and even Vietnam, the American solution to increased manpower demands has always been to increase draft levies rather than systematically mobilize its reserves. Our reserves have never been systematically and completely mobilized. Moreover, given their state of readiness, it is unclear that mobilizing existing reserves would help very much. For example, only 6 percent of the Army National Guard's units were regarded as "fully ready" in a nationwide test; 25 percent were "substantially ready"; 37 percent were "marginally ready"; and 32 percent were judged as "not ready." The Army Reserve itself had only 14 percent of its units fully ready, 24 percent substantially ready, 27 percent marginally ready, and 35 percent not ready at all.[19] An evaluation of Army Reserve combat battalions revealed that five of ten combat battalions would not be able to perform their missions, four of ten would have great difficulty in accomplishing their mission, and only one in ten would have only minor difficulties. None was found to be fully capable of performing the mission for which they were organized.[20] More than half the Army Reserve unit commanders who responded to the study stated that the quality of the enlisted men in their units was much lower than that needed to accomplish their mission. Moreover, of reserve company-size units, 35 percent were not ready to perform their mission and 27 percent were only marginally ready. The Army Reserve consists of about 3,000 company-size units, including 1,618 combat-support companies, 1,018 training companies, and 321 combat companies. None of these units is truly combat-ready by even the most marginal definition of the term.

Reserve forces are useless unless they can deploy to the battle area. If one examines the readiness of what the army calls "early deployers," units that are expected to be immediately available for deployment, it is clear that many cannot perform their missions. Fully 29 percent, or almost a third of the units designated as early deploying units, are simply not ready to deploy. Only 21 percent are regarded as "fully ready," 26 percent as "substantially ready," and 24 percent as "marginally ready." If the affiliated units which would be required to deploy with the early deploying units are examined, 88 percent of these units are either "marginally ready" or "not ready" at all to deploy; only 2 percent were designated as "ready to deploy."[21] From almost any perspective, then, American Army Reserve forces in being are inadequate not only in size but also in training, qualified manpower, and ability to deploy.

Very few replacements would flow to Europe, and if they did, they would arrive too late. Even if an adequate number of men could be found to replace the approximately 39,540 men in the European maneuver battalions, the question remains if the existing 77 C5As and 175 C-141 aircraft would be adequate to move the numbers needed as well as the one division that would have to be transported within ten days. If casualties amounted to 5 percent per day for the 39,540 in the maneuver battalions alone, then 2,000 soldiers, trained and ready, would have to be found each day. If air and missile interdictions, chemical weapons, and some nuclear fire affected all of the Seventh Army, approximately 200,000 men, then 10,000 replacements would have to be sent in each day from the first day of combat, or 60,000 to 300,000 per thirty-day period, depending on the intensity of battle and the skill of U.S. commanders. CONUS could not cope with losses of such magnitude.

Material wastage would be enormous. If the 1973 Mideast War tells us anything at all, where some 50 percent of the 3,000 tanks available to all sides were lost, then tank losses would tend to be even higher in Europe. With 20,000 Warsaw Pact tanks and 7,000 NATO tanks committed, the following attrition might result. For NATO there would be 5 percent tank and other combat vehicle losses per day; a 50-percent loss by the tenth day; and 3,500 tanks and approximately 750 U.S. Army main battle tanks remaining. The Soviets would lose 10 percent per day for ten days. But with reserves of 18,000 to 20,000 and annual production of 4,000, the Soviets would retain at least 50 to 60 percent of their original force in the attacking armies, or 10,000 to 12,000, maintaining 2-3:1 superiority over NATO. Most American available armor, about 60 percent, is in reserve in CONUS, and annual production is 300. The three divisions of armor and other equipment reserves in Germany might have an uncertain fate since the locations are well known to the Soviets. The seventy or so (actually seventy-seven but not all fly) C5As can transport one main battle tank each. If we assume that each made fifteen trips in thirty days, 1,050 tanks could be delivered together with crews and, presumably, a basic load of ammunition. Thirty-five tanks per day could be delivered if the airfields were not under attack or already destroyed, while losses among the Seventh Army 1,367 main battle tanks would probably run to sixty-eight per day (5 percent per day). Less than half the minimum necessary heavy air transport would be available; the same lack would exist for air troop transport, with no reasonably secure air bases to land the men and equipment.

The Soviet challenge has been tested in two mobilization exercises: "Nifty Nugget" and "Proud Spirit." One informed report on the fall 1978 exercise "Nifty Nugget" explains how the response of the United States and its forces to Soviet threat was tested. By computer simulation and responding to mobilization demands, "an army of some of the best trained soldiers in the United States was sent to the plains of Central Europe. It probably died there.... It had been equipped with some of the most lethal, most advanced high technology weaponry on the planet, but it did not have enough shells, missiles, fuel, food, spare parts or replacements to survive more than a few weeks... the army was attrited to death."[22] A subsequent mobilization exercise, "Proud Spirit," held in the fall of 1980, revealed major, if not crippling, shortcomings in war planning that predicted future catastrophe in Central Europe.[23] Hence, the same near catastrophic errors show up on two staff exercise occasions. This fact strongly suggests that the U.S. Army, as well as the nation, continues to be unable to respond to a deadly land challenge.

Combat Scenarios

A number of other places might offer military engagements in the national interest. The United States would fight these conflicts pretty much with the army it has today. Prospects for deep reform, like quick victory against the Soviet Army, are not bright. The areas of possible combat appear to be Southwest Asia, East Africa, and Central America. The force designed to cope with extra-European contingencies is the Rapid Deployment Joint Task Force (RDJTF). Army elements are an airborne division, air assault division, infantry division, mechanized division, armored brigade, air cavalry brigade, and two ranger battalions, or a total of forty-four maneuver battalions. The armored element has some 270 tanks, one battalion of which is a light tank battalion. Also earmarked is a Marine Amphibious Force (MAF) (6,000+) which is not committed to NATO. The ground fighting forces are supported by twelve tactical fighter squadrons, two tactical reconnaissance squadrons, and two tactical airlift wings, as well as three carrier battle groups, one surface action group, and five aerial patrol squadrons, which are in part committed to NATO. Of the forty-four army maneuver battalions, forty-one are also committed to NATO.

The first problem to be considered in any combat scenario is that the United States has no strategic doctrine to guide military intervention. The Vietnam policies of search and destroy, fire zones, unlimited napalm and bombing assaults, forced population concentrations, or any associated indiscriminate force would not likely be tolerated in any future engagement. Inevitably, military action would be under severe constraints from the viewpoint of political policy. The problem, however, is that annihilation or total war is the American tradition of war. Russell Weigley makes a convincing argument that the "American way of war since the U.S. Civil War has been a strategic concept of annihilation perfected by Gen. U.S. Grant."[24] But the methods of World War II and Vietnam will not do. First, the massive material battles of 1941-1945 or the operational methods of Vietnam would not be required in the likely area of engagement, the Third World. Next, the tactics for fighting in a multiplicity of differing areas have not been spelled out. Finally, in order to strictly control intervention, all operations would of necessity involve intricate political, cultural-religious, and economic problems and decisions. Detailed and continuous political and social scrutiny of all operations requires that political officers have intimate knowledge of a variety of areas, particularly Moslem countries. American military forces, especially the army, simply do not train officers of this quality. As it stands now, the United States would introduce large numbers of troops into highly explosive Moslem areas with little notion of their religion, politics, or sociology. The cost could be extraordinarily high.

An army's ability to fight depends not only on its internal organizational and personnel strength, which, as we have seen, may well be judged to be seriously deficient for the American Army, but also upon the types of conflicts in which it engages. Where and whom it chooses to fight are just as important in determining success and failure, and indeed perhaps more important, as its material stocks of war supplies. The Vietnam experience, in which a superpower was fought to a draw by a third-rate military force, seems a clear example of this principle.

Three types of combat scenarios are envisioned for the U.S. Army over the next twenty years. The first and most often discussed is the *Conventional War in Europe* scenario. Interestingly, this scenario is the least likely to occur. It is far more likely that the United States will intervene in the Middle East or the Caribbean-Latin America. With regard to the *Middle*

East, substantial numbers of U.S. ground and air forces could be sent to any number of Middle Eastern nations, first, to restore a friendly regime destabilized through domestic revolution or insurgency. Thus, for example, U.S. forces could be used to rescue a Mubarak in Egypt or a Hussein in Jordan or the Sultan of Oman. Second, U.S. forces could be put into action to stop a Soviet advance or to counter the use of Soviet troops in concert with some nationalistic revolution. Soviet intervention to destabilize Saudi Arabia, to incite and support Baluchistani nationalist sentiments, or even blatant aggression in Iran—all of which are aimed at the West's vital oil supply—would almost certainly provoke a U.S. response.

Intervention in the *Caribbean-Latin American theater* is projected to be very probable, within the next two decades, given America's history in that part of the world, especially Cuba and Central America. Intervention is most likely to be provoked, as in the Middle East, by the sudden collapse of a key U.S. ally to insurgency or by a conventional-style civil war. Thus, the United States could become involved in (1) a short-term conventional intervention such as occurred in the Dominican Republic in 1967, or (2) a long-term counterinsurgency campaign against entrenched guerrilla movements such as those now evident in El Salvador, Nicaragua, and Honduras.

Conventional War in Europe

In the debate about the readiness and ability of U.S. forces in Europe, it is often forgotten that U.S. forces would fight in that theater of operations only as part of a larger NATO force. Accordingly, the United States would not have to "go it alone" against the Soviets. But even as part of a larger European-NATO force, U.S. ability to meet its combat commitments in Europe is in serious question.

Three recent assessments of U.S. combat strength in Europe—"Nifty Nugget," "Proud Spirit," and the Laird Report—point to very important deficiencies in equipment, manpower, ammunition, resupply and evacuation capability, and reserve strength. Even with a twenty-day warning time (which would be an unlikely condition) the most the United States could do would be to reinforce with one division but it would be plagued by equipment shortages. On balance, it seems unlikely that the United States could meet its combat commitments to NATO in sufficient time or numbers to stave off a concerted Soviet assault against the West.

Fortunately, the chances for European intervention are remote, at least for the foreseeable future and barring any further irrationality in U.S. foreign policy toward the Soviets (for example, the recent "full court press" announced by the Reagan Administration). Indeed, official doctrine recognizes U.S. combat shortcomings in the European theater and sees the force as a "tripwire" that would invoke the U.S. tactical and strategic nuclear deterrent. In this sense, U.S. forces in Europe and the ability to respond to Soviet attacks are not credible on conventional grounds alone.

Middle East Scenarios

One highly probable scenario for the Middle East envisions the intervention of combat troops to rescue a besieged regime from domestic revolution or, as was done in Iran in 1953 and Lebanon in 1958, to destroy a domestic revolution and restore a friendly regime. Providing that the areas of intervention would be near the Mediterranean coast where U.S. carriers, naval forces, helicopters, and resupply ships could be brought to bear, the United States could carry out its missions in these areas. U.S. forces could easily deliver one marine division and its entire combat support in a relatively short time and could sustain it on the ground for long periods. In addition, carrier-based aircraft would assure control of the skies. If truly pressed, the Rapid Deployment Joint Task Force could be brought to bear, although this would stretch U.S. supply and transport facilities. However, inasmuch as any attempt to stop a coup or restore a friendly leader would be a rapid operation (probably not exceeding two months), U.S. forces would be able to execute and sustain operations of this kind, as long as naval support—combat and supply facilities—could be provided.

The second Middle East combat scenario—one involving a U.S. response to Soviet attack or large-scale Soviet troop and material support to some domestic revolutionary force—would not be as easily handled as the first. Such a confrontation would likely take place in areas where the Soviets have significant advantages in lines of supply, numbers of combat troops, and rapidity of movement. Thus, a Soviet thrust into Saudi Arabia, Iran, or in Baluchistan would present the United States and the West with a fait accompli within a matter of a few days—weeks at the outside: Soviet forces sitting atop the objective. The problem for the West would then be to dislodge them.

In such a scenario, the United States would have to rely essentially on the RDJTF to establish a point of entry or bridgehead. This objective would present real problems since the RDJTF is critically short of everything from manpower to uniforms. In addition, it is by no means certain that the RDJTF could actually deploy more than one division, and there is some doubt that it could sustain the airlift (if there were airfields to land in) to deliver its equipment. Thus, the RDJTF would require support from U.S. naval carrier groups, especially in the Persian Gulf. It would especially need its air cover and marine forces. On balance, U.S. forces would find it very difficult to sustain such a role for any period of time.

Any Soviet move against the Persian Gulf would probably provoke a Western response as well, however. This could help compensate for U.S. inabilities, but it would also raise the spectre of a direct clash between Warsaw Pact and NATO forces. Barring such a clash, U.S. forces by themselves would, be unable to dislodge Soviet forces in the Gulf under most conventional scenarios.

Latin America and the Caribbean

In any reasonable scenario of military intervention in the Western Hemisphere, the United States maintains an overwhelming conventional military capability and could easily defeat any conventional force. As Argentina, Chile, and most certainly Brazil acquire a limited nuclear capability, however, the future will probably even the balance somewhat. Such a capability, while in no sense a match for similar forces on the U.S. side, would alter the circumstances under which the United States could realistically expect to employ large-scale conventional forces without involving some nuclear exchange against its forces. Fortunately, U.S. economic and diplomatic as well as military power will likely remain sufficient to make the use of large-scale conventional intervention unnecessary except in rescuing a friendly regime by the short-term application of force against a domestic revolution.

The second Latin American scenario is less favorable, for the ability of U.S. forces to sustain a long-term counterinsurgency campaign with its forces, even in concert with a "friendly" government, is quite limited. Following Vietnam, the United States dismantled most of its unconventional war forces. At present, those forces number only nine understrength battalions, most of which are stationed outside the hemisphere. Moreover, most of the "hearts-and-minds" functions (political and psychological war capabilities) have been lost or transferred to reserve units where they have either disappeared or been allowed to atrophy. Furthermore, the United States, having failed to come to grips with revolutionary war in Vietnam, has still not developed a workable doctrine on employing its troops in such a war. One of the many tragedies of Vietnam was that failure in a strange combat environment led the army to reemphasize its conventional European role and to neglect its unconventional warfare capability. As of this writing, that capability—including troops, weaponry, and doctrine—is sorely inadequate where it exists at all. Thus, even if the political support for such a war were forthcoming, which now seems unlikely, the technical military means for accomplishing it are not in place.

Ability to Fight—The Personal and Group Dimension

Immediately following the end of the Vietnam War, the United States abandoned conscription and returned to its traditional way of raising an army, the all volunteer force. The AVF was established as a reaction to the perceived discrimination of the draft during the Vietnam War. In an effort to quiet the campuses (whose students, paradoxically, were largely draft exempt by 1969), President Richard M. Nixon returned to the all volunteer force. The rationale was that the AVF would be more closely representative of American society and more equitable in levying the burden of military service. In point of fact, the AVF has turned out to be the opposite of what was intended. Since 1973, the American soldier has been less representative of mainstream America than he was under the draft. At least 36 percent of the soldiers in the army are black and if Pentagon projections hold, by 1985 over 50 percent of the enlisted strength of the army will be black. Percentage-wise, there are three times more blacks in the armed forces than in the population at large.

While reliable data about the percentage of other minorities serving in the AVF are hard to come by, at least one prominent sociologist has suggested that over 40 percent of the army is being drawn from minority groups.[25] There is no doubt that America's army is far less representative of American society than it would be in an army raised by a relatively equitable draft. Because the army draws disproportionately from the lower strata of Ameri-can society, the quality of raw recruit material drawn into the military is somewhat lower than what we would find under a draft. The average recruit today tends to have definable intellectual and behavioral shortcom-ings which present great difficulties in transforming him into a good soldier.

One of these most obvious difficulties is the clear decrease in mental skill levels which recruits bring to military service. According to the army's own studies, the possession of a high school diploma is one of the key indicators in predicting a soldier's successful completion of his tour of duty and level of performance. While over 83 percent of American youth obtain a high school degree, only slightly more than 42 percent of the army's soldiers have obtained this degree legitimately.[26] The number of high school gradu-ates entering the army declined every year from 1976 to 1980.

The low quality of raw recruit material attracted under the AVF is also revealed by examining results of the army's own qualification tests. These tests, the Armed Forces Qualification Tests (AFQT), measure intelligence along the dimensions of math and verbal skills. During the Vietnam era when the draft was operating, fewer than 10 percent of the troops in the army fell into Category 3B or below. (Category 3B includes anyone who scores 31 percent or lower on the AFQT; Category 4 is reserved for those who score less than 20 percent of a possible 100.) In 1980, at least 59 percent of the soldiers fell into Category 3B or below. The figure may even be higher, for there is evidence that the army may have "misnormed" these scores to its own advantage. Until 1980, the Pentagon commonly cited the figure of 9 percent as the number of soldiers falling into Category 4. In that year, a study was ordered to compare the AFQT scores under the AVF with those from World War II, Korea, and Vietnam. The analysis showed that the scores had been misinterpreted against their original data base. When the AFQT scores for the army were corrected, an official report noted that the number of Category 4 soldiers had risen from 9 percent to 46 percent. Moreover, the corrected scores showed that 37 percent of the soldiers also fell into Category 3.[27] The new data demonstrate that 83 percent of the soldiers in the army in 1980 were Category 3B or below.

The decline in educational and intelligence levels is graphically evident when reading skills are examined. In 1973, the average American soldier read at the eleventh grade level or about the equivalent of a high school graduate. In 1981, the reading ability of the average soldier had dropped to the fifth grade level, or about one grade level for each year since the AVF was established. This decline has forced the army to undertake prodigious efforts to rewrite its training and instructional manuals for less intelligent troops. With warfare more and more sophisticated, the need to read and comprehend has become crucial: soldiers must be able to understand, operate, maintain, and repair increasingly sophisticated weapons. In addition, the soldier's ability to understand his environment, the regulations that govern him, and his mission depends upon his ability to read and expose himself to information.

The recruits' low quality has affected the army's attrition rates. Because many soldiers cannot adapt to military life and, indeed, because they cannot attain the required skill levels, a substantial number of first-term soldiers never finish their tour of service. In 1980, 37 percent of army enlistees failed to complete their first tour of service.[28] The attrition rate now approaches four soldiers in every ten. Perhaps most disturbing is that most of the attrition can be traced to combat arms units. The highest rate is found in infantry units, which account for 13 percent of the army's total attrition. Another 7 percent comes from artillery units. Attrition is plaguing the army at its most vulnerable point: it is attacking the strength of its vital combat power.

Because the army must compete with the civilian economy for qualified manpower, it seems to be attracting only those who cannot find other employment. Jobs that require a higher mental ability are going unfilled at critical levels. In 1979, the army had the following manpower shortages: 51 percent of its authorized radio operators; 95 percent of its heavy anti-armor weapons crewmen; 44 percent of its cavalry scouts; and 29 percent of its authorized armor crewman for its M-60 tanks. The number of critical Military Occupational Specialty shortages is even higher in the more highly skilled areas of specialist operations. For example, the army is 73 percent short of the chemical operations specialists it needs to go into battle, 66 percent short of medical specialists, 70 percent short of operating room specialists, 84 percent short of clinical specialists, and 63 percent short of its authorized electronic warfare specialists.[29] Clearly, the high mental requirements in the increasingly technological areas of military operations have resulted in grave shortages in the army's combat and combat-support structure. Paradoxically, these shortages are occurring at precisely the time when the U.S. military structure is attempting to modernize its forces and is making major investments in new sophisticated weaponry.

The number of recruits in Category 3B or Category 4, their low reading comprehension levels, and the small number of high school graduates in military service taken together constitute strong evidence that the AVF soldier is unqualified and ill-prepared to meet his military responsibilities in an army increasingly characterized by complex weapons and high technology. The degree to which the army can continue to function with such personnel as well as high attrition rates is problematical.

Under most imaginable conditions, the cohesive, trained, well-led small unit will retain discipline, confidence, esprit, and cohesion and will perform with those immediate responses to threat ingrained by incessant training and battle drill. If, indeed, the United States were to fight the next war with today's army, its army would not be demonstrably different from that which failed in Vietnam, though to give the current Chief of Staff great credit some changes are in the offing. General Edward C. Meyer has directed a slow but "sure" move to a regimental system. Some twenty company-sized units have been directed to be part of the COHORT system, with eighty more slated to be committed by 1983. COHORT will require the soldier and his officers to remain part of one unit, the company, for most of a given tour (three years).

Any limited company unit replacement system poses some problems. The immediate problem is that, since the battalion is the basic maneuver element of the army, one COHORT company of three line companies in an otherwise rapidly turning over maneuver battalion reduces the host battalion commander's command and control. He cannot transfer the COHORT soldier in his unit or remove the officers except for grave reasons. In a sense he is saddled with a unit immune to certain disciplinary measures. The command, control, and morale problems are obvious. There are still wider plans for unit replacement, however. In January 1982, General Meyer announced a shift in unit replacement from company to battalion; this change is eminently reasonable because of the key tactical function of the maneuver battalion. Battalions will be imbedded in a "regimental" system with permanent home division bases rotating on a three-year schedule between home and overseas. The organization and location of home divisions and brigades are not scheduled to be changed.[30]

Any regimental system threatens the huge bureaucracy which has a vested interest in continuing the existing individual replacement structure. With changeover of 85 to 159 percent per year, jobs are guaranteed in the administration of such a constant flow of humanity. If the regimental system is instituted, it will eventually mean far fewer transfers, less availability of choice command slots, less upward mobility, and less promotion for careerists. Hence, a mesalliance of senior officers and civil bureaucrats will likely seek to cripple COHORT.

Faced with the All Volunteer Force and using a market philosophy rather than national obligation as the basis of its recruitment policy, the army has been transformed from a profession and duty into an occupation or job. Moreover, since the army is no longer a socially representative force as it was during World War II, it has become alienated from the parent society. Charles C. Moskos has observed:

The rising minority content in the Army actually makes a more pervasive shift in the social class bases of the enlisted ranks. There can be no question that since 1973 the Army has undergone a social transformation in its enlisted membership....To foster politics that accentuate the tracking of lower-class youth into the military, especially the ground combat arms, is perverse....It is to ask what kind of society excuses its privileged from serving [as it did in Vietnam and continues to do so today].[31]

While the American upper classes have by and large accepted the obligations of political, social, and civic service, they have seldom if ever linked their privileges to military obligation and duty.[32] Volunteer Army (VOLAR) has reduced the ordinarily thin representation of privileged classes to a vanishing proportion. The effects are plain: data indicate that the army does indeed take in the deprived, the marginal, and the alienated soldier, but unlike older military units, it not only fails to negate the sense of estrangement and hostility through its own socialization but through the system it uses it also perpetrates an alienated army.

Alienation and Social Class

The higher the education class, the less the alienation.[33] College graduates constituted 8.5 percent of the army during World War II; 3.9 percent during Korea; 2.6 percent during Vietnam; and 1.9 percent in 1980. The 10.9 figure for those with "some college" in 1973 had fallen to 8.9 percent in 1980.[34] Among the "100,860 serving their first term as enlisted men in the 'combat arms' of the Army...the ones who fight—how many possessed degrees from any college, of any quality, anywhere in the United States? Twenty-five. Not 25 percent, but 25 people...of the 340,000 enlisted men who in 1980 were serving their first term, a total of 276 had college degrees."[35]

Studies have shown that socioeconomic status rather than race was the single most important contributing factor to the higher casualties among minorities in Vietnam.[36] The social status of the enlisted ranks of today's army is even lower than during Vietnam. Large numbers of these soldiers tend to be mistrustful of their society, of their peers and superiors. They are difficult to train, even more difficult to lead, and, under many circumstances, highly resistant to being shaped and molded into cohesive, disciplined, combat-effective units. Major Stephen D. Westbrook has uncovered a threat to "combat readiness and general military efficiency—socio-political alienation." Westbrook correctly attributes the condition of alienation to the outer society, the effect it has on the underprivileged and, therefore, the quality of soldier the army is forced to accept. His sample consisted of 425 soldiers assigned to maneuver battalions in CONUS and revealed the following attitudes:

- Eighty-six percent believed that most people would take advantage of them if given the chance.

- Sixty-one and 69 percent respectively believed that there were few dependable people and that people were not concerned about others.

- Fifty-eight percent believed that politicians lied, and 41 percent believed that most high government officials could not be trusted, with 37 percent uncertain.

- Fifty-two percent believed they could not count on their officers and NCO's, and 43 percent thought they accomplished nothing as soldiers.

- Forty-four percent of the soldiers did not believe their own platoons would make every effort to reach them if cut off in battle, with 21 percent unsure.

- Thirty-two percent, with 18 percent unsure, did not believe that their leaders in battle would go through what they made their men experience.[37]

Westbrook writes that the recruits bring these attitudes into the army with them and that the attitudes persist. He asks whether such an army can stand. Will it disintegrate? Will it exhibit flight instead of determined resistance? Will it quickly surrender upon reverses? If forced by the leadership into psychologically intolerable situations, will it respond with mutiny, assassination of officers, and desertion?

Barracks Culture

The barracks of the army have the qualities of a slum with associated indiscipline, a permanent drug culture, hostility to "straights," "lifers," NCOs, and officers, and mirror "alienation." Violence, crime, and drug usage of a hard and wide range are epidemic. The officer corps and the NCOs are indifferent, uninformed, or fearful of acting, and largely ignore the loss of discipline, cohesion (except the cohesion of a collectivity of "stoneheads" and junkies), and self- and unit pride. Indeed, they seem alienated from their men. "Some commanders give little attention to the boys in the barracks because they regard the 'boys' as unworthy of their time and effort...the barracks are actually only a halfway house to and from the civilian community." Without doubt, the officers are indifferent. "Many soldiers sensing this indifference, quickly turn their quarters into poster covered dope havens." Not knowing what to do, with authority stripped from them by the Department of the Army, officers observing the "erosion of social restraints and traditional values...aware that the drug problem is probably uncontrollable, have focused their attention on career progression."[38]

All successful military socialization systems share certain characteristics:

- Long-term military professionals assigned to units with long lives and sense of the "regiment," coupled with appropriate rituals and traditions.
- Standardized, rigorously enforced training, incessant battle drill in the unit of permanent assignment.
- Swift and certain elimination of the unfit.
- Implicit and explicit codes for leadership behavior strictly and continuously enforced.

None of these standards fits the U.S. Army. If traditional standards were enforced, alienation towards the outer society might well continue but alienation toward the army would cease. As history well documents, successful armies have recruited the alienated, the socially hostile, and the anomic, and have somehow transformed them into effective individuals, soldiers as well as members of formidable units, be they legion or regiment.

Intelligence Levels

In a civilization tied to quantification, much is made of standardized testing. AFQTs, Scholastic Aptitude Tests, Undergraduate and Graduate Record Examinations, the Miller Analogies Test, and dozens of personality and adaptability tests have assumed great importance. For all the deadening educationese connected with testing, there are clear associations between intelligence, education, training, and soldierly performance. The AFQT originated in World War II when it was administered to 12 million males in the armed forces. Until 1980, this test was the base against which all testing was measured. In 1982, the *Army Times* noted that in 1980, using 400 test sites around the nation, 12,000 civilian men and women were tested.[39] For the first time in thirty-five years, the armed forces had a contemporary comparative instrument with which to evaluate the military potential of recruits. While the air force and the navy experienced a measurable rise in quality of recruit, the army did not. The AFQTs taken in World War II and 1980 were compared and showed that today's youth and those of thirty-five years ago demonstrated about the same aptitude distributions. Hence, the newer tests were valid for evaluation purposes. "The Pentagon Study shows that contemporary youths have about the same aptitude distribution as the

World War II reference group."[40] Some 40 percent of contemporary males scored in the two highest categories, compared with 36 percent of those serving in World War II. However, army recruit accessions fell far below the standards of achievement for the society at large or the other services. In Category I the army recruitment achieved 2.0 percent compared to 4.9 in the civil youth cohort; for Category II, army 21.2 percent and civil cohort 34.6; in Category III army 42.5 versus civil 29.3; and in Category IV 54.5 versus 22.9. Thus, some 23 percent of army recruits scored in the top two categories compared with 37 percent of the civilians. More disquieting are the data reflecting black achievement: 95.1 percent of black males scored in the lowest two categories compared to 49.9 percent of white males. These data are of singular importance since in 1980 the army's enlisted ranks were 32.8 percent black, up from 18.1 percent in 1972.

The army is increasingly becoming a minority force, and there is some connection with alienation, social representativeness, intelligence, and performance. The level of recruit quality is even more important since, as we know, the army does not now have a reliable and institutionalized system of military ("regimental") socialization.[41] That the modern army recruit is qualitively lower than that of the World War II recruit is clear. Indeed, it is lower than the army of Vietnam since for all its final dismal behavior that army was at least tempered by the limited social representativeness of the draft. (In 1964, 34 percent of army recruits were above the sixty-fifth percentile. In 1979, 84 percent were *below* the sixty-fifth percentile.) While life in any battlefront is of a low order, its nature exacts a terrible price from those who do not bring to it a very high grade of adaptability, command of the skills and disciplines of the soldier, and military behavior historically associated with excellence. Unambiguously, the new American soldier is poorly equipped intellectually and may as well be poor in spirit if alienation is any measure of that sad condition. Recent data show that 87 percent of Medal of Honor winners scored above average on AFQT tests. Clearly, low intelligence means low combat performance.[42]

Training

In the end, poor training combined with poor spirit and low intelligence condemns soldiers to death, often a lonely and solitary one. The soldier, surrounded by the remnants of disintegrated units, is shattered by forces and conditions for which he was inadequately and irresponsibly prepared. "The Army Training Study," conducted by the Department of the Army in 1978, produced the following findings about contemporary training:

- Training is not seen as the Army's actual primary peacetime mission. It is one of several competing missions.

- Many units in the Army are not training today to the standards necessary to win when outnumbered on the modern battlefield.

- Training distractors have nurtured general tolerance of low training standards by many officers and noncommissioned officers.

- Many trainers (officer and noncommissioned officer) do not know current training philosophy—they do not know how to train.

- There is no coherent, overall training system known and practiced across the Army.

- High turnover, and in particular, internal turbulence mitigate [sic] against achieving the high training readiness required to execute our mission.[43]

In units with 20 percent turnover per quarter, or 80 percent per year, no amount of additional training time can maintain combat-readiness. By the standards of the "Training Study," virtually no army unit is combat-ready.

When the foreseeable battle scenarios are considered, it is presumed that units committed to the European theater or to the Near East, or even Central America will be individually prepared and unit trained. Material and manpower inferiority, political uncertainties in the Persian Gulf, and logistical vulnerabilities aside, if what the "Training Study" has found is true no amount of material abundance, political certainties, and logistical solidity will suffice. Army training produces "21/28 percent of (tank) gunners in EUSAREUR-CONUS respectively [who] did not know where to aim when engaging a target." Category IV soldiers, some 43 percent of the enlisted strength, are unable to learn the Redeye ring profile (that is, they cannot aim and hit with the shoulder-held anti-aircraft missile designed for close-in air defense). Armor units are the core for any defense in Central Europe, and therefore, the quality of armor crewmen is crucial. Instability is endemic in tank units tested. Data show that the average change in a tank crew, one or more members of the four crewmen, occurs every 3.3 months. Basic armor training graduates who had been in the tested armor unit from two to twenty-five weeks had "little or no training on basic armor crewman skills since joining the unit." "Training that had been conducted did not result in proficiency." As expected, the "Training Study" found that in the absence of constant refresher training such skills that had been learned decayed. "Of thirty tank units tested in EUSAREUR and CONUS less than 70 percent of authorized strength were on the average present for daily training. Generally tank crew proficiency is 40 to 50 percent below the norm specified for acceptable levels of combat skills." "The majority of enlisted accessions in test samples are mental categories III and IV, personnel who require enhanced initial training and more frequent refresher training to maintain proficiency," which they do not and, under the existing system, cannot get.

Tests in key skills reveal that "Nine out of every 10 who operate and maintain the Army tactical nuclear weapons in Europe flunked basic tests of their military skills...[failing] basic tests were 88 percent of the artillery crewmen, 89 percent of the tracked-vehicle mechanics, 82 percent of the Hawk surface-to-air missile crewmen and 77 percent of the computer programmers...[testing] 371 tank gun repairmen in 1979, only one passed...in NATO competition, hand picked American crews finish dead last with dismal regularity...while allied tankers racked up scores of 70 percent or better with the same equipment...[and] in six of 11 U.S.-based divisions the troops were rated as 'not combat ready'."[44] Unquestionably, while the army requires more modern equipment, the ability to deliver and sustain field armies in remote places, and to conduct sustained operations is limited.

Morale and Discipline

A soldier's sense of military effectiveness and attitudes both toward other soldiers and the leadership have historically been a measure of effectiveness. These attitudes are a product of the military atmosphere in which soldiers find themselves and the manner in which they perceive their leadership. Some of this condition is highlighted in the problem of alienation and the military drug culture, both of which are products of poor training, ineffective leadership, and inadequate socialization. Shorthand for this ambience is "a morale problem," the failure of "esprit." The issue centers on morale. Morale describes a condition of pride, confidence, surety in military skill, mutual trust, and knowledge of the mission, together with the confidence that what must be done can be done. Soldiers were asked, "Are the soldiers in your unit or organization proud to be members of your unit"? The response for first-term soldiers in the army was positive for only 36.2 percent. For 1979 and for all enlisted soldiers with any length of service, 37.9 were positive with 62.1 percent negative. For the years 1974 through 1979, almost no change was shown in the survey samples.[45] Associated with low morale is a multiplicity of problems. Table 5 exhibits a wide spectrum of problems consistently and historically linked to poor morale and low performance. Where officer leadership ranks number eleven in an order of problem severity, a majority across other ranks lists it as a major problem.

One significant category is the 83 percent of officers who list "Low Ability Personnel" as a problem. Morale, discipline, Junior NCO leadership, and officer leadership equally command majority focus as core difficulties. The army has addressed the issue of morale and discipline in Human Readiness Report Number 5. Prepared in 1979, its findings were rejected by then Secretary of the Army Clifford Alexander. In a summary of Human Readiness Report No. 5 John Fialka writes:

Table 5
Officer Assessments of Various Personnel Problems, U.S. Army

Problem	Percentage Who Indicate a Current Problem in Their Unit/Organization (data collected during April 1979)					
	Officers In Troop Units		Commanders		All Others	
	Pct.	(Rank)	Pct.	(Rank)	Pct.	(Rank)
Junior NCO leadership	84.4	(1)	85.2	(1)	49.4	(8)
Alcohol abuse	79.7	(5)	81.7	(2)	55.7	(6)
Family problems	83.4	(3)	78.2	(3)	59.7	(3)
Marijuana abuse	73.8	(8)	76.7	(4)	41.5	(11)
Low ability personnel	83.3	(4)	74.7	(5)	63.8	(2)
Motivation	84.4	(1)	74.4	(5)	59.1	(3)
Discipline	76.8	(7)	69.5	(7)	54.5	(6)
Morale	78.0	(6)	67.5	(8)	73.0	(1)
Senor NCO leadership	69.8	(9)	64.9	(9)	47.6	(10)
Esprit	65.8	(10)	53.6	(10)	59.1	(3)
Officer leadership	59.1	(11)	51.7	(11)	50.9	(8)
Racial conflict	50.7	(12)	39.1	(12)	38.6	(13)
Hard drugs	49.1	(13)	40.7	(12)	30.9	(13)

Sample size: 3,000

Source: DA Headquarters, 1979 data.

- Only 39 percent of enlisted men in Europe agreed that their units would do well in combat.

- Three key indicators of unit climate, enlisted attitudes, have been declining since 1976 with the lowest readings in Europe.

- Soldier motivation is the lowest in Europe.

- While reportable incidents of crime and indiscipline have dropped sharply since the beginning of the AVF part of the decline has been related to the use of the expeditious discharge. The soldier is removed rather than punished.

- Over a third of enlistees leave the Army, 35.2 percent, before their first three year enlistment is completed.

- Officers see the declining competence of their junior NCOs as an extremely serious problem.

- Only 40 percent of the soldiers believe their officers care about their welfare.

- Fewer than 45 percent of the enlisted men believe that their officers are competent.[46]

Drugs

A recent buzz-word in the Department of Defense is the "management of discipline." This means that many serious disciplinary infractions are no longer punished but are swept under the social rug by "expeditious discharge." The army gets rid of those with whom it cannot cope. Will this practice be followed in future war? Will soldiers react to the fact that serious infractions of discipline, especially combat discipline, will not result in rapid and painful punishment but serve instead to get them out of battle? Clearly, when criminal and unmilitary conduct results in reward, many will act in a criminal and unmilitary fashion.

The drug problem, persisting since Vietnam, appears slowly to be eroding combat-effectiveness, and it is doing so with higher military "tolerance." A 1981 House Appropriations Committee investigation found that the military does not pursue "swift and sure" punishment for drug abuse. Contributing to the dismal picture is a heavy reliance on the prevailing philosophy that the "problem" is a discipline matter and, therefore, best handled by unit commanders. Commanders who aggressively pursue illegal drug use generate high arrest statistics which top commands often interpret as indicative of a "problem" unit. Here the old managerial demon of career concern may cause commanders to ignore the problem and falsely report levels of drug usage and traffic. The impact of drug use has been notable:

- In 1980, drug abuse accounted for 32 percent of the 534 job disqualifications in the nuclear weapons personnel reliability program.
- European Command Headquarters officials stated that the equivalent of four combat infantry battalions was lost...because of drug abuse.[47]

Table 6 shows the comparative use of alcohol and drugs among military and civilian groups. With the exception of amphetamines, the match is quite close. Ironically, some of the military and not a few military sociologists have rejoiced that the values of the U.S. Army and the civil society are so complementary. This is a peculiar perversion of *tu quoque*. In any case, "Work Impairment Because of Drug Use During the Past 12 Months" was 22 percent in the E-1 to E-5 population. Since the lower enlisted troops make up the majority of combat troops in the army, the effect of drug impairment upon 20 to 30 percent of the force in combat can only be malignant.

Drug use among West German civilians is at least as high as among civilians in the United States. Yet, the West German Army has managed to insulate its forces from the corrosive effects of this pathology. The U.S.

Table 6
Comparison of Military and Civilian Drug Use (in percentages)

Drug Used Last Thirty Days	Military Rate	Civilian Rate
Marijuana Hashish	40	42
Amphetamines	10	4
Cocaine	7	10
Hallucinogens	5	5
Barbiturates	4	4
Tranquilizers	3	3
Heroin	1	1
Alcohol	84	82

Source: Data contained in Table 6 was extrapolated from a report by Burt Associates on military drug use done for the mlitary in 1980, portions of which appeared in a newspaper article in *Army Times*, December 15, 1980, p. 4.

Army has not, and cannot, largely because it has abandoned traditional discipline, has created an army of strangers, has permitted a leadership indifferent to its men, and has insisted on maintaining a training, socialization, and disciplinary system that rests in individualism. To the extent that the army does *not* have different values from the general society, it will be ineffective and will be defeated or destroyed. The problem of the drug traffic, indiscipline itself, is to be laid entirely at the feet of those responsible, the officer corps. The more senior the officer and the more responsible his position, the more responsible he is for these conditions.

The American NCO

The American noncommissioned officer (NCO) corps is structured around the model found in traditional European armies. The objective is to create a professional NCO corps that can act as a basic transmitter of values and military technique to the soldier. In the classical model, such a corps is expected to be a stable, career, long-term corps that would not be overly subject to personnel turbulence or attrition. Because the American Army has historically relied upon a volunteer system to fill its ranks, it has tended to stress the development of a stable professional NCO corps to serve as the primary organizers and managers of military skills and values at the small unit level. In time of war, these NCOs form the basis of an experienced training and combat cadre able to rapidly train large numbers of conscript soldiers.

The American Army has had very little difficulty in maintaining a career NCO corps either in the volunteer period prior to World War II or even in the draft armies of that war, Korea, and Vietnam. However, since the return of the volunteer system following the Vietnam War, the personnel problems attendant to that system have had a large impact upon the nature and quality of the NCO corps. The American NCO corps has been unable to attract and maintain a sufficient number of soldiers in the corps itself. The army is short aproximately 11,000 noncommissioned officers when measured against its authorized strength of 259,064.[48] Many of these shortages occur in the "top five" zone, that is, among the most senior NCO grades above E-5 rank. These experienced NCOs are crucially important to the operation of any army, and the inability of the American corps to attract and retain them is a serious problem.

What effect has the generally low quality of recruit material had on the NCO corps? The overall quality of the American NCO corps, expressed in terms of its ability to learn and train its troops, has dropped off considerably. There are several reasons for this decline. In an attempt to meet the shortage of NCOs, the promotion process within the corps itself has been accelerated. As a consequence, NCOs are less well trained and less experienced than they were before. Few NCOs are given sufficient time in grade to acquire the experience and skills they are expected to transfer to their men. The Rosenblum Report undertaken in 1979 for the army's Training and Doctrine Command (TRADOC) demonstrated that the American NCO receives considerably less training and experience than his counterpart in the armies of Britain, France, Canada, and West Germany.[49]

The intelligence level of the American NCO is dropping considerably, much as that in the AVF at large. The reasons seem related to accelerated promotion and to the pool of candidates from which eventual NCOs are selected. Since first-term reenlistments in the AVF have been declining for years, the problem is rooted in the type of people who stay in long enough to reach the rank of NCO. A series of studies reveals that soldiers in the lowest mental skill categories, namely, Category 3B and 4 which now comprise almost 80 percent of the army, tend to remain in the military more than any other group once they have completed their first tour. [50] These soldiers who have managed to complete their first tours of service but also have the lowest scores on the AFQT are reenlisting in higher percentages than any other group. And it is from this group that most future NCOs will come. Because low ability soldiers seem more willing to reenlist and to stay in service, a transmission belt has been created between this group and the

NCO corps. As a consequence, the overall quality of the army's NCO corps has been dropping over a ten-year period.

Evidence of this decline is presented in the Rosenblum Report which documents the problems of quality in the NCO corps. The report notes that the decline in NCO quality has required the introduction of self-pacing instruction even in the once-prestigious NCO academies. The report points out that self-teaching and self-pacing have not worked well and that, compared to European armies, the quality of the American NCO's training and skill levels has continued to decline. In addition, self-pacing seems to have increased both discipline and attrition problems within the NCO corps.

The difficulties that the American NCO corps has in training its soldiers are again reflected in the "Army Training Study" of 1980.[51] This study noted that one of the major problems in training the soldier adequately can be traced to his sergeants and corporals who generally know little more about military subjects than those they are trying to train. NCO quality and training are further reduced by the long list of extraneous duties and frequent assignment rotation that are both a cause and effect of the overall NCO shortage. Thus, as a result of the shortage of NCOs, the low quality of NCO recruits, and the poor training and trainability of NCOs, many NCOs have been unable to perform the critical function of any NCO corps: the training of their own troops. Ultimately, this condition affects the ability not only to fight well in battle, but also to operate the new and more sophisticated and complex equipment that is entering the army's inventory. The skills to operate and maintain that equipment have to be continually updated, sometimes on a yearly basis. The inability of NCOs to adequately train their men in the skills of war represents a major shortcoming not only of the NCO corps but also of the units themselves who cannot master the skills necessary for survival on the battlefield.

Over the last fifteen years, the West's most experienced and battle-hardened NCO corps has gradually slipped to the point where many of its members are genuinely unqualified and ill trained. In a report completed in 1979 by John Fialka, officers identified the most severe problem facing their units over the five-year period of the study as the quality of leadership at both the junior and senior NCO ranks. Both officers in troop units and unit commanders throughout the army cited the low quality of junior NCO leadership as the first ranking problem. No less than 84.4 percent of officers in troop units identified the low quality of junior NCO leadership as the major problem facing their units. With regard to commanding officers an even greater number, 85.2 percent, ranked junior NCO leadership as the major problem with which they had to deal in their units. The data for senior NCO leadership quality are not significantly better; 69.8 percent of the officers in troop units regarded senior NCO quality leadership as a major problem in their units, as did 64.9 percent of commanding officers generally.[52] The army's own studies seem to point clearly to an officer corps (especially those officers in troop units and who hold positions of command) that perceives the quality of the NCO corps as decidedly low.

The American Officer

By assessing the American officer corps throughout ten years of war in Vietnam, we can measure some of its character and performance today. The American officer in Vietnam has been subjected to considerable scrutiny in a number of books and articles written by scholars, military men, and even the military establishment itself.[53] Almost all of these studies conclude that the quality of officer leadership in Vietnam, especially at the small unit level, was poor. Several serious problems that emerged within American battle units can be traced directly to poor officer leadership. Among these problems were high rates of desertion, refusal of units to engage the enemy, a series of mutinies, a consistently high drug use rate, and, most serious of all, the assassination of officers by their own men. These events are mute testimony to the officer's general inability during Vietnam.

Ten years after the end of the Vietnam War, many of the problems that emerged during that war concerning the officer corps remain, and with the introduction of the AVF some of these problems have actually worsened. Hence, the ability of the American officer to perform well in future wars can be cast in some doubt.

The American officer corps is plagued by a shortage of officers. The army has a total of 84,447 serving officers, a number which comprises 11 percent of the total force. Although the number of officers as a percentage of total strength has declined, the officer corps remains far too large as well as maldistributed in rank. Generally, to be effective field armies must never exceed a ratio of officers to men of more than 5 percent. By this standard, the American officer corps is twice as large as it should be. Moreover, its ratios are maldistributed. During Vietnam, the army fielded one officer for every 8.5 soldiers. This ratio was far too high, exceeding the World War II ratio of one officer for every 9.4 soldiers. Today that ratio is even more disproportionate, with the army fielding one officer for every 6.8 soldiers.[54] Although the American Army has a large officer corps at the same time it suffers from an acute shortage of officers in certain ranks, most noticeably in the junior ranks from which the commanders of small combat units are drawn. The army is having great difficulty in retaining young officers, especially combat arms officers. The army is holding on to only 60.5 percent of its officers beyond their first tour of duty (the lowest retention rate since 1975), and the rate continues to decline. Although retention is slightly better (66.7 percent) in the combat arms, it still represents a five-year low.[55] Curiously, the rate has declined steadily following the introduction of the AVF and improvements in salaries and benefits.

The magnitude of the officer shortage is serious. According to official army projections, the corps requires the entry of approximately 10,500 new junior officers every year. In 1980, that number fell to about 8,000 actual entrants from all sources, including ROTC and West Point. Thus, the army is short approximately 2,000 officers, or about 20 percent of the force complement necessary to man a force of 700,000. These shortages are felt most importantly at the junior ranks. The army has no lack of general officers or of the major, colonel, or lieutenant colonel ranks. The shortages are most acute and most damaging at the lieutenant, first lieutenant, and captain ranks, precisely at those points where officers are needed to train and command killing combat units of platoon and company size. In 1980, the army projected that it would be short 5,900 captains; captains normally occupy critical combat leadership positions. By accelerating promotions and reducing the experience required for its first lieutenants, the army estimated that by 1982 it could reduce the shortage of captains from 5,900 to 3,740. This would, of course, precipitate an even greater shortage of first and second lieutenants, a shortage that could have grave consequences inasmuch as the Army has already reported 20 percent fewer lieutenants than it needs to man the force. Moreover, by accelerating promotions in order to solve the captain shortage, it is very likely that the quality of captains will decline much as that of the lieutenants has.

The very high turnover rate in the American officer corps continues to produce turbulence as it did in Vietnam. For example, General George S. Patton, Jr., commander of the 2nd Armored Division in Germany, noted that in the twenty-six months in which he was that unit's commander he witnessed the turnover of five assistant division commanders, or at a rate of 400 percent. During the same period, he witnessed the changing of three chiefs of staff for personnel, three chiefs of staff for intelligence, three chiefs of staff for operations, and four chiefs of staff for supply. Focusing on his field commanders, General Patton had six different brigade commanders, three divisional artillery commanders, and two different division support commanders. In addition, he saw the turnover of three maintenance battalion commanders, four cavalry squadron commanders, and two engineer battalion commanders.[56] Taken together, there is every reason to believe that the rate of assignment turnover among officers who hold critical command and staff positions is so high as to raise serious questions about their ability to train and adequately prepare their units to fight effectively.

The severe assignment turnover is not idiosyncratic; rather, it is the logical consequence of certain institutional practices that make frequent assignments a requirement for the officer corps to function within the bureaucratic environment defined for it. Certainly, a major cause of officer turnover is that the army has too many officers to begin with and far too many field grade and general officers. As noted above, the American officer corps is at least twice as large as it needs to be. The increased number of staff officers, together with the unrealistically short twenty-year retirement system, forces an officer to move from one assignment to another. The American Army simply does not allow captains, majors, or lieutenant colonels to serve long periods without necessarily competing for promotion and new assignments. This "up-or-out" policy forces an officer to pass through a number of "gates" or "tickets" within a twenty-year period in order to qualify for promotion or, indeed, even to qualify for his retirement benefits. An officer cannot remain in a specific job or assignment for long periods as he can in the Canadian, British, German, French, Israeli, and even the Soviet Army and continue to perform effectively in that assignment. The system of promotion, evaluation, and retirement compels an officer to move or else be dismissed.

The American officer corps is characterized by amateurism. Placing officers with little experience in a series of unit assignments—especially combat command assignments—assures that large numbers of officers in critical posts will have little or no experience in their jobs. At the platoon and company level, this condition is exacerbated by the shortage of officers in these ranks and by the policy of accelerating the promotion of second lieutenants, who themselves are inexperienced, to higher grades. Few officers are well trained for the positions they occupy; moreover, few are allowed to remain in their positions long enough to acquire that experience. Evidence of amateurism can be found most readily at the small unit level, that is, at the battalion commander level and below within a division. A study of the 8th Infantry Division done in 1980 reveals that 65 percent of the battalion commanders in the division had not served with troops for ten years or more before taking command of their battalions.[57] One battalion commander had not been in a troop unit assignment for seventeen years prior to assuming command of his battalion.

Given these difficulties, considerable problems of quality may emerge. As viewed by his men, the American officer leaves much to be desired. When officers themselves were asked if "officer leadership" had been a problem in their units "during the last six months," 53.7 percent responded yes, and 20.6 percent felt that the problem was getting worse. Only 8.7 percent thought the problem was improving. Those officers who served in troop units had even worse perceptions of officer quality. Of officers serving with troop units, 59.1 percent felt that the quality of officer leadership was a problem for them and 23.1 percent thought that the problem was getting worse.[58] When the commanders were approached, 51.7 percent thought that the quality of officer leadership in their units was a problem and 18.4 percent saw the problem as deepening. A total of 19.5 percent felt that the problem was at least stable. Of officers in combat units, 57.0 percent thought that the quality of officer leadership in their units was a problem in the preceding six months and 22.8 percent thought that the problem was increasing.[59]

All of these statistics suggest that the American officer corps may have serious leadership weaknesses. In many cases, even the officers do not perceive their peers as of good quality; they also suggest that this low quality is creating problems within army units.

With regard to the troops' views on officer quality, the number of soldiers who believed "my officers care about my welfare" fell to 40 percent, a decline of 10 percent over the last five years. Only 45 percent of the soldiers thought that their officers were "competent" compared to 60 percent who thought so five years before. Similar data emerged from the Westbrook Study in 1980. There 52 percent of the soldiers interviewed believed that they could not "count on their officers to look after their interests," while another 20 percent were unsure. In addition, 37 percent thought that their officers were not concerned about them in any meaningful way; 28 percent believed that "most officers cannot be trusted." Devastatingly, 32 percent of the soldiers did not think that their officers would be willing to suffer the same hardships and risks in battle that their men would have to undergo. Finally, the 1978 CBS poll of soldiers in the Berlin Brigade found that 53 percent of the troops interviewed would be unwilling to follow their officers into battle.[60] It is difficult not to conclude that the troops see the American officer as incompetent and genuinely unconcerned about his men.

The critique of the officer corps made of it during Vietnam remains valid today. To the extent that these practices hinder or prevent the development of effective combat leadership, they still cut across and reduce the quality of officer leadership. Whenever the soldiers and even other officers evaluate officer leadership in the American Army, the continual judgment is that the officer corps is of low quality and is more managerial than military, and has clearly failed to develop many of the skills leading to effective combat units. To the degree that the organizational problems that crippled the officer corps during the Vietnam War remain unchanged a decade later, the corps may perform as badly in the future as it did the last time it took to the field of combat.

Conclusions

American forces generally do not seem well prepared to fight the kind of war that would most likely occur in the late twentieth century, the counterinsurgency type. U.S. forces could prop up or rescue friendly regimes in the Western Hemisphere and the Middle East littoral area with great chance of short-term success; they could not realistically stop a determined Soviet thrust in the Persian Gulf area, however, without raising the spectre of a nuclear confrontation. In Europe, the situation is problematic in that any NATO-Warsaw Pact clash immediately threatens nuclear war.

In an age of large U.S. defense budgets, little of the money is being allocated to increasing the ability of U.S. forces to respond to the most

38   RICHARD A. GABRIEL AND PAUL L. SAVAGE

likely contingencies they will have to face. Most of the money is being placed in high technology equipment and, of course, in strategic weapons and their accompanying delivery systems. The United States is apparently returning to a condition that existed in 1960. Then the United States sustained a large nuclear strategic posture while its conventional forces were allowed to deteriorate. In Vietnam, U.S. forces found themselves totally unprepared for such a war. The same situation seems to be confronting U.S. forces today and will continue to do so until political leaders tailor force structures to their logical scenarios of employment. To date, that linkage is clearly out of balance.

Notes

1. Lewis Fry Richardson, "The Statistics of Deadly Quarrels," *The World of Mathematics*, vol. 2 (New York: Simon and Schuster, 1956), pp. 1254-63. Despite its regularity and despite evidence to the contrary, Americans treat war as an aberration.

2. T. N. Dupuy, *A Genius for War: The German Army and General Staff, 1807-1945* (Englewood Cliffs, N.J.: Prentice-Hall, Inc., 1977).

3. Russell F. Weigley, *History of the United States Army* (New York: Macmillan Co., 1967), pp. 556-69. Data reflect U.S. Army strengths up to 1966. The use of the words "Thin History" is Weigley's.

4. See Martin van Creveld, *Fighting Power: German Military Performance, 1914-1945*, submitted to Office of Net Assessment, Department of Defense, Washington D.C., December 1980. Citing Dupuy, *A Genius for War*, that "German units, at a divisional level were superior to Allied units by a factor of 20-30 percent," van Creveld accounts in detail for German combat superiority over the U.S. Army, notably in World War II. Germany's superiority rested in the total concentration on combat and battle staff excellence, together with the factors contributing to the "institutionalization of excellence." Americans treated soldiers as objects of managerial or human engineering.

5. Franklin C. Spinney, *Defense Facts of Life*, unpublished staff paper.

6. The British Army lost 45,000 men in the first sixty minutes of the Battle of the First Somme and over 500,000 in the later Flanders battles alone—all in approximately two years. In the two world wars, 3,575,548 Germans were killed in action. If we use a multiplier of four for total military casualties, Germany had war losses of 14,302,548 in the two world wars. The United States has not experienced losses of this magnitude.

7. *Dupuy, A Genius for War*, passim.

8. John Collins, *Strategic Balance: USA-USSR* (New York: McGraw-Hill, 1980), an update by DA headquarters, May 1982.

9. *Warriors to Managers, The French Military Establishment Since 1945* (Chapel Hill, N.C.: University of North Carolina Press, 1981), pp. 346-60, passim. If NATO remains intact, a total of 630,000 men, 10 armored divisions, 17 mechanized divisions, and 2,150 aircraft can be committed; these figures exclude French forces.

10. Collins, *Strategic Balance*, p. 198.

11. Ibid.

12. James E. Dorman, consultant, *The US War Machine* (New York: Crown Publishers, 1978), p. 260.

13. Collins, *Strategic Balance*.

14. Dorman, *A Genius for War*, section by LTC Donald B. Vought and LTC J. R. Angolia, "The United States Army."

15. "An Overview of the Manpower Effectiveness of the U.S. All-Volunteer Force," Report by the Comptroller General, (April 14, 1980), Washington, D.C.: U.S. Government Printing Office, p. 3.

16. Critical Problems Restrict the Use of National Guard and Reserve Forces," GAO Report, July 11, 1979, Washington, D.C.: U.S. Government Printing Office, p. 4.

17. Ibid.

18. Ibid.

19. Ibid., p. 56.

20. Ibid., p. 24.

21. Ibid., pp. 48-58.

22. John J. Fialka, "The Grim Lessons of Nifty Nugget," *Army* (April 1980): 14-18.

23. John J. Fialka, "The Pentagon's Exercise 'Proud Spirit': Little Cause for Pride," *Parameters* 11 (March 1981): 38-41.

24. Captain James A. Bowden, USA, "The RDJTF and Doctrine," Unpublished paper, 1981, p. 17. Bowden states that doctrines of military annihilation are less than useful for limited war. Such doctrines are by definition self-contradictory.

25. Richard A. Gabriel, "About Face on the Draft," *America* (February 9, 1980): 95; and Charles Moskos, "How to Save the All-Volunteer Force," *The Public Interest* (Fall 1980): 74-89.

26. Gabriel, "About Face on the Draft," p. 95. Note that the army's official figures for 1980 show the number of high school degree soldiers as 72.3 percent. However, this figure includes those who were awarded a degree *after* entering the service. Degrees may be obtained through at least eleven programs operated or recognized by the army. Many of these equivalency programs actually require much less than a "genuine" high school degree.

27. *Aptitude Testing of Recruits*, Washington, D.C.: Office of the Assistant Secretary of Defense (Manpower), (July 1980), pp. 1-12.

28. Staff study prepared for Congressman Robin Beard, 1980, p. 3.

29. "Active Duty Manpower Problems Must be Solved," GAO Report, November 26, 1979, pp. 1-29.

30. *Army Times*, June 25, 1982, pp. 1 and 23.

31. Charles C. Moskos, "Making the All Volunteer Force Work: A National Service Approach," *Foreign Affairs* (Fall 1981): 20.

32. Richard A. Gabriel and Paul L. Savage, *Crisis in Command: Mismanagement in the Army* (New York: Hill and Wang, 1978), pp. 81-82.

33. Alienation is a much abused and ideologically loaded word. Stephen D. Westbrook, Major USA, defines it as a condition of estrangement or separation. This definition is consistent with historical usage and is measurable. See Stephen D. Westbrook, "The Alienated Soldier: Legacy of Our Society," *Army*, December 1979: 18-23.

34. "This is Your Army," DA headquarters, December 29, 1980.

35. James Fallows, *National Defense* (New York: Random House, 1981), p. 127.

36. "Symposium," *Armed Forces and Society* 6, No. 4 (Summer 1980): 590.

37. Westbrook, "The Alienated Soldier," pp. 18-23, passim.

38. Larry H. Ingraham, "The Boys in the Barracks," unpublished, Washington, D.C.: Walter Reed Army Institute of Research, 1978; and for a measurable definition of slum sociopsychopathology, see Edward C. Banfield, *The Heavenly City Revisited* (Boston: Little, Brown and Co., 1974).

39. *Army Times* March 8, 1982, pp. 1 and 14.

40. Ibid., p. 14.

41. John Keegan, *The Face of Battle* (New York: Viking Press, 1976) should be required reading for all professional soldiers. The fact that diverse human beings have been pressed successfully into a military mold over the centuries, under inordinately difficult conditions, places American combat flabbiness in a poor light.

42. *Army Times*, June 21, 1982, pp. 1 and 21.

43. "Army Training Study," TRADOC publication 1978. In this study, senior officers usually commented that such conditions were those of 1979 and that "things have changed." In this connection, one should consult the 1979 followup study of the *Army War College Study on Leadership* replicating the 1970 study, where little or nothing has changed in the ethical ambiance of the army. See also all comments on training in "Army Training Study."

44. Jack Anderson, "Our Military's in Trouble," *Boston Globe*, Parade Magazine, February 14, 1982. This sometimes questionable, if not sensationalist and shrill, source illustrates the increasing awareness in popular journalism that the army has entered a troubled period. Sensationalism notwithstanding, Anderson's data are correct. He suggests no solution since these are both sophisticated and exotic. See Gabriel and Savage, *Crisis in Command*, passim.

45. DA headquarters, *Quarterly Sample Surveys of Military Personnel.*

46. John Fialka, "The Report No One Wants to Talk About," *The Washington Star.* December 15, 1980 (Reprint).

47. "Report Attacks Tolerance of Military Drug Problem," *Army Times*, March 28 1982, p. 27.

48. Human Readiness Report no. 5, p. 8.

49. The Rosenblum Report is actually a two-year study undertaken by TRADOC in 1978-1979 on the quality of troop training and NCO quality. It emerged formally in a briefing given in 1979 under the title "Comparative Training Strategies." The information contained here and attributed to the Rosenblum Report was obtained from John Fialka's notes and memoranda for record. (Fialka attended that briefing.) The official version of the report is unobtainable. Citations hereafter refer only to the Rosenblum Report.

50. John Fialka, "Re-Enlistments Higher Among Low IQ Recruits," *The Washington Star*, January 24, 1981, pp. 1 and 4.

51. John Fialka, "GI Proficiency at Low Level New Study Says," *The Washington Star*, February 3, 1980, p. 2; the Rosenblum Report makes the same point.

52. Ibid.

53. Douglas Kinnard, *The War Managers* (Hanover, N.H.: University Press of New England, 1977); Cincinnatus, *Self-Destruction: The Disintegration and Decay of the U.S. Army During the Vietnam Era* (New York: W. W. Norton Co., 1981); Ward

Just, *Military Men* (New York: Alfred A. Knopf, 1970); William R. Corson, *The Betrayal* (New York: W. W. Norton, 1968); William Hauser, *America's Army in Crisis* (Baltimore: Johns Hopkins University Press, 1973); and Gabriel and Savage, *Crisis in Command*.

54. John Keeley, "So Many Competing Demands," *The Washington Post*, July 6, 1981, pp. 4–5.

55. Human Readiness Report No. 5, p. 12; see also "Commissioned Officer Retention Rates," Washington, D.C.: DA (Public Affairs), October 9, 1980, p. 2.

56. Letter to the Editor by Major General George S. Patton, Jr., *Army Magazine* (May 1981): 7.

57. Louis Sorley, "Turbulence at the Top: Our Peripatetic Generals," *Army* (March 1981): 14–24. (See especially p. 21.)

58. Human Readiness Report No. 5., p. C-3.

59. Ibid.

60. Westbrook, "The Alienated Soldier," p. 20.

Selected Bibliography

"The Army Lacks Quantity and Quality." *The Boston Globe*, September 1, 1981, p. 1.

Bacton, Julius W. "First Class Army...4th Class Living Conditions." *Army* (November 1980): 22–26.

Cincinnatus. *Self-Destruction: The Disintegration and Decay of the U.S. Army During the Vietnam Era*. New York: W. W. Norton Co., 1981.

Corddry, Marion. "The Doctor Shortage." *Army* (May 1979): 18–24.

DAPE-MPE Information Paper. "This Is Your Army, 1981." December 29, 1980, pp. 1–10.

"Defense Affirms Readiness Lag." *Army Times* (September 29, 1980).

Department of the Army. "The Army Training Study." Washington, D.C. August 8, 1978.

Department of Defense. " 'Cover Up' of Manpower Crisis Alleged." *Armed Forces Journal* (April 1979): 8, 26.

Fialka, John. "Army Views Manpower Situation as a Crisis." *The Washington Star*, March 31, 1980.

———. "Can the US Army Fight?" *Washington Star Series*, December 1980.

———. "The Grim Lessons of Nifty Nugget." *Army* (April 1980): 14–18.

———. "The Pentagon's Exercise 'Proud Spirit': Little Cause for Pride." *Parameters: Journal of the U.S. Army War College* 11, No. 1 (March 1981): 38–41.

———. "A Question of Quality." *Army* (June 1980): 29–32.

———. "Re-Enlistments Higher Among Low IQ Recruits." *Washington Star*, January 24, 1981, Section A, pp. 1 and 4.

Gabriel, Richard A. "About Face on the Draft." *America* (February 9, 1980): 95–97.

———. "Combat Cohesion in Soviet and American Military Units." *Parameters: Journal of the U.S. Army War College* 8, No. 4 (1979): 16–27.

———. "The Quality of Troop Leadership in Soviet and American Armies." FII/OACSI. Washington, D.C., July 1980.

——— and Savage, Paul L. *Crisis in Command: Mismanagement in the Army*. New York: Hill and Wang, 1978.

————. "The Environment of Leadership." *Military Review* (July 1980): 55-64.

Goldrich, Robert L. "Historical Continuity in the U.S. Military Reserve System." *Armed Forces and Society* (Fall 1980).

Heymont, Irving. "Can Reserve Units Be Ready on Time?" *Army* (March 1978): 23-26.

Ingraham, Larry H. "The Boys in the Barracks." Unpublished. Washington, D.C. Walter Reed Army Institute of Research, 1978.

Kinnard, Douglas. *The War Managers.* Hanover, N.H.: University Press of New England, 1977.

Moskos, Charles C. "Desertion Rates." Department of Defense Statistics, January 1981. (Per thousand listed personnel and FY 1979 by race and sex.)

————. "How to Save the All-Volunteer Force." *The Public Interest*, No. 61 (Fall 1980): 74-89.

Patton, George S., Jr. Letter to the Editor. *Army* (May 1981): 7.

Philpott, Tom. "U.S. Combat Capability Given Low Marks." *Army Times* (October 6, 1980).

Pirie, Robert, Jr. "Why Military Aptitude Tests Really Do Matter." *Armed Forces Journal* (July 1981): 70.

Smith, Paul. "Military, Civilian Rates Parallel: Survey Shows Extent of Drug, Alcohol Use." *Army Times* (December 15, 1980): 4 and 68.

Sorley, Lewis. "Turbulence at the Top: Our Peripatetic Generals." *Army* (March 1981): 14-24.

Toomepeau, Juri. *Soldier Capability and Army Combat Effectiveness.* Washington, D.C.: U.S. Army Recruiting Command, 1980.

U.S. Comptroller General. *Critical Manpower Problems Restrict the Use of National Guard and Reserve Forces.* Washington, D.C., U.S. General Accounting Office, July 11, 1979.

U.S. General Accounting Office. "Attrition in the Military." February 20, 1980, pp. 10-12.

————. "AWOL in the Military: A Serious and Costly Problem." Report to the Congress. FPCD-79-52, March 30, 1979.

————. Report by the Comptroller General of the United States. "An Overview of the Manpower Effectiveness of the All-Volunteer Force." (Unclassifed sections used only), April 14, 1980.

Westbrook, Stephen D. "The Alienated Soldier: Legacy of Our Society." *Army* (December 1979): 18-23.

Canada

Charles Cotton

Canada's land forces remain unique among the armies of advanced industrial nations. The Canadian "Army" is an integral part of the unified and integrated Canadian forces. It shares a common terminology, rank system, uniform, initial and advanced training establishments, and headquarters superstructure with the air and sea components of the military in Canada. Defense arrangements in Canada have been in a state of continual evolution since unification was embarked upon in the mid-1960s, but the last few years have been characterized by increasing stability in the land force, with the regimental system—inherited from historical associations with the British Army—providing the institutional bedrock.[1]

A number of difficulties confront the analyst who would describe and evaluate the Canadian Army as it is now constituted. First, the concept has not been tested in battle, as Canada's last major operation was in the Korean War. Second, it is not always easy to define the structural relationships involved in planning, personnel, and financial functions (as opposed to combat) associated with the army, since these functions are coordinated at higher levels by National Defence Headquarters in Ottawa. Third, because of the unification of the Canadian military, the number of formal positions in the army does not necessarily reflect the number of army personnel, especially in the combat-support and support roles of the land force. Theoretically at least, the support personnel in Canada's military are employable and deployable in all three operational environments. This fundamental facet of a unified force concept can create strains which might undermine the cohesion of operational units. Notwithstanding these complexities in analysis, however, this chapter provides a descriptive evaluation of Canada's land forces.

The views and opinions expressed in this article are those of the author and do not in any way represent the official views and policies of the Canadian Department of National Defense or the Royal Military College of Canada.

Canada's military traditions have been largely influenced by her hinterland status to three great empires: the French prior to 1763; the British from 1763 to 1945; and, most recently, the American since the end of World War II. The institutional characteristics of the Canadian army are, to a considerable extent, the product of Canada's long association with Britain (first as a colony and later as an active member of the Commonwealth) and the collective defense arrangements which developed in the Cold War and detente era. From the British connection came an army culture and institutions centered on the regimental system, as well as an abiding distinction between professional soldiers and a territorially based citizen militia. Since World War II, the professional segment of the army has expanded as Canada's standing commitment to collective defense has increased.

Before the Cold War, Canada relied mainly on the maintenance of a small regular army and a militia to meet her requirements for land defense. For much of the period from 1867 to the onset of World War II, the militia, although comparatively large in numbers, was poorly trained and equipped. In 1939, for example, the regular army consisted of 4,169 men in all ranks, while the militia consisted of 51,418 in all ranks.[2] The onset of major conflicts in 1914 and 1939 caught Canada unprepared for major land operations, but it was in these two conflicts that Canadian troops earned an international reputation for combat-effectiveness.

In World War I, Canada fielded a corps of four divisions which fought on the Western Front and which earned a reputation as an effective assault force on the basis of its performance at Vimy Ridge. A total of 619,636 men and women served in the Canadian Army in World War I, with casualties totaling 59,544 killed and 172,950 wounded. In World War II, Canada produced a field army of five divisions which fought in Northwest Europe and which shared in the stiff fighting in Italy in 1943-1945, and from France into Germany in 1944-1945. At its height, the Canadian Army in World War II totaled 730,625 men and women, 22,917 of whom were killed and 52,679 wounded.[3]

With the onset of the Cold War, the Canadian government opted for a peacetime standing army much larger than that of the past. The size of the army more than doubled between 1950 and 1953, rising from 20,652 to 48,458, with most members having had combat experience in World War II.[4] During the Korean conflict, Canada deployed an infantry brigade to Korea. Since that time, no Canadian troops have been involved in major combat operations, although there have been a number of deployments involved with peacekeeping forces of the United Nations (UN). The size of the army has shrunk since the 1950s. At the present time, approximately 29,000 of the 82,000 members of the Canadian forces can be classified as army, although the number of troops in actual field formations is smaller.[5]

Voluntary Recruitment

All personnel in the Canadian Army, regardless of regular or reserve status, serve on a voluntary basis. The same applies to all other segments of the Canadian forces. With the exception of limited conscription in the two world wars of this century, Canada has consistently recruited her military manpower on a voluntary basis. (Even limited conscription created severe strains with the country in both wars.) It is highly unlikely that any government will introduce some form of compulsory military service, or national service, in the foreseeable future, and Canadian military planners have learned to live with the vagaries of an all volunteer force.[6]

The acceptance of voluntary recruitment and participation within the Canadian community affects the army more than the other two segments of the armed forces, although higher personnel costs generally draw funds away from equipment procurement. The combat arms have consistently experienced problems of manpower supply, since combat trades are not a popular career choice for the youth of an affluent industrial democracy. Attrition in the army generally, and especially in the combat arms, remains a destabilizing factor in the readiness and cohesion of operational land units. A more subtle process is also involved: the need to be "attractive" to recruits exerts pressures toward the convergence of army institutional practices with the wider society. Canadian Army leaders, aware of these consistent but subtle pressures, retain a collective concern that operational considerations have priority.[7]

Another salient feature of the Canadian situation involves that nation's dual language and culture: in Canada, French and English have equal status in law. This culture is formally recognized within the military, and Canadian soldiers have the opportunity to pursue careers in their mother tongue. In some units of the army, French is the working language, and one of the three brigade-sized groups in Canada is a French formation. The nucleus of the French segment of the army is found in the Royal 22 Regiment, the "Van Doos," with a home station in La Citadelle, Quebec City. Currently, three battalions of this regiment are on active regular service with the Canadian Army.

There are no indications that the cultural and linguistic duality within the Canadian Army undermines its cohesiveness or political effectiveness, despite the fact that separatist tendencies are apparent in the wider society, especially in Quebec, the home province of most French units. In training and staff functions, officers and NCOs of both languages work side by side, using, for the most part, English as the working language. Most courses and training manuals are available in both official languages. Again, the costs of this duplication draw funds from equipment procurement, but the social and political rationale for it is almost without exception accepted by Canadian military personnel.

Civilian Control

Civilian control of the military in Canada is taken for granted, and the army, along with other segments of the military, is responsive to civilian political control, consistent with its British heritage. This control extends beyond strategic decisions regarding force size and deployment to such matters as unification, the employment of women, and the linguistic issue mentioned above. Simply put, the army is responsive and loyal to Canada's parliamentary authority. Its internal political role in Canadian society is minimal, and its use internally is reserved for situations when civilian authorities perceive they cannot maintain social order in specific areas. Occasionally, army units are "called out" to quell prison riots, or to fight forest fires and floods under the umbrella of "aid to civil power." The most significant recent involvement of army units in the internal life of Canadian society occurred in 1970 when the federal government invoked the War Measures Act and deployed several army units in central Canada as a result of incidents by a group of radical Quebec separatists. During this situation, the so-called October Crisis, army units showed a high degree of restraint and professionalism, a consequence, perhaps, of extensive experience in U.N. peacekeeping operations.

The Canadian Army does not have an active role in nation-building at the present time, although it does get involved in fighting national disasters. It does some work in developing the transportation infrastructure of the isolated northern regions of the nation, but this is not a principal role. In the early stages of Canada's history, however, the army did play an important role in national development.[8]

Recent Combat Experience

As mentioned earlier, Canadian troops have not been involved in combat operations since the Korean war when Canada deployed a brigade group as part of the 1st Commonwealth Division in the United Nations force. One unit distinguished itself in protecting the withdrawal route through the Kap'yong Valley in April 1951, the 2nd Battalion Princess Patricia's Canadian Light Infantry. For their stand, they were awarded a U.S. Presidential Unit Citation, a badge they continue to wear today.

Overall, the Canadian performance in Korea upheld the image of Canadian units as cohesive and effective military formations that could most usefully employ a part of larger multinational formations. In spite of a large land mass, Canada has a small population. Yet, three decades have passed without the army being involved in active combat operations. In three decades it has shrunk in size to the point where it is hard pressed to meet its commitments.

Composition

The regular land component of the Canadian forces consists of two separate formations, both of which are under the command and control of National Defence Headquarters in Ottawa: *Mobile Command*, with headquarters in Saint Hubert, Quebec, consisting of just over 17,000 personnel; and the *land element of Canadian Forces Europe*, with headquarters in Lahr, Southern Germany, consisting of 3,200 personnel in a mechanized brigade group. Mobile Command is, essentially, the army component of the Canadian forces, and it maintains the training establishments oriented specifically toward land warfare, notably, the Combat Training Center in Gagetown, New Brunswick. Personnel in deployed units in Germany receive their initial training and experience in Mobile Command, which provides the manpower source for the brigade in Germany. Although units rotated to Germany before unification, the tendency in the past decade has been to go with individual, or small group, rotation on an as-required basis. The potential negative effects of this practice are offset to some extent by the fact that brigade combat units in Germany are affiliated with regiments stationed in Canada.

In addition to these two major army formations, there is a reserve militia which contained 14,727 personnel in 1980. Militia units are dispersed throughout the country and are recruited locally, although, increasingly, the regular force is controlling leadership development in reserve units. The militia units are under the control of the commander, Mobile Command. Although nominally designated as "Regiments," most of the 198 militia units in Canada are approximately the size of a reinforced company. In the event of a large-scale war, however, they would provide an infrastructure for mobilization of a much larger force.

The militia in Canada is closely linked to regular force elements. It is organized into five areas across the country, with regulars supporting militia staff at area headquarters. Its de facto role is to enhance the deterrence capabilities of the regular force and to support its ongoing tasks and activities. It is not seen as a potentially effective fighting force, but rather as a manpower pool for the regular units. In 1980, for example, militia personnel were serving in many regular positions in Mobile Command, including fifty militia personnel who were in Cyprus to augment a regular artillery unit (5e Regiment d'artillerie légère du Canada). The militia also supports and augments units in Germany: in 1980, 179 militia personnel participated in field exercises in Germany on a "fly-over" basis.[9] This support role of militia units represents a significant change from the historical pattern where the small regular component supported a large citizen militia. It effectively means that Canada's modern militia is not, by itself, a deployable, combat-effective force of any consequence.

Mobile Command, commanded by a lieutenant-general, constitutes the army in Canada and controls all maneuver combat units outside of those deployed in Germany. The commander of Mobile Command is defined as the head of the army. The command consists of three major brigade-sized formations and of close air support units which are under the operational control of Mobile Command. Two of the formations are designated as 1 Canadian Brigade Group (1CBG), located in Calgary, Alberta, and 5e Groupe-Brigade du Canada (5eGBC), located in Valcartier, Quebec. As the nomenclature indicates, the first is an English formation, and the second, French. The third formation, designated as the Special Service Force, differs from the other two in its makeup and employment. It is located centrally in Petawawa, Ontario. Each formation is commanded by a brigadier-general. In addition to these major formations, Mobile Command includes two training units: the Combat Training Center in Gagetown, New Brunswick, which provides virtually all specialized land combat training; and the Canadian Airborne Center in Edmonton, Alberta, which trains personnel in airborne operations including paratroopers.

Each of the two basic brigade groups in Canada has a balance of three infantry battalions, one armored regiment, one artillery regiment, one combat engineer regiment, a combat service (support) battalion, and a combat signals squadron. Each also includes a tactical helicopter squadron for close air support. The infantry units consist of battalions of regiments which represent the career affiliation of their members, a virtual copy of the British regimental system.

The configuration of the Special Service Force is basically the same as the brigade groups described above, except that the infantry component of the force consists of three commandos of the Canadian Airborne Regiment (CAR), as well as one standard infantry battalion of approximately 650 of all ranks. The CAR is an air mobile and air droppable force which can be used as a "quick reaction" force in isolated settings and in U.N. scenarios. The entire force is considered airportable, and thus units are typically equipped on a lighter scale than those of the two standard brigades. In addition, components of the artillery, engineers, and logistics support units in the Special Service Force are trained in airborne operations.

In addition to the three brigade-type formations, Mobile Command in Canada contains the 1st Canadian Signals Regiment (1CSR) located in Kingston, Ontario. This unit provides the infrastructure of command communications, and is separate from the three major maneuver formations. The signals regiment would provide the support for a task force headquarters if one were to be deployed outside Canada. It is co-located in Kingston with the Canadian forces training school for communications.

The combat-support ratio in Mobile Command is very close to 1:1 (see Table 7). As Table 7 shows, 47 percent of the command is composed of combat troops, with 53 percent support. Interestingly, only 10.1 percent of

Table 7
Canadian Combat[a] and Support Personnel, Mobile Command, 1979

Category	Number	Percent
Combat officers	930	5.3
Support officers	858	4.8
Combat enlisted	7,322	41.7
Support enlisted	8,448	48.2
TOTAL	17,558	100.0

[a] Includes armor, artillery, and infantry.

Source: Charles A. Cotton, *Military Attitudes and Values of the Army in Canada*, Canadian Forces Personnel Applied Research Unit, Report 79-5 (Toronto, 1979) p. 44.

the command are officers. In actual units this percentage would, of course, be lower, as many of the officers are in headquarters staff positions.

The second major land formation in the Canadian forces is 4 Canadian Mechanized Brigade Group (4CMBG) of some 3,200 troops, with its headquarters in Lahr, Southern Germany. It represents the land component of Canadian Forces Europe (CFE), a land and air formation under the direct control of National Defence Headquarters in peacetime. In the event of war, however, operational control of the overall force would be transferred to NATO. In the case of 4CMBG, operational control would pass to the Commander Central Army Group (CENTG), and 4CMBG would in all likelihood form a reserve in one of the two southern corps of CENTAG.

The brigade in Germany is fully mechanized and manned with experienced troops at all levels. Its basic structure is similar to the standard brigades within Canadian territory under Mobile Command control. The only significant difference is that it contains one less infantry battalion, having two compared to the three in Canadian home brigades. As of 1980, 4CMBG comprised the following units (see Table 8). With the exception of an additional infantry battalion, the structure of 4CMBG is similar to that of the brigades in Canada described above.

The units of 4CMBG remain permanently in Germany, and individual personnel are rotated to fill positions, with the standard tour length being two years. Comparatively speaking, the Canadian contribution to NATO in Germany is quite small, a situation which has prompted some to observe that Canada is not pulling its weight in this area, in either numbers of troops deployed or equipment. In the past five years, however, the Canadian government has made a serious effort to increase capital spending on new equipment. In the army's case, the most notable purchase has been the reequipping of the armor unit in Germany with the German Leopard tank.

Current operational planning in the event of a crisis period in Europe is

Table 8
4 CMBG Units, by Type and Number of Personnel, Canadian Army, 1980

Type	Unit	Personnel
Artillery	1st Regiment, Royal Canadian Horse Artillery	500
Armor	Royal Canadian Dragoons	450
Engineers	4 Combat Engineer Regiment	190
Communications	4CMBG Headquarters and Signal Squadron	200
Infantry	3rd Battalion, Royal Canadian Regiment	570
	1st Battalion, Royal 22 Régiment	570
Services	4 Service Battalion	500
Medical	4 Field Ambulance	100
Police	4 Military Police Platoon	80
Air support	444 Tactical Helicopter Squadron	90

for an augmentation of 4CMBG with an additional 2,400 troops from Canada. The troops are identified and deployable at short notice, but there may be problems with this concept as a recent Senate review of defense manpower in Canada has indicated.[10] Canada has never fully carried out a test of augmentation plans aimed at manning the units in Germany to their full operational levels. It may prove very difficult to transport designated troops in Canada to Germany during an emerging crisis. At the same time, the augmentation deployment of Canadian-based troops to 4CMBG during a crisis would reduce the numbers at home, which could prove a problem if Canadian territory were also threatened.

Weaponry

Canadian troops have long received high marks for professionalism and training, and low marks for their equipment. This situation is changing slowly as the government continues a program of reequipping the military which it began in the late 1970s. Most of the major items of equipment in the Canadian army are procured from foreign sources since Canada does not have an industrial infrastructure for major weapons systems. Some equipment is manufactured in Canada under license, and most of the soldiers' personal equipment is procured in Canada.

As a general rule, the units in Germany (4CMBG) receive priority in equipment allocations. The brigade in Germany remains the most mechanized of the four brigade-sized formations in the Canadian Army, but that level of mechanization is a matter of degree rather than type. The basic inventory of equipment in the Canadian Army remains relatively standard across formations, and is outlined in Table 9.

Table 9
Basic Equipment in Canada's Army

Type	Equipment
Artillery	• 105mm L5 pack howitzer (Italy) used in airborne airportable roles • 105mm C1 (M1A1) towed howitzer—Canadian base units • 155mm M109 (USA) self-propelled howitzer—NATO unit
Armor	• Leopard C1 medium tanks, deployed in NATO unit • Lynx AFV (M113 ½ USA), reconnaissance • Cougar AFV, combat fire support in Canadian-based units • Grizzly APC, new acquisition for mechanized infantry • APC, M113 (USA) mechanized infantry, used in NATO units
Anti-aircraft	• Blowpipe LLAD SAM (UK) • 40mm Bofors (Sweden), used in air defense in NATO base
Support weapons	• Mortar—81mm L5 (UK) • Heavy machinegun—0.50 Browning HB M2 (USA) • Heavy anti-tank—106mm M40 A1 recoilless rifle (USA); SS11 ATGM (France); TOW (USA), main system in use
Small arms	• Pistol—9mm Browning (Belgium, made in Canada) • Submachine gun—9mm Stirling (UK, made in Canada) • Rifle/automatic rifle—7.62mm NATO FN/C1 (Belgium, made in Canada) • General purpose MG—7.62mm Browning 1919 (USA) • Light anti-tank—66mm LAW (USA) • Medium anti-tank—84mm Carl Gustaf (Sweden)
Aircraft support	• Observation helicopter—CF 136 Kiowa (USA) • Tactical transport—CH 135 Twin Huey (USA) • Medium helicopter—CH 147 Chinook (USA) • Tactical fighter—Northrup CF5 (USA)

As a general rule, minor items of army equipment are manufactured within Canada, either from Canadian designs (clothing is a case in point) or under license from foreign manufacturers. Major items in the equipment inventory, however, are typically bought off the shelf from foreign sources, since Canada does not have a major arms industry. This approach might make resupply problematic in the event of major operations, although all equipment is derived from reliable NATO sources. Canada does not have a large inventory to replenish the equipment of units committed to war.

Typically, units are equipped with the available equipment, and a limited reserve is maintained. In short, the equipment is procured for a standing army, and not in terms of a mobilization establishment scale.

Canadian troops are completely equipped with mechanized transport, either of the tracked or wheeled variety. The degree of armor protection for troops varies from unit to unit, as well as within units, since, apart from the NATO brigade, infantry units may have one or two mechanized APC companies, with others equipped with light trucks. One of the priorities in land equipment procurement in the past few years has been to update troop transport capabilities in the army. To this end, new light trucks and heavy 5-ton trucks of American design, built in Canada, have been procured.

Overall, equipment procurement for the Canadian Army has increased in the past five years, but budgeting restrictions coupled with rising personnel costs have limited the number of items purchased in each instance. This perhaps is one of the deepest dilemmas of the all volunteer force; personnel costs continually drain away funds from the purchase of needed equiment. The country may reach a point where the technology in place is inadequate to the professional competence of the troops using it. Frustrations can set in, as highly trained troops are confronted with outdated equipment, causing many to leave the military. This attrition raises personnel costs, and thus the vicious circle is complete. This problem has been recognized in recent years, however, and the reequipment of the army, as well as the air and sea components, has been given priority.

Employment Scenarios

The Canadian Army is primarily trained and equipped to participate in high-intensity operations on the Central and Northern Fronts of the NATO European theater. In its organizational format, tactics, and equipment, it is designed to articulate with the larger NATO formations in which it will participate in the event of an outbreak of hostilities. It is unlikely that Canadian troops will become involved in high-intensity operations on their own soil, given the fact that a land invasion of Canada is highly improbable in the current strategic climate. (In any event, Canada does not have enough troops to defend her large land mass.) Beyond operational employment of Canadian troops in NATO operations, the Canadian Army is likely to be committed to peacekeeping duties with the United Nations and, to a lesser extent, to internal security operations within Canada. Both of these employment scenarios are of the low-intensity variety, involving minimal force.

NATO Scenarios

At the present time, Canadian troops are slated to participate in NATO operations in two separate sectors: the Central Front; and north Norway, or the northern flank of NATO. The commitment to the Central Front—4CMBG augmented by an additional 2,400 troops—has already been described above. The Canadians would form part of the strategic reserve in CENTAG, assuming that augmentees could be airlifted into Germany without difficulty. The size of the Canadian commitment to the NATO Central Front is a matter of some debate in Canada, and a recent Senate review recommended that the number of troops committed be increased to approximately 10,000 by 1987.[11]

Canada also maintains a force of some 4,000 troops for employment in north Norway. This force is designated the CAST force, for Canadian Air-Sea Transportable force, and is largely composed of elements from the Special Service Force based in central Canada. All troops allocated to the CAST force are "multi-tasked," that is, they also have other commitments within Mobile Command. One example of this conflicting tasking lies in the fact that one of the battalion groups in the force is also Canada's contribution to the ACE (Allied Command Europe) Mobile Force. This unit is stationed in Canada like the remainder of the CAST force, but would be flown into Denmark if Warsaw Pact forces attacked Denmark first before Norway. It would be withdrawn from Denmark and committed to Norway if subsequent developments led to combat in Norway. Either way, the commitment would be reduced since troops cannot be fighting on two fronts at the same time.

The recent Senate review of defense manpower in Canada raised questions about the viability of the CAST force as a strategic concept for Canada. Although one segment of the CAST force is airportable and air droppable, with a fair prospect of reaching positions before Soviet forces could occupy them, the remainder must be transported by sea and has a lower probability of deploying to the combat zone in sufficient time. There is doubt, too, that sea transportation would be adequate in a crisis situation.

Despite these limitations, the CAST force components are regularly involved in exercise in Norway and in Canada's North. For example, 1,200 Canadian troops participated in exercise "Alloy Express" in northern Norway during March 1982. The primary arms units involved from Canada were from the Special Service Force and included an infantry battalion, as well as artillery, helicopter, and logistics units, representing Canada's Armed Mobile Force (AMF) commitment. Canadian troops are trained in winter warfare as a matter of course, and they adapt readily to the NATO northern flank environment.

Peacekeeping Operations

Canadian troops have extensive experience in low-intensity UN peacekeeping operations,[12] but not all of it is satisfactory from a Canadian viewpoint. Although combat troops remain committed to UN operations in Cyprus, the tendency in recent years has been for Canada to provide the technical and logistics expertise for operations, while less developed nations provide combat troops. This has been the case in the Middle East in the past few years.

Peacekeeping represents a peculiar form of military employment, one which troops trained for more intense combat operations adapt to without great difficulty. It is an important strategic activity for Canada since, in the longer term, a stable world order is in the national interest. It also has other outcomes which help to exercise and motivate the members of a peacetime force, for it has provided Canadian troops with a foreign deployment of a quasi-operational post. But it should be remembered that peacekeeping is not combat, and the experience gained is not likely to be transferrable.

Some Canadian troops will likely continue to be deployed under the UN flag, although Canada is becoming increasingly sensitive to further requests for troop commitments. (The frustrating deployment of Canadian observers to Vietnam did little to offset this sensitivity.) It would seem that peacekeeping, which had its heyday in the 1960s, will increasingly take second priority to the NATO focus in the coming years.

Internal Security

As already noted, Canadian troops do not play a large role in the maintenance of social order within Canada. Outside of the October Crisis of 1970, large numbers of troops have not been employed in this capacity in recent years. Canada is, relatively speaking, an extremely stable democracy, with a history of military subordination to civil control. It is unlikely that internal security operations will be an important employment scenario for Canadian troops in the coming decade.

This low probability is important from another point of view: if all Canadian troops designated for deployment with NATO forces were actually put into the field into Europe, there would be precious few troops left behind to guard the homefront. Those remaining would number no more than two battalion-sized groups, numerically incapable of internal security operations on a significant scale. This points up the essential problem with Canada's army: the number of troops available is inadequate to meet the existing paper commitments. The problem is not one of quality but rather of quantity.

Quality of Manpower

Overall, Canadian Army personnel are highly trained volunteers with a reputation for military professionalism within NATO. On an individual basis, they are among the best trained, best paid, and most motivated professional troops in the Western Alliance. The basic problem is that there are too few of them to make more than a marginal contribution to collective defense in the West.

Troops

Canadian combat troops serve an initial engagement of three years, and the recruitment of sufficient numbers of combat arms troops has been a consistent personnel problem in the 1970s. Recruits are assigned to a regiment, and, typically, their regimental affiliation remains with them as long as they remain in the combat arms, including later phases (if they remain) at the NCO level. Attrition is a perennial problem, and trained troops are lost early in their career. Figures for the 1970s indicate that the five-year retention rate for combat arms troops was approximately 22 percent.[13]

The recruitment and retention of combat arms soldiers have received considerable attention from army leaders and from National Defence Headquarters in Ottawa. A new plan was introduced in 1976 whereby combat recruits were offered the opportunity to enter a technical or logistics support trade after a three-year stint in the combat arms. (Canadian youth find employment in noncombat specialties a much more attractive option.) A nucleus of combat leaders is retained and is given accelerated promotion under this plan, which is proving effective in helping to man the combat arms.

One of the continuing concerns at the troop level in units is personnel instability, a situation that weakens the cohesion of units. This instability is partly the result of the higher attrition rates noted above and partly the result of the individualized training system which is the norm in the Canadian forces. Army officers, aware of the negative impact of personnel instability and individualized training, have taken steps to increase unit stability and collective training.[14] In fact, leaders at all levels are concerned with the development and maintenance of cohesion. In this situation, the stabilization of leader-led relationships is seen as a critical focus for manpower policies,[15] since leader instability weakens the motivation of junior troops.

Another current problem centers on the motivation of support troops for service in a land combat-support role. Support personnel in the unified forces have an opportunity to serve in all three operational environments, as well as on static support bases which serve all types of units. Research has shown that, given a choice, most support troops would prefer service in a nonland setting,[16] and the supply of combat-oriented support troops, including officers, has been recognized as a problem in Canada. (Interestingly, former combat troops reassigned to support elements are motivated for army service.) Increasingly, personnel slated for land service are given indoctrination and training in army philosophy and tactics. Canadians are coming to see that the image of a support tradesman who can function effectively in land, air, and sea is an impractical concept for a modern force.

While at the very junior troop levels, there are problems of career motivation and attrition, the mainstay of the Canadian Army is its nucleus of experienced and highly motivated career NCOs who provide key elements of continuity and training resources within regimental life. The career NCOs are, in many respects, the backbone of the army and its disciplinarians. Research has shown that this group exhibits a vocational orientation to military service, as well as strong identification with the regimental system which provides the social infrastructure of Canada's army.[17] There is a tendency to promote younger troops to the NCO ranks these days, but NCOs typically have more than twelve years of service. Training for senior NCOs (including warrant officers) is systematic and intense, and produces a highly qualified unit leader.

Within combat units, the top NCO occupies the role of regimental sergeant major, the individual who maintains discipline with units and advises the commanding officer on matters related to the troops. This role, derived from the historical affiliation with Britain, is a key one in maintaining unit cohesion and represents the culmination of the enlisted career ladder.

Overall, Canadian military policy focuses on structural avenues to increase unit cohesion and operational motivation. Included are policies concerned with socialization into unit life, collective training, and the rotation of subunits rather than individuals. These concerns confront the leadership of all Western volunteer armies, and only time will tell whether the problems of recruitment, attrition, and junior troop career motivation will be reduced to manageable levels in the future. The leaders of Canada's army have recognized the problems, however, and are taking steps to deal with them.

Officers

The less than 2,000 combat arms officers in the Canadian Army are intensively socialized in the regimental ethos, even though some of their training occurs in unified training schools. Early training and experiences center on units, and these influence their collective self-image and role orientation. They define themselves as professional soldiers, and they display a vocational orientation toward military service. Collectively, their professional concern centers on the operational integrity of Canada's land forces, and they are generally negative toward civilianizing trends in the wider Canadian military.[18]

Training for officership occurs both in unified training institutions and in uniquely army institutions. Initial training for all officers in the Canadian forces occurs at the Canadian Forces Officer Candidate School in British Columbia, where general military knowledge and skills for all officers are imparted. Subsequent to this schooling, combat arms training for officers takes place at the Combat Training Center in New Brunswick. Following completion of training in an arm, the first posting of the junior officer is to an operational unit, where he occupies a junior leadership role at the platoon or troop level. Subsequent training is intended to equip him for more advanced combat leadership roles and/or staff duties. Staff training for army-oriented officers is given at the Canadian Forces Land Command and Staff College in Kingston, Ontario, where captains and majors take an intensive six-month course in all aspects of land warfare. Completion of this course is the basic prerequisite for advanced duties in army settings, and participants include support officers as well as combat arms officers.

Further staff training is taken at the Canadian Forces Command and Staff College (CFCSC) in Toronto, where majors from all segments of Canada's unified force undertake a year-long course designed to equip them for higher level staff and command responsibilities in the military. Individuals with an army background take a land segment within the course, along with a common segment for all students. Selection for this course is competitive and is a prerequisite for further promotion. Selected Canadians take equivalent courses in other countries, while there are a number of foreign students in the Toronto CFCSC course.

The final level of formal officer staff training occurs at the colonel level and involves a year's course at the National Defence College, which, incidentally, is co-located with the Army Staff College in Kingston. Students in this course include a number of civilians from government, academia, and the private sector. Attendance of the National Defence College course is typically the prerequisite for subsequent promotion to general officer status.

The formal, that is, staff, training of Canadian officers parallels that given in other Western societies, notably the United States. The formal training, however, complements regimental unit-level socialization and employment which provides the stable center of the combat officer's career. In this setting, critical values are shaped and reinforced, and Canadian officers remain firmly committed to the continual requirement for regimental loyalties in a modern bureaucratic force. Regimental insignia are worn up to, and including, the rank of colonel, and at various stages in the officer's career he will return to employment in a field unit. This provides the infrastructure for the development of collective solidarities, as well as for cohesion between NCOs and officers, since both groups interact continually over the career life cycle. It is not uncommon, for example, for a unit commanding officer and regiment sergeant major to have begun life together as a platoon leadership team fifteen years earlier. Thus, officership for the combat arms officer is inextricably linked to the collective fate of the members of a particular regiment.

Partly because of the centrality of regimental affiliation in Canada's army, individualization and careerism do not seem to be pervasive among officers. Since the officer is linked together through time with NCOs and troops, the calculative individual becomes recognized early on. The result is a relatively cohesive collection of units, officered by a group of individuals who take their professional responsibilities seriously, and who find social supports for their professional identity within the boundaries of regimental life.

Combat arms officers in the Canadian Army share a consensus that their primary concern is training for warfare, and thus they, as a group, consider the army's operational effectiveness to be the primary criterion in policy development and training. The role of the combat officer as leader is central to his self-conception, and in recent years a number of documents and symposia have been produced which deal with the process and ethics of combat leadership. Combat officers are sensitive to the dysfunctional consequences of civilianization for combat-effectiveness, and the combat development process in Canada's army has, as one of its fundamental assumptions, the proposition that army combat institutions must be unique and differentiated from civilian life-styles and managerial assumptions.[19] In short, there is a great deal of concern with sustaining a unique army ethos within Canada. For example, a conference of all serving army generals on the "Army Ethos" was held in Quebec City in April 1981.

If combat arms officers in the Canadian Army exhibit a high degree of corporateness and professionalism oriented toward land combat, there is more ambivalence evident among support officers. Support officers are members of the unified functional support classifications in the Canadian forces, and as such they are liable for service in land, air, *and* sea environments. Recent research has shown that a significant minority of support officers serving in army settings do not identify with service in land operational settings.[20] At times, this bifurcation in attitudes can create underlying strains in the army's daily life and might reduce its cohesion in actual combat operations. This phenomenon has been recognized, and steps have been taken to increase the land indoctrination and training among segments of the support classifications liable for service in land environments. Until they reach senior rank levels, the identified segments typically serve in land units, and their training is oriented to that end. They do, for example, attend the CFCSC course described above.

Overall, Canadian Army officers exhibit a collective concern with the maintenance of a distinctive army ethos within the structural context provided by the regimental system. They are proving resistant to the incorporation of managerial jargon and fads from industrial psychology into land combat practices and doctrine, although they are receptive to technical advice from graduate-trained specialists in the behavioral services. The combat arms officers are supported in these concerns by the long-service NCOs who share regimental affiliations with them. At the leadership level, there are apparently no major weaknesses in the Canadian Army.

Conclusions

This profile of Canada's volunteer land force has examined a number of critical dimensions: size, organization, deployment, equipment, culture, and quality of troops and leaders. Canada's army remains unique among the armies of industrial nations of either the Eastern or Western blocs, in that it is part of a fully unified and integrated military system, adopted in the 1960s. To date, the concept has not been tested in battle, nor have other nations adopted the Canadian concept of a single unified force serving in three distinct operational environments. Perhaps only battle will provide the critical data to fully evaluate the military validity of the Canadian concept. In the interim, Canadians have been professionally engaged in the fine tuning of their defense arrangements. There is no doubt that there have been institutional "growing pains," but accommodations have been made to the unique contingencies of each environment.

Canada's small volunteer army exhibits a high degree of professionalism, expecially in its leadership cadres, and, increasingly, a renewed corporate identity founded upon a longstanding regimental tradition. A distinctive army ethos has been retained and solidified during the more than fifteen years since unification was enacted. The army's strengths include its continuing reliance on traditional concepts of leadership, service, and organizational style. Despite the erosive impacts of civilianization and prolonged peace, the army retains the elements of a cohesive, combat-oriented force. It has taken time to articulate and implement this model in the context of a liberal society at peace and a unified military system, but the prognosis is good.

Other strong points of the army are its leadership cadre, at both the officer and NCO level, its professional esprit and training, and its institutional infrastructure. These qualities will continue to be the foundations of Canadian Army professionalism in the coming decades. Its weaker points are also likely to continue into the future. These are a lack of numbers and of major items of land combat equipment, and problems of recruitment, retention, and motivation at the junior troop level. In some respects, this same list confronts the three major Western volunteer armies in Canada, Britain, and the United States. The cost of combat personnel for the standing detente force draws fiscal resources away from capital equipment procurement, and the tendency in the long run is to reduce troop strength. In the long run, one moves toward fewer but better paid troops. They are not, however, necessarily better motivated. For one thing, they are likely to be stretched thin in relation to commitments, and frustration can result.

In the future, Canadians will have to confront these areas and make critical decisions at the highest levels of force management and the political arena. The choice between troops and equipment is, in some respects, a chronic issue for military planners. It will also be necessary to balance the criterion of operational integrity against the incentives and life-style pressures in attempting to meet manning levels for junior combat troops. The position of Canadian combat officers, however, is clear: the operational integrity of units has first priority in this area. The question that remains is whether a sufficient number of volunteers can be attracted into the land force.

A more difficult problem to be faced in the near future is the degree to which existing commitments can be met by the existing number of overextended troops and units. The recent Senate committee on military manpower confronted this issue and concluded that increases in troop strength and the number of units were of immediate necessity. Regardless of the quality of leadership and the degree to which heroic traditions remain an influence in the ongoing life of the army, numbers do count, as does the up-to-date material to equip them. It is in this regard that we find the really crucial issues which confront Canada's army as we move toward the year 2000. Given adequate troop and equipment levels, there is no doubt that the Canadian Army would be a first-rate land force, within the context of Canada's relatively small population.

Notes

1. See, for instance, C. A. Cotton, R. K. Crook, and F. C. Pinch, "Canada's Professional Military: The Limits of Civilianization," *Armed Forces and Society*, 4 (1978): 365-89. On the place of the regimental system in the Canadian Army, see D. Loomis, "The Regimental System," Mobile Command Headquarters, Saint Hubert, 1975.

2. Data taken from *Defence Canada 1980*, Department of National Defence, Ottawa, 1981, catalogue No. D3-6/1981, pp. 16-17. This publication has been issued annually for a number of years and is a good source of descriptive material on the organization of Canadian defense.

3. D. J. Goodspeed, *The Armed Forces of Canada 1867-1967*, Directorate of History, Canadian Forces Headquarters, Ottawa, 1967.

4. *Defence Canada 1980*, p. 17.

5. Standing Senate Committee on Foreign Affairs, *Manpower in Canada's Armed Forces* (Ottawa: Houses of Parliament, January 1982).

6. Cotton, Crook, and Pinch, "Canada's Professional Military." This article provides a useful overview of the structural characteristics of the unified force in Canada. Also see T. C. Willett, "The Military and Social Control in Canada," in R. J. Ossenberg, ed., *Power and Social Change in Canada* (Toronto: McClelland and Stewart, 1980.)

7. See, for example, the discussion in "The Development of Collective Training in the Army," *Canadian Defence Quarterly* 8, No. 1 (Summer 1978): 8-15. Also relevant is D. S. Loomis and D. T. Lightburn, "Taking into Account the Distinctness of the Military from the Mainstream of Society," *Canadian Defence Quarterly* 10, No. 2 (Autumn 1980).

8. Many of the early settlers were British troops. See Goodspeed, *The Armed Forces of Canada*, and G. Stanley, *Canada's Soldiers* (Toronto: MacMillan of Canada, 1974.)

9. *Defence Canada 1980*.

10. Standing Senate Committee on Foreign Affairs, *Manpower in Canada's Armed Forces*, pp. 19-20.

11. Ibid., p. 16.

12. See Paul Martin, *Canada and the Quest for Peace* (New York: Columbia University Press, 1967). Also see *Defence Canada* for various recent years, and J. H. Allan, "The Future of Peacekeeping for Canada," *Canadian Defence Quarterly* 8, No. 1 (Summer 1978).

13. Cotton, Crook, and Pinch, "Canada's Professional Military," Table 8.

14. See the sources cited in note 7 above.

15. On this point, see the data cited in Charles A. Cotton, *Military Attitudes and Values of the Army in Canada*, Canadian Forces Personnel Applied Research Unit, Report 79-5 (Toronto, 1979).

16. Ibid., pp. 40-43.

17. Ibid., Table 8, p. 58. The same degree of support is found at the officer level of the army.

18. Charles A. Cotton, "Institutional and Occupational Values in Canada's Army," *Armed Forces and Society* 8, No. 1 (Fall 1981): 99-110.

19. See the interview with Lieutenant General J. J. Paradis, commander of Mobile Command, in the *Calgary Herald*, January 9, 1980, p. E2. Paradis spoke out against civilianization of the Canadian Army and argued for a renewed concern with a vocational definition of soldiering. Also see Loomis and Lightburn, "Taking into Account the Distinctness of the Military from the Mainstream of Society."

20. Cotton, *Military Attitudes and Values of the Army in Canada*, Table 6, p. 42.

Bibliography

Burns, E.L.M. *Manpower in the Canadian Army*. Toronto: Clarke Irwin, 1956.

Byers, R. B., and Gray, C. *Canadian Military Professionalism: The Search for Identity*. Toronto: CIIA, 1973.

Cotton, C.A. "Institutional and Occupational Values in Canada's Army." *Armed Forces and Society* 8, No. 1 (Fall 1981): 99-110.

———, *Military Attitudes and Values of the Army in Canada*. Canadian Forces Personnel Applied Research Unit, Report 79-5. Toronto, 1979.

———, Crook, R. K., and Pinch, F. C. "Canada's Professional Military: The Limits of Civilianization." *Armed Forces and Society* 4 (1978): 365-81.

Dickey, J. *Canada and the American Presence*. New York: New York University Press, 1975.

Eyre, K. C., and Eyre, C. "Canada." In John Keegan, ed. *World Armies*. Facts on File. New York, 1979.

Goodspeed, D. J. *The Armed Forces of Canada 1867-1967*. Directorate of History, Canadian Forces Headquarters. Ottawa, 1967.

Gray, C. *Canadian Defence Priorities*. Toronto: Clarke Irwin, 1972.

Kellett, A. *Combat Motivation*. Operational Research and Analysis Establishment, ORAE Report R77. Ottawa, 1981.

Loomis, D. S. *The Regimental System*. Mimeographed. Mobile Command Headquarters Saint Hubert, 1975.

Porter, G. *In Retreat*. Toronto: Deneen and Greenberg, 1978.

Preston, A. "The Profession of Arms in Postwar Canada." *World Politics* (January 1970).

Senate of Canada. *Manpower in Canada's Armed Forces.* Report of Standing Senate
    Committee on Foreign Affairs. Ottawa: Houses of Parliament, January 1982.
Stanley, G. *Canada's Soldiers.* Toronto: MacMillan of Canada, 1974.
Willett, T. C. "The Military and Social Control in Canada." In R. J. Ossenberg, ed.
    Power and Social Change in Canada. Toronto: McClelland and Stewart, 1980.

England

Dominick Graham

Today's British Army is a professional force with strong regimental loyalties, excellent discipline based on self-respect, a noncommissioned elite, and energetic junior officers. For most of this century its peacetime strength, about 175,000 men, has been scattered across the world. Only in the last ten years has it been "brought home," though it still serves in many climes, albeit in small numbers. Compared to 1914, today the army has fewer infantry and more engineers and technicians. The seventy-five battalions in the Expeditionary Force of 1914 had been the marching corps of the army. There are now only fifty-six battalions in the army against more than double that number in 1914.

The army was not and never has been Britain's senior service. The British public has always thought of the navy as the nation's first line of defense. As a demonstration of naked power, the Dreadnought was much more impressive than the soporific stamp, jingle, and rattle of infantry columns on the march.

Except during the Battle of Britain, when they heard anti-aircraft gunners in action, even if they did not see them, civilians have only read about the deeds of their army. They have an offhand regard for it partly because for centuries it has only fought overseas. Thus, many of its famous campaigns, except in India, have depended on ships for transport and supply. It is not surprising, then, that in the legend about British strategy the hard-fought victories of Marlborough, Wellington, and Haig in continental Europe were sometimes regarded as a result of strategic miscalculations that might have been avoided. The proper strategy was to have the British provide ships, money, and supplies to its allies, preferably for cash, and, if need be, a small expeditionary force to fight in out of the way places against the enemy's second team.

How curious, then, that amphibious doctrine developed in war has been so quickly forgotten in peace. One reason for the amnesia on this subject was that, until 1908, neither the army nor the navy had a General Staff to record historical lessons, to evolve doctrine, and to make plans in peacetime.

In World War I, only the army had a General Staff. After discordant experience in strategic planning during this war, it was proposed that a single Ministry of Defense should replace the three separate ministries. In 1936, a minister for the coordination of defense was appointed to establish priorities during the early stages of rearmament. In April 1940, the prime minister, Winston Churchill, absorbed that minister's responsibilities and directed national defense himself. And although the direction of military strategy by the chiefs of staff committee under the chairmanship of the prime minister was satisfactory, each service was running the war from a separate ministry. After the war, in 1945, a minister of defense was responsible for strategy and for directing the budgeting of the three services. The defense minister's role and powers were progressively increased thereafter, until, in 1964, the Admiralty, War Office, and Air Ministry were combined in one ministry, and the responsibility for the central direction of the three services was given to one man with a joint services staff.

The British Army has always been a professional army. The public of a country that never conscripted its manpower for the army at least, in peace or war, willingly indulged its contempt for conscripts by praising its regulars. The army frowned on the idea of national service only because it did not have the resources to train a rotating reserve force as well as a force of seven divisions that was ready to go to war. Indeed, the funds and training cadres were insufficient to equip and train the Territorial Army—the successor to the militia and the volunteers—to a standard high enough for it to meet a first-class enemy unless a six-month breathing space were permitted after the outbreak of war. The British believe that their regulars are greatly superior to conscripts, and they are generally unimpressed with the way others train conscripts. They are quite aware that the German conscript receives as much training in two years as the British regular in four. They also know that on mobilization the army would have to absorb more than 60 percent of its war establishment in reserves.

Today's army has survived despite a protracted rear guard action during Britain's withdrawal from overseas. It has adopted new weapons and techniques while it suffered continued financial retrenchment, and it has performed as creditably in front of its allies, on exercises, as it has on its people's television screens in live action in Northern Ireland. It has become an integral part of a truly tri-service force. Table 10 lists the roles the army has played in various countries in the last twenty years. The table clearly demonstrates the army's experience as a fighting regular force.

The British Army was surprised by the militance and chaos of the postwar world. In the National Service Act of 1947, which became effective in January 1949, the focus was still mainly on the threat of war on the Continent rather than on irregular conflicts overseas. The act reflected a distorted understanding of what the British contribution had been in the past:

Rapid developments in modern warfare will rob the country of that breathing space—measured in years rather than months—by virtue of which alone in the past two wars it has been enabled to build up its war-like strength and thus overcome its enemies. There will no longer be six months to train the reserve.[1]

In its view, the national servicemen were to provide an immediate force in being in Europe while the regulars served overseas where combat duty was required. Circumstances were not to permit this arrangement.

The Korean War in June 1950 found an army already overextended and the country spending as much as was wise on defense. National service had to be extended to two years, reservists had to be called, and time-expired men retained. The forces that would have been run down to an all-service total of 0.682m by April 1951 had to be raised to 0.8m. It was calculated that defense expenditure would be quadrupled by 1953-1954. The army was to be built up to ten active and twelve reserve divisions. A decline in regular recruiting had been reversed partly by better pension conditions for those already serving, a new three-year engagement for those straight from the street, and pay increases. But it was no longer a matter of retraining veterans from the war but of attracting younger men from the labor force. The likelihood of combat was an attraction, but recruitment fell back almost to 1949 levels in 1951 only to double in 1952 to 53.2 thousand in response, perhaps, to the performance of the Commonwealth Division in Korea. The strength of the army was almost 350,000 in that year.[2]

The nuclear factor began to enter British strategic calculations in 1952. A year and a half after the first British atomic weapon was exploded in the Monte Bello Islands in 1952, a Defence Review observed that maintaining the technical lead over the Soviets was paramount and that in the future the Royal Air Force (RAF) and the research and development of guided weapons that would eventually deliver nuclear bombs would have priority over the army, on which expenditure would decline. It was the government's intention to return to long-term regular engagements for the force in Germany which would act as a tripwire that activated nuclear weapons. An all-regular army was also required to bring force to bear quickly in Cold War and limited war situations outside Europe.[3] This line of thought was taken further in 1957, after the fiasco at Suez had brought a change of government, although not a change of party. The truth was seen that Britain and France could no longer indulge in major operations against even a second-class foe, not because they could not win battles but because the Exchequer could not pay the rental fee.

A regrouping was attempted that would thin out British forces overseas.

Table 10
Roles of the British Army, 1961-1982

Serial	Date	Location	Event	Casualties
44	1961	KUWAIT	Support to Amir against threatened Iraqi invasion	
45	1961	BAHAMAS	Threat of invasion	
46	1961	ZANZIBAR	Elections. Aid to civil power	
47	1961	BELIZE	Hurricane Hattie. Aid to civil power	
48	1962	BELIZE	Belize Freedom Fighters—Guatemalan incursions	
49	1962	BRITISH GUIANA	Riots in Georgetown	
50	1962	HONG KONG	Refugees from China	
51	1962-1966*	BORNEO	Indonesian confrontation	
52	1963-1966*	MALAYSIA	Brunei disturbances	
53	1963	SKOPJE	Earthquake—Yugoslavia civil assistance	
54	1963-1966	SWAZILAND	Reinforcement—strikes	
55	1963	ZANZIBAR	Elections. Aid to civil power	
56	1963-to date*	CYPRUS	Greek-Turkish communal strife and UN operations	114 killed; 182 wounded
57	1963	BRITISH GUIANA	Communal riots and state of emergency (can count as two ops)	
58	1964	ZANZIBAR	Revolution	
59	1964	TANGANYIKA		
60	1964	UGANDA	Army mutinies (can count as one op)	
61	1964	KENYA		
62	1964-1967*	ADEN	Radfan ops and Aden terrorists	181 killed; 1,321 wounded
63	1965	MAURITIUS	Riots	
64	1965	EL SALVADOR	Earthquake. Aid to civil power	
65	1965	BECHUANALAND	BBC radio transmitter guard—Rhodesia crisis	
67	1965	MALAYA	Flood relief	

69	1966	HONG KONG	Disturbances
70	1966	SEYCHELLES	Unrest. Aid to civil power
71	1966	BRITISH HONDURAS	Border operations
72	1966	HONG KONG	Floods
73	1966	VIENTIANE	Floods—Laos
74	1966	BASUTOLAND	Famine relief
75	1966–1967	LIBYA	Evacuation of British nationals and rundown of bases in Beghazi, El Adem, and Tobruk
76	1967	HONG KONG	"Red Guard" riots
77	1968	SICILY	Earthquake. Aid to civil power
78	1968	BERMUDA	State of emergency
79	1968	MAURITIUS	State of emergency
80	1969–to date*	NORTHERN IRELAND	IRA campaign (271 killed; 3,025 wounded (to date))
81	1969–1971	ANGUILLA	Political unrest
82	1969	BERMUDA	Black Power Conference
83	1969–1976*	DHOFAR/OMAN	Assistance to Sultan in suppressing externally supported rebellion
84	1970	TUNISIA	Floods. Aid to civil power
85	1970	JORDAN	Medical relief
86	1970	PAKISTAN	East Bengal floods. Aid to civil power
87	1971–1972	MALTA	Withdrawal and return
88	1972	QE2	Bombscare—Para drop
89	1972	BRITISH HONDURAS	Reinforcement
90	1973	QE2	Guard against Arab threat
91	1974*	CYPRUS	Evacuation British, etc., nationals, Turkish invasion
92	1976–1977	BRITISH HONDURAS (BELIZE)	
93	1982	FALKLAND ISLANDS	War

* Award of campaign and/or U.N. medals.

Combing out nonoperational units would be possible with the phasing out of national service. The British contingent in Germany was reduced from 77,000 men to 64,000 in twelve months, and further reductions would follow. Commitments in the Middle East and Far East would be shared with Baghdad Pact, SEATO, and ANZAM countries, although British responsibilities in the Persian Gulf, the Arabian Peninsula, and East Africa would be fulfilled. In order to enable the new strategic reserve that would form in the United Kingdom to respond to calls for assistance, the RAF fleet of transports would be increased.

The army entered a period in which it strove to adjust to what promised to be a new defense era of high technology and management techniques rather than leadership. It had to shed officers and noncommissioned ranks that would reduce its strength by half in five years. At the same time, a modern family of weapons appeared to replace the obsolescent ones that had survived since 1945. The shadow over reequipment was the rising cost of nuclear weapons and delivery systems. Budgetary success depended largely on reducing the figure of 100,000 men still serving in the Far and Middle East and reducing the force in Germany from 64,000 to 55,000.[4]

The policy aimed at making the army into a small, compact, hard-hitting force. The attempt to achieve this goal marks a distinct period in the army's history since 1945. By its end it was intended that the army should number between 165,000 and 180,000 men. Pay and conditions for the newly enlisted regulars, who would replace the national servicemen completely by 1962, would be improved and the image of the soldier in the public's imagination altered. The army was going to be competing with industry for technicians as never before and with the other services as well.

The physical and mental capacity of the recruits entering the army in the 1960s had improved vastly over that in 1914 or 1939. Food rationing in the 1940s, the employment of mothers, and higher wages in the family had all had beneficial effects. The army was now able to select its recruits and to pay them better after it had grown leaner and meaner. Although the plan was good, Britain's economy could not support the army it deserved, and it was clearly necessary to retrench again.

In 1964, infantry regiments were grouped into divisions for recruiting and administrative purposes, and a number were encouraged to amalgamate into larger regiments with up to three battalions. The Territorial Army, the descendant of the emotive militia of the eighteenth century, was scrapped altogether. So was the Army Emergency Reserve. From the remains a new Territorial and Army Volunteer Reserve (TAVR) was constructed. The new organization was 50,000 strong and would reinforce the British Army of the Rhine (BAOR) if war broke out.[5]

Just before the Labour government was defeated in 1970, the uneasy relationship between Catholics and Protestants in Northern Ireland blew up into what was to be a long campaign against the Irish Republican Army

(IRA). The forces employed there increased from two infantry battalions and elements of an armored reconnaisance regiment to a maximum of twenty-seven major units during "Operation Motorman" in July 1972. For much of the time in the next decade, between seven and fourteen major units would rotate for four months at a time between the United Kingdom, Germany, and Northern Ireland. An Ulster Defence Regiment had to be formed, and the Royal Ulster Constabulary was reorganized. In the meanwhile, the army had to take over police duties and adapt methods that it had perfected in several different parts of the world to the United Kingdom where the police, the politicians, and the civil service were ill versed in the procedures and nuances of "low-intensity warfare."

But Northern Ireland had not yet become a long-haul when the new Heath government, in its first defense review, ritually declared that it was "determined to...make good as far as possible the damage of successive defence reviews." It observed that the previous administration had "run down units with great traditions to a point that would have left an inadequate provision for unforeseen commitments." And the TAVR had been "so reduced that it no longer includes any uncommitted reserves." Northern Ireland illustrated "the shortage and undermanning of regular units."[6]

In fact, except that it retained cadres of some of the regiments that had been scheduled for disbandment with the purpose of restoring them when manpower and funds were sufficient, the new government continued much the same policy as its predecessors. That was not surprising considering that the factors were unchanged. The distribution of the army by January 1 indicated how far the previous measures had gone:

United Kingdom	101,300
Germany	53,000
Mediterannean and	
Middle East	10,400
Far East	19,200

The decline in recruiting that had partly been the result of the previous economies was corrected by improving pay and conditions along the lines already suggested by the Labour government, and also by the upsurge that typically occurred whenever there was a job to be done, even in Northern Ireland.

In 1974, Labour returned to power and in typically forthright language reasserted its intention to concentrate its defense efforts in Europe. It agreed that the Conservatives had had the same intention but had been more willing "to counter threats to stability throughout the world. So...the government...inherited a defence programme of world-wide political and military commitments" and military forces stretched to contribute to all the major areas of the alliance.

This statement was disingenuous for it could not have been made but for Northern Ireland. Its real intention was to serve notice that the government now intended to pull in its horns in Europe, too. Pressed by its left wing to cut defense spending and aware that the poor performance of the economy might be partly blamed on defense spending, which was still absorbing a larger percentage of the gross national product (GNP) than in other European countries, it felt justified in cutting British commitments still further. Britain would withdraw from supporting NATO in the Mediterranean by 1976 and concentrate her efforts on the Central Region, the Eastern Atlantic, and the Channel, on the nuclear field, some specialist forces, and the U.K. base.

This time, the cuts fell on amphibious forces. Royal Marine commandos, helicopter and commando ships which also carried Royal Artillery units, and assault ships, as well as the Joint Airborne Task Force, already reduced to a mere two parachute battalions, were disbanded. Of three parachute battalions, only one would now be fully operational. The U.K. Mobile Force was to be reduced to one brigade from two, and the battalions absorbed elsewhere. The total strength reduction of the army was to be 15,000, which included some artillery regiments that had been made redundant by reorganizations in the composition of divisions in Germany. This was the latest of several games that had been played with the organization of BAOR since the late 1950s; each was economically motivated but thinly disguised as tactically designed. The government also withdrew from a number of joint research and development projects including the RS 80 long-range artillery, which had reached definition stage with Germany and Italy, and the Anglo–French light helicopter. It also reduced followup orders of the Anglo–Belgian tracked combat recce family of vehicles.

In 1979, the Conservatives returned to grapple with identical problems. Despite all the rhetoric, the reduction of the army had reached its limit. In 1981, there were actually four fewer artillery regiments, two fewer engineer regiments, one fewer commando, and one more infantry battalion than in 1974. All the parachute battalions were operational. After a reduction to 4.75 percent, defense expenditures had risen again to 5.2 percent of GNP. The army was still overextended, but the strain on it of the worst period in Northern Ireland had not recurred. The TAVR which provided BAOR with 30 percent of its mobilized strength was enlarged again. The security of Europe in the event of a Soviet invasion still depended on nuclear forces, including tactical ones. (See Table 11 for a description of British Army Combat Units and Equipment.)

Perhaps the new factor in the situation was that the extension in the reach of Soviet strength overseas was likely to require the British, rather than any of their other European friends except the French, to restore at least some of Britain's maritime forces. She was still the only truly maritime power in Europe.

Table 11
British Army Combat Units and Equipment

Units	
corps, armored, artillery division headquarters	6
armored regiments	10
armored reconnaissance regiments	9
infantry battalions	48
Gurkha infantry battalions	5
parachute battalions	3
special air service regiment	1
missile regiment with Lance	1
air defense regiments with Rapier	3
artillery regiments	18
engineer regiments	9
army aviation regiments	6
Total Manpower:	163,681

Equipment	
Tanks	
Chieftain medium tanks	900
Scorpion light tanks	271
Armored Vehicles	
Saladin armored cars	243
Scimitar armored cars	290
FV438 armored fighting vehicles with Swingfire anti-tank weapons	178
Ferret cars	1,429
Fox scout cars	200
FV 432	2,338
Saracens	600
Spartan APC	60
Artillery	
105mm pack howitzers/light guns	100
Abbot 105mm guns	155
M-109 155mm sp	50
M-107 175mm	31
M-110 203mm sp/howitzers	16
Anti-Tank/Air Defense	
Lance, Carl Gustav 84mm, 120 mm rcl;	
Milan, Swingfire atgw	
Striker with Swingfire	
L/70 40 mm AA; Blowpipe, Rapier/Blindfire sam	
100 Scout, 7 Alouette II, 20 Sioux, 150 Gazelle,	
and 20 Lynx helicopters—configured anti-tank	

Based on data taken from *1981-82 Military Balance*, International Institute for Strategic Studies, London, 1981, pp. 30-32.

Combat Ability

In June 1981, the Defence Review made the familiar point that "the best way of enhancing the deterrent effect of our armed forces" was to "raise the nuclear threshold" by giving "more resources to their hitting power in combat." Whether the British economy is any more capable of sustaining the effort required for that and also for aiding the United States and the French overseas, as in the past, is open to question. What is not in question is that the army will continue to perform at a high level of efficiency whatever revenges the whirligig of time brings. While there has been no fighting in Germany, the British Army has been as efficient and smart as ever. It is also small and capable only of taking its place beside allies of less certain quality. Elsewhere in the world, however, the army has been tested in conflict more continuously than any other Western army, and it has not been found wanting.

The British Army is the most experienced army in dealing with strata of conflict from the Borneo frontier war in support of Malaysia against Indonesia, through the protracted Malayan Emergency against a Communist attempt to take over the state, to keeping the peace between Greeks and Turks in Cyprus and the Protestant militants, the IRA and its Catholic supporters in Northern Ireland, and the Falkland Islands. (Number of casualties and campaign medals awarded are given in Table 10.)

In playing its role in the Malayan Emergency, the army benefited from its experience in Palestine which immediately preceded it. It found that low-intensity operations could be successfully conducted only if the civil authority made the policy on the spot through a combined directing staff of civilians, police, and military which met daily. The conflict in Malaya was soon acknowledged to be essentially political, and the police, who lived with the populace, were more important than the soldiers in keeping the peace, as they are in normal times. Indeed, as far as possible the aim was to maintain the rule of law through the courts and elected representatives, and to minimize the use of force. The target of police and soldiers was the enemy's infrastructure rather than his order of battle. It was intelligence rather than bullets and high explosives that achieved success. Significantly, close cooperation among the three agencies was developed under the direction and guidance of men who had learned the meaning of interservice and civil-military teamwork in World War II and also knew Malaya intimately. They succeeded largely because they were able to follow a consistent policy, without interference from London, once agreement was reached that the aim of the operation was independence for Malaya. Thanks to revenues from the export of tin and rubber, the interests of the British Exchequer were subordinated to the needs of the emergency.

In Borneo, bush operations against an insurrection supported from across the Indonesian frontier by Indonesian troops were brought to a standstill in circumstances that made a press blackout possible. The operations were done on a shoestring by small units, helicopter-borne, on foot, or using small boats. Classical ambushes, surprise marches, and excellent jungle tactics made it the most successful and least advertised of British postwar campaigns.

The British were less successful where the political purpose was uncertain. For example, a large concentration of force between 1945 and 1948 failed to suppress the Jewish national war for Palestine. Poor cooperation with the Palestine police, which failed to provide good intelligence, and unclear military policies about what was properly a military operation or a police operation were exploited by a Jewish command that had studied British methods and practiced sound doctrine. Above all, the political will to stay was lacking. Once it became clear that the British were going, the game was up for the army. For there could be no peaceful handover to a friendly government; the enemy was already in the saddle. Similarly, in the retreat from Aden, the political successor was not ensured, and the army had to attempt to control a struggle for succession between 1964 and 1967. In that struggle it suffered 92 dead and 510 wounded, a much higher figure than the 59 dead and 123 wounded suffered in Malaysia during the confrontation with Indonesia during 1962-1966. In the conventional operation against Egypt in 1956, which was brought to an end by unusual cooperation between the United States and the Soviet Union but reached its military objectives, at a cost of 16 dead and 99 wounded, the political direction was disastrously uncertain. In the months that followed, morale in the army was low and the mood angry. The realization that the country no longer had the capacity to mount a major conventional operation even against a second-class opponent was underlined by the White Paper in the following year which, recognizing the fact, initiated a redundancy plan for a reduced army which created a mood of uncertainty in the next few years.

Trouble in Northern Ireland, which began in 1969 after the major reductions and withdrawals that began in 1964 were completed, has been a running sore for the army ever since. In the earlier years, the army had to operate with a crippled Royal Ulster Constabulary. Two rules of low-intensity operations— that the police should be effective and that the courts should be able to operate normally—were broken. Hence, the army had to do police work. To this blow was added a second problem for the army. The political direction was taken out of the hands of resident civilians, so that the troika that was so successful in Malaya had only one sound leg in Northern Ireland. Finally, the press and the public, which naturally did not understand the rules of low-intensity warfare as did the army, turned its wavering light on the scene and had to be educated slowly about what was going on. At the same time, the army, treading warily and making many mistakes on the way, learned how to handle the press and to adjust its operations to a second front—the political war of ideas. In general, the British public was pleased and proud of its men who could be seen on television screens whenever a Bloody Sunday or Bloody Friday inadvertently occurred, and were impressed by the phlegmatic and fair-minded manner in which they dismantled bombs, managed excited mobs, and pacified hysterical residents who expressed what appeared to be eccentric views on life and times.

Remarkably, while the grind of four- or five-month tours in Northern Ireland bore heavily on families, it did not affect recruiting. Indeed, recruiting benefited for a time. The opportunity for units to be operational without distraction, for twenty-four hours, for weeks on end, was invaluable training for officers and NCOs, and as a result the ranks drew closer together.

Officers

There has, of course, been a democratic revolution in Britain since 1945, when the first Labour government with an absolute majority came to power. Since then, measures such as a consolidated wage for servicemen were passed in response to the need to make army life as comparable to civil life as possible. Much more freedom was afforded to men in the ranks when off-duty, messing was greatly improved, and accommodation was made more comfortable. When off-duty, officers and men had always played games together, but field sports, such as skiing, climbing, and sailing, were increasingly done together in the spirit of equality in the 1960s and 1970s. The officers were once taken exclusively from the public schools and from a minority of them. Immediately after the war, the Labour government expressed its intention to enable young men from all backgrounds, as well as the ranks, to achieve commissioned rank. The two prewar military academies, Sandhurst and Woolwich, were combined, and education there was made free. All students were called "officer cadets," and the distinction between "Gentlemen Cadets," whose fathers paid for their education, and "Army Cadets," who were selected from the ranks and had to pay nothing, was abolished.

In fact, the original sources of officer material dried up as opportunities for making money and achieving distinction appeared to be greater in commerce, industry, and the public service than in the army. Furthermore, the officers who were required in the army that was being visualized after 1957, and that it has now largely become, required the kind of education that only the engineer and artillery cadets at the Royal Military Academic at Woolwich had received in 1939. It was considered whether Sandhurst should offer a degree course, but in the end the academy went in the other direction. The course was reduced in length, and efforts were made to recruit directly from the graduates of universities. From 1971, those receiving short-service commissions attended for six months only, while those taking regular commissions continued for a another five months. About 40 percent of the cadets came directly from schools, 30 percent from the ranks of the army, and 14 percent from Welbeck College (a kind of junior college run by the army); the rest were direct entry officers from universities. The Military College of Science was then available for those who were selected to take degrees after entering the army, and a certain number of places were reserved at universities, as had been the case before the war, for engineers and some others.

The recruiting of other ranks has had its ups and downs, depending on comparative pay and conditions in civil employment, the current world situation, and the most recent government White Paper, which foretells cuts or expansion. Men prefer to enter a service that is expanding, receiving new equipment, embarking on important operations, and is receiving good rather than bad publicity. By and large, the best recruiters are active soldiers who are leading satisfying lives. The most consistently successful part of the enlistment machinery has been the Junior Leaders (Boys) Units into which fifteen and sixteen year olds are enlisted. Typically, for every fifteen soldiers enlisted, five more entered as boys. In 1972, 20 percent of recruits were fifteen years old, 14 percent were sixteen, and 23 percent were seventeen. These units are particularly important for the technical arms.[7]

The schools of higher education, such as the staff and joint services colleges and the arms schools, have been completely reorganized since 1945. A system of arms schools did not even exist in 1939. A few officers attended Staff College, but only those reaching senior positions and expected to become general officers attended the Imperial Defence College. Now it is almost essential to pass the staff college course to be promoted beyond major. Next is a National Defence College which replaced the Joint Services Staff College in 1971. Its symbol is the Cormorant—a bird of voracious appetite that smells fishy, although it operates effectively on the land, the sea, and in the air.[8] In 1979, the Joint Services Warfare School moved to the same location and operated under the same commandant. At the top is the Royal College of Defence Studies. In 1970, it replaced the Imperial Defence College which was established in 1927. Seventy-five attend its year-long course, of which only thirty are British service officers.

Conclusions

The British Army has perhaps fought more small campaigns since 1945 than any other Western army. Its capacity to work out of ships, or aircraft, in primitive conditions, and in small units and formations is unsurpassed as the Falklands War demonstrated. It has a long tradition of excellence at that level and an ability for detailed planning which such operations demand. At the clandestine end of the spectrum, the Special Air Service has been successful in operations that are paramilitary and close to being police operations. The army's regular enlistment, as well as the scope consequently allowed NCOs at the section level to take responsibility in the field, is vastly superior in these kinds of operations to conscript or short-service enlistment. Being traditionally a small army, for which the great wars of this century were exceptional rather than typical combat situations, it is peculiarly suited to the type of irregular and low-intensity warfare that has predominated, in its experience, since the Korean War ended.

Americans may ask how the British have avoided the disciplinary problems that have beset their own army. To attempt to prove why something has not happened is, of course, fruitless. It would be of value to explain some factors that produce equilibrium in the British Army that are not precisely present in others. That they endure through the decades suggests that they suit the British temperament in one form or another. It is not necessarily true that what's sauce for the goose is sauce for the gander.

The British Army has never regarded itself as a cadre for a national army that will fight a major war. Rather, it has been a small professional force fighting almost every year of its life somewhere on the globe, in so-called peacetime. Consequently, it has generally avoided theory and untested doctrine in favor of down-to-earth practical soldiering. This philosophy has been strengthened by the experience of being outnumbered by enemies and, generally, being more impoverished than friends. Minimum force has been required because, in general, that is all that has been available.

The symbols of permanence, of continuity, have survived amidst change because they serve a useful purpose. The regimental system with its old Cardwell-linked battalions, a curse to the army before 1914 because it was unworkable in war, has given way to larger infantry divisional groupings that are halfway towards a corps of infantry but retain distinguishing characteristics and a family spirit. The artillery, which was the largest single regiment in the army, has turned to regional recruiting to give its individual regiments some territorial base. The British have always been acutely aware that units above an optimum size will suffer from poor morale and that efficiency should not be equated with administrative convenience. It has resisted the managerial revolution in that respect.

Finally, and by no means exhaustively, the British Army has never regarded itself as consisting of civilians, whether managers or technicians, in uniform. All are soldiers; and as professionals they are apart from those who punch the clock beyond the gates. Physical recreation is part of training, but it goes on around the clock. Where it used to be association football, hockey, and rugby football for other ranks, and hunting on horseback or shooting tigers for the officers, now it takes every form from climbing Everest, traveling over land from Patagonia to the Arctic, to sailing around the world. It is for officers and men alike.

The Falklands Postscript

Military administrators since 1945 had striven to concentrate British resources in defense of continental Europe where they would be deployed in conjunction with their allies. The achievement of that aim had been delayed by continual emergencies outside Europe and, in the 1970s, by the one in Northern Ireland. In the latter years, amidst the reductions in all services, defense commentators and serving officers continually questioned whether Britain was still capable of undertaking operations overseas, on her own, against an enemy equipped with modern weapons. The short answer from politicians was that another Suez-type situation would not arise. The country's foreign policy was designed to avoid such armed confrontations. If it should occur, in Belize for instance, the single reserve brigade in readiness in the United Kingdom would suffice.

Military planners are not given to the belief that all will go "right on the night," however. Consequently, exercises that rehearsed the rapid reinforcement from Britain of the northern tier and the central sector of NATO included far-reaching plans to coopt and adapt merchant shipping for military use, for small assault landings and the kind of tri-service operations that the British, alone among the European allies of the United States, were supposed to be able to mount. Fortunately, the planners in the Ministry of Defence had revised and tightened up their plans in 1981 and were satisfied that they could put ashore a force of about two brigades a considerable distance from home.

There remained, as there always do in war, questions that would not be answered until fighting began. For how long could Britain maintain a fighting force, say on the other side of the Atlantic? How effective were the complex weapons systems that it would carry with it?

In April 1982, the Falklands were invaded by the Argentine. In late May came the landings by Royal Marines and two battalions of the Parachute Regiment. There followed reinforcement by three battalions of the 5th Brigade, the reserve held in the United Kingdom. By mid-June the Argentine Army had been defeated. During the sea and land operations, a remarkable public debate occurred in the United Kingdom about equipment and methods. Most of it concerned the Royal Navy, for the spotlight was on the sea and air operations until the last three weeks. Voices regretting the submergence of British services in NATO were heard again. The navy, they said, was not properly equipped for assault landings. It lacked a large carrier. The words of Dennis Healey, "Assault landings are a thing of the past," were recalled, and he was admonished that planners ought never to use the word "never." Naval air was less effective than it should have been because radar surveillance had not been effective. Why was the British AWAC not yet ready? Had better early warning been supplied, shipping would not have been lost and the VSTOL Harriers would have been more effective against enemy aircraft. More ship-to-air missiles were needed, and even more machineguns would have been useful. It was curious that Port Stanley Airport had not been closed to Argentine C-130 aircraft even on the last night of the land assault.

Naval weaknesses were weaknesses in one leg of the tripod on which a combined operation rested. The army felt them in the loss of heavy helicopters and in a shortage of landing craft which extended the period during which a landing was vulnerable to air attack. But criticism of the equipment and performance of the land forces against an enemy that was about equally equipped was almost completely absent. That may have been due partly to the press censorship that was applied after an outcry against the liberty allowed the press initially. But while it is too early to discover details of the professional lessons that have been learned, we can make some initial observations that may stand the test of time.

The Chieftain battle tank and heavy guns were not employed, and the Scorpion light tank, well suited to the boggy ground, did not play a prominent part in the fighting. Therefore, armored doctrine was not tested. The artillery 105mm howitzers and light guns, the latter with a long range of 18,000 yards and an effective shell, were both satisfactory but, being dependent on helicopter lift, would not have been able to sustain an extended siege against Port Stanley. Although 400 rounds per gun had been dumped, all but twenty or thirty rounds had been consumed by the end. The vital role of the Blowpipe and Rapier SAMs, revealed in the Middle East fighting, was demonstrated by a Western army for the first time. The British learned, however, that all weapons must fire at aircraft, and one aircraft, at least, was destroyed by a machinegun. Infantry movement depended on the capacity of the men to hump 80 pounds on their backs over rough moorland. Point sections used helicopter lift for reconnaissance and the seizure of key points ahead of the advance. Night fighting was a feature of British tactics in taking main positions. The superiority of the Marines, parachute battalions, and 5th Brigade over the Argentines in this department was most marked. Use of infiltration tactics by sections was standard procedure. And, in the phase when they closed with the enemy, the well-worn truth that all enemies behave much alike until you get within 50 yards of them, was relearned. This was particularly evident in the flat terrain between Darwin and Goose Green.

The professionalism of the British troops was impressive. More than 12,000 Argentinians surrendered to seven battalions. These numbers surely suggest that counting heads and examining the capabilities of weapons listed in reference books is a poor way of evaluating armies. We seem to have to relearn that lesson time and again. It is tough, realistic, and frequent training, as well as battle experience, that produces adaptable soldiers who can meet the unexpected and who can speedily and faultlessly perform the numerous tasks required in the battle zone and behind it. The quality of that training cannot be quantified in the pages of the *Military Balance*. If it has been effective, it will result in professional performances in action. That means performing effectively the first time in action, before troops have become veterans. A second opportunity does not always come. Only professionals will get it right on the first night.

Notes

1. Cmnd 6743, February 1946.
2. Cmnd 7327, February 1948.
3. Cmnd 6923, October 1946.
4. For the passage on Palestine, see David Charters, "Insurgency and Counter-Insurgency in Palestine," unpublished thesis, London University, 1980, pp. 45-47 passim.
5. Charters, "Insurgency and Counter-Insurgency."
6. Cmnd 7631, February 1949.
7. Cmnd 4891, 1972.
8. Henry Stanhope, *The Soldiers: An Anatomy of the British Army* (London: Hamish Hamilton, 1979), p. 74. Stanhope's book is quite the best and most detailed source for the British Army since 1945, if not the only one of its kind.

Bibliography

Adan, A. *On the Banks of the Suez.* Los Angeles, Calif.: Presidio Press, 1980.

Anglesey, Marquess of. *A History of the British Cavalry, 1816-1919.* London: Leo Cooper Co., 1973.

Barclay, C. N. *The First Commonwealth Division: The Story of the British Commonwealth Land Forces in Korea, 1950-1953.* Aldershot, England: Gale and Polden Co., 1954.

Barnett, C. *Britain and Her Army, 1509-1970.* Harmondsworth, England: Pelican Books Inc., 1974.

Blaxland, G. *The Regiments Depart: A History of the British Army, 1945-1970.* London: William Kimber, 1971.

Carew, T. *The Korean War: The Story of the Fighting Commonwealth Regiments.* London: Pan Books, 1970.

Featherstone, D. F. *All for a Shilling a Day.* London: Jarrolds Inc., 1966.

Foss, M. *The Royal Fusiliers.* London: Hamish Hamilton Ltd., 1967.

Horne, A. *To Lose a Battle: France 1940.* London: Macmillan & Co., 1969.

Keegan, John. *The Face of Battle.* London: Jonathan Cape, 1976.

Skelley, A. R. *The Victorian Army at Home, 1959-1899.* Montreal: McGill Queens University Press, 1977.

Winter, D. *Death's Men: Soldiers of the Great War.* Harmondsworth, England: Penguin Books, 1979.

France

Steven T. Ross

Traditionally, French leaders have regarded continental power politics as their primary concern, and the army's essential mission was to prepare for and wage campaigns in Europe. Overseas ventures, though important, could never by themselves decide the nation's fate, but continental diplomacy and war could and did determine the destiny of France.

Louis XIV enlarged and reformed the French Army, transforming it from a semifeudal institution into an obedient instrument of the royal will. He used the army to pursue a policy of continental aggrandizement. Louis also constructed a large fleet and encouraged overseas trade and colonization, but geographical factors, expansionistic dynastic ambitions, and the existence of European enemies led him to devote most of his military resources to continental operations. Several of his wars had colonial and maritime components, but the results of continental battles and campaigns were decisive in determining the success or failure of his search for hegemony.

The Sun King's successors were also Continentalists. France continued to maintain a large fleet and expanded the colonial empire, but the main thrust of French foreign and military policy remained European. Most French regiments served and fought in Europe where the monarchy continued to seek additional territory and influence. Overseas garrisons were relatively small, and the French often protected their colonies from British attack by seizing strategic territory, the Low Countries with their invasion ports, or Hanover, the home of Britain's monarchs, which they could relinquish in return for a restoration of colonial losses.

The French Revolution changed the nature of war but not the army's continental focus. The Royal Army, led by aristocrats, who commanded a rank and file composed of long-service volunteers drawn from society's lower orders, gave way to a mass citizen army. The Republic adopted universal conscription and picked its officers on a basis of loyalty and talent.

The army reflected the society that created it and became a powerful and effective instrument of both the Republic and the Empire.

Despite drastic changes in structure and organization, the army's fundamental role remained continental. French leaders did occasionally wage overseas campaigns, but the fundmental issues of the day—the Republic's survival in the face of hostile coalitions, French revolutionary expansion, and the extent and power of Napoleon's Empire—hinged on the results of European military operations.

During the Restoration and July Monarchy, there were no major wars in Europe, and France became involved in a major military effort to conquer Algeria. French military and political leaders, however, continued to regard the European scene as the nation's area of primary concern. The post-1815 army became virtually a closed society, a state within a state, and adopted a stance of strict political neutrality in domestic affairs. Most troops were peasants conscripted by lot. The officers came from the middle class and from the ranks, and the military tended to be physically and intellectually isolated from civilian society. Within their garrisons, however, military men continued to study Napoleon's campaigns and prepared themselves for conventional large-scale European wars rather than for small-scale colonial expeditions.

The army's stance of political silence, *la grande muette*, enabled it to survive the revolutions of 1830 and 1848. It accepted Louis Napoleon's coup and the subsequent transformation of the Second Republic into the Second Empire. Napoleon III changed the army into a long-service professional force, pursued the conquest of Algeria, and invaded Mexico. His primary efforts, however, were continental, and his army's most significant campaigns were waged in Europe. Defeat in his last major war doomed the Empire and led to the painful advent of the Third Republic.

The Republic restored the citizen conscript army and regarded the military as the nation's shield against renewed German aggression and as the instrument of revenge. French national survival and status as a great power depended upon the army's ability to protect the state from German attack.

The Republic also greatly expanded the French Empire, but an important factor in imperial ventures was the search for resources and manpower to throw into the scales against Germany. Most of the troops used overseas were colonial levies or Foreign Legion regiments. These formations were led by officers from the Metropole, but the manpower was not French. Metropolitan divisions remained at home where they prepared for a major war with Germany.

After 1871, the army began to attract increasing numbers of aristocrats into the officer corps. The aristocrats saw in military service a way to serve France without adhering to republican ideals. Although the officer corps became steadily more Catholic and conservative, the army as a whole retained its position of political neutrality. There was never any serious danger of military support for Fred Boulanger, and although the Dreyfus affair involved many high-ranking officers in a serious miscarriage of justice, the army as a whole remained aloof from the scandal and its ramifications. The military never seriously threatened the political system, and the overriding importance of French security ultimately minimized the impact of the affair on military institutions. The army remained the nation's indispensable shield.

During World War I, the Western Front was the only battle zone where France would win or lose the war. After the mobile war had stagnated into static trench combat, the French nation transformed itself into a huge machine designed to sustain the army. French leaders reluctantly agreed to several peripheral campaigns, and French divisions fought at Gallipoli and Salonika. Divisions from the Western Front also reinforced the Italians after Caporetto. Military and civilian leaders, however, shared the belief that the Western front was decisive, and most French divisions stayed and fought in France.

As the bloody, indecisive conflict dragged on, the French like other belligerents displayed signs of war weariness. In 1917 the army mutinied. Over half the divisions experienced acts of collective indiscipline. Basically, the troops refused to launch further suicidal attacks, but they never declined to defend their own positions and the soil of France.

The problem of countering a new German drive for hegemony dominated French military thought during the interwar years. The Republic sought to limit the size and armaments of the German Army. French military men also advocated the separation of the Rhineland from Germany but had to settle for permanent demilitarization of the region. Realizing that in terms of population and industrial resources Germany had greater war potential than France, the Republic created a series of alliances in Eastern Europe and constructed a series of strong defensive works along the Franco-German border. The army also had to crush rebellions in Morocco and Syria, and the fear of Communism became pervasive in the officer corps. By the mid-1930s, many officers were convinced that France was on the brink of civil war, and some of them became involved with clandestine right-wing organizations that were preparing to strike down what they regarded as a political regime that was slipping steadily to the left. Most of the officers, however, remained loyal to the tradition of political silence and focused their attention on the problems of the security of Metropolitan France.

The army basically agreed with the government's reluctance to offer early resistance to the expansionist policies of the Third Reich. Thus, when World War II began, France had already suffered severe political and strategic defeats. Nevertheless, the catastrophe of 1940 was swift and stunning. The army had the requisite manpower, equipment, and even a doctrine of armored warfare sufficient to meet the Germans on roughly even terms. The high command, however, made a significant blunder in deploying its operational reserves. Moreover, the high command persisted in thinking of warfare in the measured terms of World War I and lacked the flexibility to respond quickly to the German *blitzkrieg*. As in past conflicts defeat in Europe was decisive, and the Third Republic collapsed. The collapse of 1940 led to the simultaneous emergence of Vichy and the Resistance. It also led to the emergence of the overseas empire as a decisive factor in the nation's future.

General Charles de Gaulle sought the liberation of France and the restoration of the nation's status as a great power. Until 1942 the vast majority of the Free French forces were colonial troops. Even after the Allied landings in North Africa and the shift of allegiance of the Vichy forces in Morocco and Algeria, most Free French soldiers were not Metropolitan Frenchmen. Juin's army in Italy was primarily colonial, and it was only after the liberation of Metropolitan France that significant numbers of Frenchmen entered the ranks of de Lattre's First Army. The Empire and its troops thus played a major role in liberating the Metropole, a fact that was to influence French military attitudes and missions for the next two decades.

After 1945, the army was purged of its collaborationist and overtly pro-Vichy elements and was sharply reduced in size. The officers sought to return to their traditional continental concerns, and the emergence of the Cold War seemed to justify this approach. France joined NATO, and elements within the army began to study the problems associated with warfare in a nuclear environment. In the early 1950s, the French Army created the Javelot Brigade. This was a small, heavily armed, highly mobile formation designed to fight a major war, including nuclear combat, in Europe. Two other divisions were organized along these lines, but concern for preparing for a major European clash was soon overwhelmed by the requirements of waging colonial warfare.

Fighting erupted in Indochina in 1946. Strong factions in the army and the government insisted that France retain control of its Asian colony. For them another retreat was unsupportable, and they felt that French prestige required the suppression of nationalist revolts and retention of the Empire. Imperialist political factions were for many years strong enough to compel any government in the Fourth Republic to adhere to their wishes.

The government, however, realized that the French public would never support a full-scale war of colonial reconquest and decided to employ only colonial and professional troops in Indochina. Although led by French officers, the units that fought the war consisted of Foreign Legion regiments, colonial formations, and long-service French troops who volunteered for overseas duty.

As the guerrilla war dragged on, the officers in Indochina began to feel progressively more isolated from the Metropole which displayed little interest in or support for their war. The officers began to see themselves as fighting a unique kind of revolutionary-guerrilla war against the forces of world Communism. Moreover, the officers developed the notion that they rather than their political leaders understood the true interests of France and Western civilization. They began to view themselves as centurions protecting the frontiers of the civilized world while a corrupt and indifferent public ignored and even undermined their efforts.

The government's decision to liquidate an unwinnable war coupled with the defeat at Dien Bien Phu convinced these men that the very people they were defending had betrayed them. They left Indochina with the firm conviction that they would never again retreat from battle with the Communist foe and would lash out against anyone who sought to force them to capitulate. Thus, the professional veterans of Indochina entered the much larger and more decisive war in Algeria with a growing hostility towards the civilian government and a determination to impose their military-political views on the civil authorities in Paris.

The Algerian conflict called forth a much greater French effort than the Indochina War. Algeria was France's oldest colony and was judicially part of the Metropole. For many, the retention of Algeria was regarded as the last stand of French claims to great power status. France never deployed more than 180,000 men at one time in Indochina. In Algeria the Republic used conscripts and ultimately stationed 400,000 men, the equivalent of twelve divisions, in North Africa. Many military men adopted the views of the Indochina veterans and came to regard the war not only as part of the anti-Communist struggle, but also as a test of the nation's will to remain a great power. Consequently, the military became progressively more willing to oppose official policy.

As the war dragged on, the government began to contemplate a compromise peace with the Algerian nationalists. The army refused to accept the idea of Algerian independence, and in May 1958 units in Algeria, backed by the European settlers, openly rebelled. The revolt enjoyed substantial support throughout the armed forces, and it succeeded in destroying the Fourth Republic and bringing to power the man who, the army believed, would keep Algeria French.

De Gaulle had made ambiguous statements that sounded as if he intended to retain French control of Algeria. De Gaulle's decision to liquidate the war and grant Algeria independence precipitated another military mutiny in 1961. The rebels had much tacit support within the officer corps, but neither the conscripts nor the public rallied to their cause. The rebellion collapsed, and although fugitive military men and many European Algerians mounted a campaign of murder and assassination in Algeria and in France, the war was ended. France withdrew from Algeria, and the Fifth Republic survived.

After 1962 De Gaulle reasserted the army's traditional continental role. He believed that only by acting as a European power could France retain her status as one of the world's major nations. De Gaulle intended to reassert France's role as an independent great power, reorient the army's doctrine and missions, and revive the tradition of political silence within the military.

Doctrine

The new course in French foreign and military policy required France to become a nuclear power. De Gaulle expanded the nuclear program that the defunct Fourth Republic had begun, and France acquired a substantial arsenal of nuclear weapons. The *force de frappe* became the keystone of the Fifth Republic's defense policy. The emphasis on nuclear weapons in turn implied a diminished role in national defense for the army and allowed de Gaulle to take steps to reestablish full civilian control over the military.

The government moved quickly to reduce the army's size. In 1959, the army numbered 804,000 men. By 1963, it contained 415,000 troops, and in 1967, the government had lowered it to 338,000. Officers whose loyalty was suspect were either forced into retirement, transferred to isolated garrisons in the Metropole, or posted outside of France. In the late 1960s, the French garrison in Berlin, the Army of the Rhine, and units stationed in Africa contained numerous officers who to a greater or lesser degree had supported the concept of a French Algeria. They were to serve out their careers in areas where their ability to make trouble for the government was severely circumscribed. The army's share of the defense budget also declined, while that of the air force and navy, because of their nuclear roles, increased.

In 1968, during the popular disturbances in France, de Gaulle issued an amnesty to his former military and civilian foes in return for military support if he felt he had to use the army to restore the government's authority. The amnesty marked the official termination of civil-military suspicions, restored *la grande muette*, and gave added coherence to French defense policy.

The goal of de Gaulle's defense policy was to sustain France's ability to act as an autonomous great power. France, he said, would defend herself by herself and in her own way. The *force de frappe* was the centerpiece of the policy of independence. French nuclear capability gave the Fifth Republic an independent deterrent. Though generally supportive of the Atlantic Alliance, France always retained the freedom to implement its own foreign and military responses to a wide variety of opportunities and threats.

The army's role under de Gaulle was consistent with the overall national objective of sustaining French independence and great power status. The army consisted of three main segments. The forces of maneuver comprised five mechanized divisions, two of which served on German soil. Equipped and trained to fight a large-scale conventional battle, the French formations, in both size and organization, resembled an American mechanized division. The second segment consisted of two Alpine brigades, twenty-one infantry battalions, three armored cavalry regiments, and an artillery regiment. Known as the defense of territory forces, these units were responsible for home defense. Their roles included providing security for military bases and vital civilian installations against foreign attack and domestic sabotage. The Gendarmerie also had an anti-sabotage and anti-subversion mission. An airborne division and an airportable brigade, together with the Foreign Legion and a number of other units stationed overseas, comprised the forces of intervention. The intervention forces were designed to sustain French influence and interests overseas, especially in former French colonies. The airborne units in France were also available as a strategic reserve in the event of a European conflict.

French leaders after de Gaulle soon faced the same dilemma as their American counterparts. Nuclear weapons might well deter a central strategic war, but they were not adequate to meet other threats, including a major conventional attack. Nor were conventional forces the sole answer since an aggressor with larger forces could always overwhelm them and again force the nation's leaders to choose between suicide or surrender. In the 1970s, French political figures and military strategists concluded that tactical nuclear weapons could fill the gap between purely conventional and all-out nuclear responses to a major attack. In 1976, President Giscard d'Estaing stated that France had to prepare to respond to a variety of tests at the appropriate levels, a concept much like the American doctrine of flexible response. The government then undertook to reorganize the army in order to integrate it fully into a coherent defense policy designed to meet a variety of contingencies.

The primary object of current French defense policy is to guard the nation's independence. France continues to reject reliance on other states and retains the freedom to decide when, where, and how to engage its armed forces. France also rejects neutralism, recognizing that the European and global power balance is an important factor in her own security. Thus, while France continues to refuse integration into the NATO military structure, the Republic remains a member of the Atlantic Alliance and welcomes the presence of American forces in Europe. France's leaders have stated that the prime European military threat emanates from the Soviet Union and its Warsw Pact allies. They have also stated publicly that France will assist the alliance in repelling any attack from the East.

Current French military strategy is founded upon the capabilities of nuclear and conventional dissuasion and combat. France seeks to dissuade an aggressor from attacking by convincing any hostile power that a major military action risks reprisals that would cause losses far in excess of any possible gain.

French leaders agree that credibility involves the ability to respond to a nuclear strike as well as to attacks where a nuclear threat would not be appropriate. Thus, large and effective conventional forces are necessary, and tactical nuclear weapons are required to bridge the gap between nuclear strategic weapons and conventional forces. The tactical nuclear weapons are supposed to protect conventional forces from being overrun by superior numbers and to provide a solemn warning that strategic forces will be released if an aggressor persists in his attacks. The French thus reject the Soviet and American view that dissociates tactical and strategic nuclear forces. The French integrate conventional, tactical nuclear, and strategic nuclear forces into a single coherent defense doctrine.

Organization

The French national defense structure is designed to provide the government with the ability to make rapid and effective political-military decisions. The defense establishment also deals with long-range issues, including weapons procurement and military organization within the broader scope of the nation's foreign and domestic priorities.

The president of the Republic is the commander of the armed forces. He alone can give the order to use nuclear weapons. The military cabinet of the president is charged with keeping him informed of all matters of military importance. The president also presides over the Council of Ministers which defines defense policy as part of the overall national policy. Finally, the president heads the Defense Council. The members include the premier, the foreign minister, the minister of national defense, the minister of interior, the minister of finance, and others as required by specific situations. The Defense Council is a decision-making body on general defense matters within the framework of national policy.

The premier is in charge of the overall conduct and management of national defense. He executes the decisions of the Council of Ministers and the Defense Council. The General Secretariat of National Defense coordinates interministerial decisions and has a crisis watch function. It also disseminates national level intelligence.

The Minister of Defense directs and coordinates national defense policy. The minister has three principal deputies: the general delegate for armaments, who is in charge of research and development and production; the secretary general for administration, who is in charge of defense financial matters; and the Chief of Staff of the armed forces.

Several autonomous directorates also report to the defense minister. The minister supervises the Information and Public Relations Bureau, the director for military security, a counterintelligence unit, the Directory of the National Gendarmerie, the comptroller general, the Directory for Nuclear Testing, and the SDECE, the foreign intelligence agency. Some defense experts feel that the defense minister has too many departments to supervise, but no program for a major organizational reform has yet been brought forward.

The Chief of Staff of the armed forces has operational control of all major commands. His main peacetime roles are to see to training, preparedness, and the formulation of war plans. The army, navy, and air force chiefs have no operational responsibilities in war. They direct training and supervise the administration readiness levels of their respective services. A Joint Staff hedquarters assists the Chief of Staff in preparing war plans, and the Armed Forces Combined Operations Center, located in an underground complex in Paris, enables the Chief of Staff to contact all separate commands, thus providing rapid and efficient command and control.

The Chief of Staff has at his disposal an intelligence apparatus, the External Relations Division, and the Military Intelligence Exploitation Center which provides strategic and military analysis. The services have their own intelligence units. The army intelligence branch, for example, is called the Intelligence and International Relations Bureau. The Chief of Staff may also receive information from the SDECE, most of whose personnel are active duty military men. The SDECE controls the clandestine acquisition of foreign intelligence and counterintelligence abroad. The SDECE also has a paramilitary capability and controls a regiment of the 11th Airborne Division. The regiment is organized in small teams and operates much like the British Special Air Service (SAS).

The French armed forces are integrated into a National Command Authority that provides for both civilian supremacy and rapid response to any crisis. The communications network and the intelligence structure provide civil and military authorities with essential information that enables the government to respond effectively to changing situations.

Nuclear Forces

The strategic nuclear forces are designed to dissuade an aggressor from launching a preemptive nuclear strike on France. They also act as a last step in an escalation ladder. Although France's nuclear arsenal is much smaller than the arsenals of the Soviet Union and the United States, the French believe that they can inflict damage sufficient to convince an aggressor that even a successful attack would be too costly to contemplate. French nuclear forces contain land, sea, and air components, a triad that guarantees a large measure of survivability.

The land leg of the French triad consists of eighteen missiles on the Albion Plateau. Nine of them are S-2 missiles with a 150-kiloton warhead and a range of 1,600 nautical miles. The other nine are S-3s with one-megaton warheads and a range of 1,800 nautical miles. The government plans to replace the remaining S-2s with S-3s, and since fixed silos are vulnerable to attack, Paris is contemplating the introduction of a mobile land-based system.

The seaborne element consists of five nuclear-powered missile submarines, each carrying sixteen missiles. A sixth submarine will carry the M-4 missile which has six independently targeted reentry vehicles. The other submarines will receive the M-4, and the government also plans to build a seventh submarine in the late 1980s, thus allowing three boats to remain on patrol at all times.

The airborne component consists of thirty-three Mirage IV-A bombers with fifteen more in reserve. There are also eleven KC135-F tankers which give the bombers a range of about 3,000 miles. The Mirage IV-As carry the AN-22 nuclear bombs with a 60-kiloton yield. Although the Mirages are getting old, the government intends to modernize them and keep them operational into the 1990s.

The tactical nuclear element consists of twenty-four Super Standard fighter-bombers and five Surface-to-Surface missile regiments armed with the Pluton missile which has a range of 120 kilometers and a yield of about 20 kilotons. The regiments are deployed in Laon, Suippes, Belfort, Mailly de Camp, and Oberhoffen. All of the Pluton bases are in the Northeast, ready to move into Germany or to the Franco-German frontier in case of hostilities. A Pluton regiment has 1,000 men and 300 vehicles. It is organized into a battery of command and services, a security and transport battery, and three firing batteries, each with two missiles. The army has a total of thirty-two Pluton launchers. The Plutons entered service in 1974 and are becoming outdated. The government is, therefore, planning to introduce an improved tactical missile, the Hades, and may undertake the production of enhanced radiation weapons.

Manpower and Equipment

The decision to employ nuclear weapons as part of a spectrum of dissuasion in order to avoid a suicide or surrender response to aggression has led the government to increase defense spending and modernize the conventional forces, especially the army. In 1975, the defense budget amounted to $13,984 billion; in 1979, $18,776 billion; and in 1980 $22,220 billion, a 14.9-percent increase or a real growth of 4.7 percent of the nation's GNP. Currently, the army's share of the defense budget is about $6.8 billion, 55 percent of which goes for operating expenses and 45 percent for capital expenditures. The 1981 defense budget has climbed to $25 billion, and the French seem to be willing to devote sufficient resources to pay for both nuclear and conventional forces.

In 1981, the active French army had a strength of 314,722 officers and men, of whom 202,990 are conscripts. The army has about 20,000 officers and 67,000 NCOs. The government expects to cut further the army's numbers and to stabilize the force at 311,000. The army's missions are to protect the nation's territory and to defend French overseas interests. In contrast to the pure Gaullism of the late 1960s, the current regime expects to support the Atlantic Alliance and regards Soviet and Warsaw Pact aggression as the most dangerous, if not the most immediate, threat to French national interests. As in the past, the army's main mission is continental, and there remains a strong secondary concern for the nation's global position.

A French armored division has a strength of 7,000 men. It has a reconnaissance squadron with six anti-tank launchers and four radars. There are two tank regiments, each with four tanks, and one mechanized infantry squadron with a total of fifty-four medium tanks and nineteen mechanized infantry combat vehicles per regiment. There are also two mechanized infantry regiments, each with two mechanized infantry, and two tank companies with twenty medium tanks, forty-four mechanized infantry combat vehicles, six 120mm mortars, and sixteen anti-tank missile launchers per regiment. The divisional artillery regiment has twenty-four 155mm guns, ten anti-aircraft guns, and six radars. The division also has an engineer regiment, a logistics regiment, and an anti-tank company with twelve anti-tank missile carriers and two radars.

The French armored division is considerably smaller than Western and Soviet formations. It is designed to operate in both conventional and nuclear environments and in many respects resembles the old Javelot Brigade concept. An American armored division has 18,900 men and 324 tanks, and a Soviet tank division contains 11,000 men and 335 tanks. Even the People's Republic of China has armored formations with 9,200 men and 323 tanks. The French division with its inventory of 148 tanks, 245 armored personnel carriers, twenty-four self-propelled guns, twelve 120mm mortars, and fifty anti-tank launchers possesses substantial firepower despite its small size. Moreover, the division is highly mobile and enjoys substantial tactical flexibility. The corps is organized to provide additional fire and logistics support. The armored division is not designed to wage an attrition battle. Rather, the unit is supposed to meet and engage an aggressor, and, if the aggressor persists in attacking, French doctrine calls for the early employment of tactical nuclear weapons.

French motor rifle divisions are also small, containing 6,900 men. There is an armored regiment with thirty-six light tanks and three motorized infantry regiments, each with four motorized, one reconnaissance, and one support company. A regiment has ninety-five wheeled armored personnel carriers, six 120mm mortars, eight 81mm mortars, and twenty-four anti-tank guided missile launchers. The division also contains an artillery regiment with twenty-four 155mm howitzers, ten anti-aircraft guns, and six radars, an anti-tank company with twelve anti-tank weapons, an engineer company, and a logistics regiment.

Like the armored division, the French infantry division is smaller than its American and Soviet counterparts. The American division has 18,500 men, 216 tanks, and 350 APCs. The Soviet division contains 10,485 troops, 188 tanks, and 308 APCs. The French division has 36 tanks, 370 APCs, 24 howitzers, 24 81mm, and 18 120mm mortars, 84 anti–tank launchers, and 58 anti–aircraft guns. It is designed to stop a limited attack or act as a tripwire for the release of nuclear weapons.

The army also has a number of special purpose divisions. The Alpine division has 9,460 men and contains an artillery and seven maneuver regiments. The parachute division has an artillery and eight maneuver regiments with 15,545 men, and the Marine division with five maneuver regiments plus artillery and support units is 8,670 strong. These divisions operate in special terrain, act as part of the general reserve, and contribute forces to participate in overseas operations.

The army's order of battle includes the First Army headquarters and the headquarters of the Ist, IInd, and IIIrd Corps. There are eight armored divisions: the 1st, 2nd, 3rd, 4th, 5th, 6th, 7th, and 10th, and four motor rifle divisions: the 8th, 12th, 14th, and 15th. There is one Alpine division, the 27th, a parachute division, the 11th, and a Marine infantry division, the 9th.

Each army corps has an 8,000-man artillery brigade that contains three anti–aircraft regiments, a nuclear artillery regiment, a self-propelled artillery regiment, a towed artillery regiment, and a surveillance and target acquisition regiment. The corps also contains a 14,500-man logistics brigade to handle supply, medical, and maintenance functions.

The army has forty-four regiments that serve with corps, army, and regional commands. These regiments include infantry, artillery, signal, engineer, chemical warfare, reconnaissance, transport, and helicopter formations. The Ist Corps, for example, contains the 4th, 6th, 7th, and 10th armored divisions. The nondivisional regiments include two mechanized infantry, two armored reconnaissance, three signal, three helicopter, two engineer, two transport, one chemical warfare, and one traffic control regiment, in addition to the artillery and logistics brigades. First Army headquarters controls two signal, one engineer, one river crossing, and one airborne long-range reconnaissance regiment. Military Region 2 in central France has two infantry, a helicopter, and a signal regiment.

Two regiments serve in Berlin, and thirteen regiments, a light brigade, and the 8,000-man Foreign Legion are designated for service overseas. The 9th and 11th divisions also contain elements that the government can deploy outside Metropolitan France.

Reserves consist of fourteen infantry divisions with a total of 215,000 men. Four of the divisions derive their manpower from various military schools. In a major crisis, most reservists would be ready for action by M + 4, and the mobilization process would be complete by M + 11. Some reservists would join active units, while the majority would get their equipment and supplies from one of the 100 mobilization centers.

Most of the army's equipment is modern and in good condition. France produces most of its own weapons, and the arms industry employs over 275,000 people. The weapons inventory includes 1,100 medium and 340 light tanks, 900 armored cars, 3,000 armored personnel carriers—about half of them tracked—800 artillery pieces, 2,500 mortars, 38,000 trucks, and 625 helicopters. The army has also realized the growing importance of anti-tank missiles. It has about 700 Milan launchers. The Milan has a two-man crew, can fire as many as five rounds a minute, has no telltale flashback, and has a range of 2,000 meters. The army has also acquired the HOT ATGM which has a 4,000-meter range and is fired from a vehicle or helicopter. There are relatively few HOT weapons, but several hundred are on order as well as 900 additional Milans. The army is also planning to acquire some 2,000 wheeled APCs, 300 tracked APCs, 190 medium tanks, and over 100 155mm self-propelled guns. The army is acquiring a new fleet of jeeps, utility trucks, and tracked scout and command vehicles. By the end of the decade, the army will have acquired over 37,000 new vehicles. Currently, the army's major shortage is modern 155mm self-propelled artillery. The armored divisions have sufficient modern guns, but some of the infantry divisions and the reserves will have to rely on older 105mm weapons for some time. A number of new weapons are in the research and development stage. Improved anti-air and anti-tank missiles and a new main battle tank are being designed for the 1990s.

The army's logistics is based on the assumption of a short war. The French believe that a war's decisive phase would occur within two to three weeks after the commencement of hostilities, and the logistics system is geared to sustain about three weeks of intensive combat. The army's 300,000 tons of stored munitions is adequate, as are other stocks of parts and equipment. The army has about 175 logistics units and over 100 depots. Most are concentrated in the Northeast, but some have been moved to the South and to the Mediterranean coast to avoid undue concentration in case of a preemptive strike. The ground forces are relatively short of fuel oil, but private oil companies are required to maintain 25 percent of their stocks as an emergency reserve, and there are over twenty-eight million barrels of oil available from French firms. The logistical system is thus consistent with the national defense policy. It is adequate for a short, high-intensity war. It can sustain overseas intervention operations for long periods, and it specifically rejects the concept of preparing for a lengthy conventional conflict in Europe.

The National Gendarmerie provides the army with additional strength. A national police force subordinated to the minister of defense, the Gendarmerie numbers 82,000 men. Its strength expanded steadily throughout the 1970s and will continue to grow in the 1980s. It has more men than the French Navy. The Gendarmerie is subdivided into a number of functional units, the largest being the Departmental Police with over 44,000 men. They are located throughout France with posts in some 3,800 rural communes. The Mobile Gendarmerie, 18,500 strong, operates in larger units and has heavy weapons including tanks and APCs at their disposal. The

2,900 men of the Republican Guard are a ceremonial unit which also provides security for the Republic's leaders. Some 3,000 Gendarmes serve overseas; small contingents guard airports and patrol coastal waters; and there are also special anti-terrorist detachments and a parachute unit. In a crisis, about 100,000 reservists are available. In wartime, the Gendarmerie supplies battle police to the army and protects vital installations from domestic and foreign saboteurs.

The Gendarmerie has in its equipment inventory 36 tanks, 120 armored cars, 188 APCs, 280 81mm mortars, 43 helicopters, 21,000 vehicles, and about 200,000 light weapons ranging from pistols to assault rifles and light machineguns. The Gendarmerie also possesses an excellent communications system. The rise of transnational terrorism, the fact that the Soviet Army has special purpose forces trained in sabotage and assassination techniques, and the existence of a large domestic Communist party—some of whose members might well support the Eastern Bloc in wartime—have increased the importance of the Gendarmerie's role in providing internal security in both peacetime and crisis situations.

Officers

No army is better than the quality of its officers and enlisted men. Given two forces of roughly equal size and similar equipment, the better trained and motivated army will usually emerge the victor. No matter how good the structure and technology, an army's capability is fundamentally a function of the quality of its personnel.

The officer corps is well trained and well educated. Most of the senior leaders have combat experience. The army recruits about 900 new officers per year. About 180 are graduates of École Spéciale Militaire de Saint Cyr, which is now located at Coëquidan in Brittany. The École Militaire Interarmes (EMI) and the École Militaire du Corps Technique et Administratif (EMCTA), both of which are also at Coëquidan, train an annual contingent of 300 NCOs to become officers. Saint Cyr has a two-year course, and courses at the EMI and EMCTA are one year long. An additional 200 NCOs become officers by special examination and another 130 by seniority. Some civilian candidates and suitable conscripts may receive direct short service of reserve commissions.

Graduates of the Coëquidan schools, especially Saint Cyr, form an elite within the army much like the "West Point Protective Association" in the U.S. military. They receive 10 percent higher pay and enjoy better promotion prospects. Admission to Saint Cyr is by competitive exam. The quota is always filled, and standards have remained high. Recruiting has become localized, and the percentage of students from the western regions is disproportionally large. The school is also becoming self-recruiting, and about 40 percent of the students are sons of graduates. The army also runs six boarding schools for the sons of living or deceased soldiers, thus enhancing the self-recruiting nature of the officer corps. The officer corps enjoys high social prestige. The officers tend to come from middle- and upper-class backgrounds and are fairly conservative in social and political outlook. The tendency towards elitism is balanced by the large number of NCOs who become officers and by a rigorous promotion system that places a premium on both academic and operational performance.

After commissioning, second lieutenants attend a service arm school for a year. The infantry school is located at Montpellier, the armor school at Saumur, artillery at Chalons or Draquignan, engineers at Angers, train at Tours, material at Bourges, transmissions at Montargis, medical at Lyon, and Gendarmerie at Melun. Captains may specialize further, and the army has special schools for management, intelligence, and atomic energy, and junior staff officers attend the École d'État-major.

Higher military education includes the École Supérieure de Guerre for field grade officers. A Command and Staff School, the École Supérieure de Guerre, is located in Paris, and officers must graduate from it in order to command major units. The École Supérieure Interarmes trains students from various service colleges in the methods of interservice cooperation. The Centre des Hautes Études Militaires stands at the top of the military education pyramid. It trains about twenty-five colonels per year for senior defense posts. The Centre is co-located in Paris with the Institut des Hautes Études de Défense Nationale for senior civil servants, and the two schools work together.

Questions of social stratification and political attitudes are less important than the basic issues of whether or not the army will obey the civilian authorities and whether or not the military will be an effective instrument of national policy.

Since 1962, the officer corps has emphasized the defense of the national patrimony and has revived the tradition of *la grande muette*. The colonial page has been turned and the corps reduced in size. Dissidents have been removed from the ranks, and new officers are carefully nurtured in the concept of nonpolitical service to the state. The educational and training system, with its emphasis on academic and operational proficiency, seems to have produced an effective and efficient cadre of junior officers. Senior officers have combat experience, as do some of the middle grade and junior officers in the Exterior Action Force (EAF). The French officers are among the most experienced in Western Europe. Moreover, command tours range from two to three years, a period that is sufficient to allow a commander to learn his job and to use his expertise effectively. None of the officers has led large units in high-intensity combat, but neither have senior military leaders from most other major armies. Save for a dramatic and highly improbable change in the nature of the government's domestic and foreign policy, the officer corps will in all probability remain obedient to the Constitution and civil authority. The officers should also be effective combat leaders.

NCOs

The NCOs appear to be a skilled and efficient group. Like the officers, they are well trained. Many of them are long-service professionals who have seen much combat. Almost all of them have advanced schooling in service schools or in the national NCO academy. French NCOs have traditionally enjoyed the reputation of being tough, durable, and competent. They play a vital role in training recruits, managing material, and developing unit cohesion. In a crisis they will probably perform effectively.

About 65 percent of the army's manpower consists of conscripts. Upon reaching their eighteenth year, all Frenchmen are liable for military service. About 450,000 become eligible each year. There are some deferments. Others are excluded as morally, intellectually, or physically unfit. Those who are drafted serve one year with the active forces, four years in the ready reserves, and thirteen years in the second line reserves. The annual contingent numbers about 250,000. The government cannot assign draftees outside of Europe. Some of the draftees elect to serve a five-year tour, but the majority return to civilian life after completing their one-year obligation. The one-year recruits fill the ranks of the units assigned to operate on the Continent.

Draftees are sent directly to their units where they are trained and perform their service duties. An instructor group from the regiment conducts basic training. A recruit may be sent off for specialist training but normally stays within the unit throughout his service. Alpine and parachute regiments conduct preinduction instruction, but even in these units, the recruit, once in service, stays with his regiment throughout his time in uniform. Training takes about six months—four for basic instruction and two for advanced work.

Some of the draftees are members of the Communist party which has a membership of about 300,000 and attracts between 16 and 25 percent of the electorate. Most officers feel that party members and sympathizers are Frenchmen before they are Communists. Communists are excluded from the most sensitive positions, but in other respects they are treated like other draftees. Neither the government nor the military regards the presence of Communist recruits as a significant security threat.

Training cadres have been educated in the methods of instructing new recruits, but since they get new conscripts about every sixty days they are seriously overworked. On the other hand, the system of keeping a soldier with his unit throughout his service time has the undoubted advantages of improving unit morale and cohesion. The excessive rotation of personnel common in many armies does not plague the French military system.

The training of technicians required to operate the complex equipment of the modern armed forces does present special problems. The army attempts to assign civilians with requisite skills to equivalent military positions. Most draftees, however, are from nineteen to twenty-two years of age and have not yet developed high skill levels. The army runs special courses for technicians, but this reduces their active service time. The army also seeks long-term volunteers for high technology positions, a policy that has had some success. Operational units perform only basic maintenance on their vehicles and equipment, and the better trained specialists serve at division and corps levels.

The army has also sought to improve reserve mobilization procedures and training. Annual exercises usually involve some reserve divisions, and there are plans to activate about three divisions each year. There are also command post exercises for reserve officers, and specialist reservists are mobilized periodically.

Conscription, if not popular, is generally accepted by all segments of society as a fundamental requirement for both citizenship and national defense. Public opinion polls regularly indicate the existence of broad popular support for conscription, and debates about the draft focus on the details, not the existence, of the draft. The demonstrations of 1968 and 1973, for example, dealt with specific issues and did not question the conscription system itself.

The officer corps favors the draft. They would like a longer term of active duty but recognize that the current conscription system provides the army with good quality recruits, costs less than an all volunteer force, fills reserve units, and brings the army closer to the people. The army employs recruits in both combat and support arms. Recruits even serve in the Pluton regiments. Draftees are not simply placed in support units but are an integral part of the military system. The officer corps does not favor an all professional force and is committed to the concept of a citizen army.

The political right also favors conscription as the most effective means of providing France with armed forces capable of enabling the nation to play a great power role in world affairs. The left, which, historically, created the mass citizen army, also favors the draft as supportive of democratic ideology. Some factions would reduce the term of active service but generally regard the draft as preferable to a professional army. The right sees the army as a force of order, while the left views it as a guarantee of freedom. Almost all political factions agree that the army and military service play a significant role in the development of patriotism and citizenship. Interpretations of what military service should do for the soldier and the nation differ, but most factions agree that military service helps nurture civic patriotism. Governments in the future may modify the terms of conscription, but France will doubtless retain some form of obligatory military service in the foreseeable future.

Deployment

To enable the army to perform its missions within the overall context of the nation's defense policies, the government in 1976 undertook a major reorganization of the structure of the land forces. The goals were to create an army capable of quick reaction to a variety of crises, to integrate tactical nuclear weapons into the army's organization and doctrine, to provide for an army that could operate in various geographical conditions, and to enhance unit autonomy. The reforms also sought to streamline the army's administrative structure and save money by eliminating redundant staff and line units.

The reforms eliminated the distinction between territorial and maneuver forces. France was then divided into six military regions, each with a central military command (see Map 1). The region commander received responsibility for mobilizing reserves and conducting exercises, and for the overall direction of all army, navy, air force, and police elements in his region during emergencies. The commander also detaches or receives combat elements as required by a particular situation, and he is in charge of disaster relief and riot control. The commander of Military Region 6 in eastern France is also the commander of the Ist Army Corps.

Each military region is divided into two to five military districts. There are a total of twenty-two districts. In peacetime, the district commander's principal function is reserve mobilization, administration, and training; he also controls all army units in his zone. If a combat division is located in his district, he is also the division commander. As a result of the reforms, one region command and seventeen staff units were eliminated. Under the old system, region and district commanders controlled only territorial and reserve forces. By giving the commanders operational authority over both active and reserve forces, the government has improved command unity and efficiency.

The army has also restructured its operational units. The basic tactical unit is now the regiment which is about the size of an American or German battalion. It contains between 800 and 1,200 men. The brigade has been eliminated, and there is no intermediate command between the division headquarters and the battalions.

The army's deployments are consistent with the emphasis on the continental mission and with the secondary role of protecting the nation's overseas interests. Of the army's total manpower, 253,000 men serve in Metropolitan France, with the major units concentrated in the northern and eastern departments; 48,500 men are stationed in Germany; and 2,700 troops form the Berlin garrison.

The First Army with its headquarters at Strasbourg controls three corps which contain all the armored divisions. The Ist Corps with the 4th, 6th, 7th, and 10th Armored divisions has its bases in Military Region 6, which

Map 1.
The Military Regions of France

HQ 1 ARMY - STRASBOURG
HQ I CORPS - METZ
HQ II CORPS - BADEN
HQ III CORPS - SAINT GERMAINENLYE
HQ MILITARY REGION 1 - PARIS
HQ MILITARY REGION 2 - LILLE
HQ MILITARY REGION 3 - RENNES
HQ MILITARY REGION 4 - BORDEAUX
HQ MILITARY REGION 5 - LYON
HQ MILITARY REGION 6 - METZ

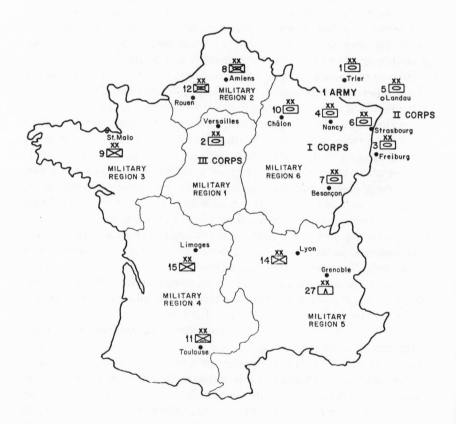

98

includes the northeastern departments. The IInd Corps with the 1st, 3rd, and 5th Armored divisions serves in the Federal Republic of Germany, and the IIIrd Corps with its single division, the 2nd Armored, is located in Military Region 1, which encompasses Paris and the surrounding departments. The 8th and 12th Infantry divisions are located in Military Region 2 along the Belgian border. They can easily reinforce the First Army. Military Region 5 in the Southeast contains the 14th Infantry and 27th Alpine divisions, while the 15th Infantry and 11th Parachute serve in Military Region 4 in the Southwest. The 9th Marine Infantry is located in Military Region 3 in western France. The infantry divisions can also reinforce the First Army, while the 11th and 9th, which have an amphibious capability, are part of the strategic reserve. Both divisions contain elements that are available for deployment overseas, but most of the regiments are designed to operate on the Continent.

Nearly 11,000 troops serve overseas either in French possessions or in former French colonies. Garrisons vary in strength depending upon local conditions and the value that Paris attaches to a particular area.

Djibouti contains the largest overseas garrison, both because of its strategic location and because of the volatile strategic and political situation in the Horn of Africa and Indian Ocean region. The force numbers about 4,000 men and includes the 13th Foreign Legion Demibrigade, the 5th Combined Arms Regiment, and the 6th Marine Artillery Regiment. French troops also serve in several friendly African nations. The 43rd Marine Infantry is in the Ivory Coast; the 10th Marine Infantry in Senegal; and the 6th Marine Infantry in Gabon. Other units, including the 33rd Marine Infantry, the 9th Marine Infantry, and the 3rd Foreign Legion, serve in French possessions in South America and the Pacific. A small force is stationed with U.N. units in Lebanon, and groups of military advisers operate in over twenty nations.

The army maintains a special command, the Exterior Action Force, to reinforce the threatened garrisons and to intervene rapidly in overseas areas where national interests may require a military response. Since conscripts cannot be employed outside Metropolitan France, all members of the EAF are long-service volunteers.

The 9th Marine and the 11th Airborne divisions, together with several nondivisional units, contribute elements to the EAF. The 9th assigns an infantry, an armored infantry, an artillery regiment, and a Command and Support Battalion to the EAF, and the 11th Parachute has a cell of three regiments, as well as a command and support unit designated for overseas intervention. Nondivisional elements include several Foreign Legion regiments, two helicopter regiments, and two parachute infantry regiments. For transport the EAF has forty C-160s with a range of 3,500 kilometers. Two of the C-160s are fitted out as airborne command ports. The army is also acquiring twenty-five improved C-160s with an aerial refueling capability that will extend the plane's range to 7,000 kilometers. The EAF

Command can use any or all of the assigned units to create a force suited to a particular mission.

The EAF is a well-trained, highly proficient force, but is a light infantry organization. It has no tanks or heavy artillery and little logistics backup. It can strike quickly and effectively, but it has no real staying power. To correct this deficiency, the army has organized a heavier unit. The 31st Demibrigade consists of an overseas infantry regiment and two Foreign Legion regiments, and is equipped with self-propelled 155mm artillery, APCs, and armored cars. It has sufficient logistics support to sustain lengthy medium-intensity operations.

Combat Scenarios

The ultimate value of an army is its ability to successfully complete its missions. The most dangerous but least likely contingency is the requirement to wage a major war in Europe. The army's ability to conduct high-intensity, continental operations forms an integral part of the national policy of dissuasion, and in the worst case, military operations on the Continent will play a crucial role in French national survival or lead to collapse and capitulation.

The French government and army agree that the only realistic threat in Europe comes from the Soviet Union and its allies. De Gaulle's all points defense concept has in practice been abandoned. The army's doctrine, training, and organization are predicated upon a threat from the East. The army has, in fact, established a close but informal working relationship with NATO. French regiments in Germany conduct joint exercises with American and Federal Republic troops; there is a Franco-American interoperability manual for communications; and French officers lecture at American service schools where they describe French methods and tactics. On numerous occasions the Republic's leaders have stated that the First Army will assist NATO in resisting any Soviet attack.

Against a major Soviet thrust into the Federal Republic, French divisions east of the Rhine with reinforcements from France could give a good account of themselves in the initial stages of hostilities. Small, highly mobile, and heavily armed, the French units could probably blunt the first echelon of a Soviet attack. The small size of the divisions would, however, preclude sustained high attrition combat. Loss rates in modern mechanized warfare are quite high, and no matter how well the French divisions fought, they would suffer a loss rate that in a matter of days or at most a few weeks would force them to retreat or face annihilation.

It is at this point in any conflict that the French government has threatened to use tactical nuclear weapons. In fact, the army is structured in such a manner as to require the employment of nuclear weapons after a brief period of conventional warfare. To avoid being overwhelmed by superior numbers, army doctrine relies almost exclusively on battlefield nuclear weapons. Moreover, the French would undoubtedly desire to use their nuclear hardware before the battle reached the national territory. Germany, not France, is the preferred battleground.

It is not possible to predict the results of employing battlefield nuclear weapons. Some believe it would produce a quick armistice as leaders on both sides contemplated the awful prospects of escalation. Others are convinced that the first nuclear explosion would be the first step on a ladder of rapid escalation towards a general nuclear war. Still others are convinced that belligerents could use tactical nuclear weapons without inevitable escalation. In any case, the unpredictability of results should convince any potential aggressor to contemplate seriously the inherent danger of launching a war.

In war, the release of both tactical and strategic nuclear weapons is a decision that rests exclusively with France. The United States and NATO have their own doctrines concerning nuclear weapons which may or may not coincide with French views. France resolutely retains independent control over the use of its nuclear arsenal.

The existence of France as an independent variable in the Western camp has distinct advantages for NATO. The Soviets may feel that they are able to calculate NATO reactions to an attack, but the independent French strategy must cause significant problems for Soviet planners. The French might not in fact fight. They might fight and not use tactical nuclear weapons, accepting defeat as preferable to escalation. They might use tactical nuclear weapons but stop short of resorting to strategic weapons, or they might do exactly what they have been saying for years they would do if attacked and treat the use of tactical weapons as a final warning prior to a release of strategic nuclear forces. Any Soviet attack scenario would have to take account of the range of probable French reactions, thus injecting greater complexity and uncertainty into any Soviet strategic design. The fact that France has the doctrine and capability of launching nuclear strikes independently from its Atlantic allies adds immeasurably to the Alliance's warfighting capacity and deterrent posture.

There is no way to predict what the French would do *in extremis*. In 1940, the Republic capitulated, although it was possible to carry on the conflict from the colonies. By contrast, in 1870 and 1871 the French resisted long after their fate had been sealed, and in 1914 after the disastrous frontier battles, the army rallied and won the Battle of the Marne. Currently, the government is planning to modernize the nuclear arsenal and intends to build a new generation of strategic and tactical missiles. In contrast to the growing antinuclear sentiment in Western Europe, protests in France are feeble and halfhearted. The small disarmament movement is closely identified with the Communist party and enjoys little popular support with the French public. Thus, the French government might not be willing to trade

Paris for Moscow or even Belfort for Minsk, but only the most irresponsible Soviet leader would say so with certainty. French dissuasion policy is clear and coherent, it is supported by the public, and consequently, it maintains a high degree of credibility.

The need to intervene overseas, especially in the Third World, is a less dangerous but more likely contingency than a major European War. The overseas regiments, the EAF, and Gendarmerie intervention groups are organized and trained to perform a wide range of tasks including hostage rescue, anti-terrorist strikes, and support of friendly regimes aginst insurgencies and cross-border hostilities.

The French government has no desire to wage wars of the scope and intensity of the Indochina and Algerian conflicts. Paris has no intention of ever again fighting a long colonial conflict. The forces of intervention can move and strike quickly, or they can render aid to a friendly regime for long periods at low levels of combat intensity. The new overseas demibrigade provides significant additional firepower, and the overseas and intervention forces can handle the most probable threats to French global interests.

In 1978, for example, the 2nd Foreign Legion Parachute Regiment went into Zaire and accomplished its mission quickly and efficiently. When terrorists seized the Grand Mosque in Mecca, the Saudi foreign minister asked the French government for help. The Intervention Group of the Gendarmerie flew to Mecca and quickly restored governmental control of the Mosque, killing most of the revolutionaries in the process. The well-trained professionals involved in overseas operations are capable of responding rapidly and effectively to most conceivable threats to the Republic's global interests.

Conclusions

France fully intends to maintain its status as a major power with European and global interests. The government intends to maintain military forces commensurate with the nation's status. Defense budgets have grown and, short of economic catastrophe, will continue to expand. Army missions are fully integrated into a total concept of national defense. The army is organized, trained, and equipped to defend the national territory against internal and external threats. It stands ready to support the Atlantic Alliance in pursuit of French national objectives, and it supports the nation's policies overseas. The army has returned to the traditional primacy of the continental mission and is a major pillar of the West's security edifice.

Bibliography

Carrias, Eugene. *La Pensee Militaire Française*. Paris: Presses Universitaires de France, 1957.

de La Gorce, Paul Marie. *The French Army: A Military-Political History*. New York: G. Braziller, 1963.

Dupuy, Trevor. *The Evolution of Weapons and Warfare*. New York: Bobbs–Merrill Co., 1980.

Fall, Bernard. *Street Without Joy: Indo-China at War 1946-1954*. Harrisburg, Pa.: Stackpole Co., 1961.

———. *The Two Vietnams*. New York: Praeger Books, 1963.

Horne, Alastaire. *A Savage War of Peace: Algeria 1954-1962*. New York: Viking Press, 1978.

Howard, Michael. *War in European History*. Oxford: Oxford University Press, 1976.

O'Ballance, Edgar. *The Indo-China War, 1946-1954*. London: Faber and Faber, 1964.

Revol, J. *Histoire de l'armee Française*. Paris: Larousse, 1929.

Talbot, John. *The War Without a Name: France in Algeria 1954-1962*. New York: Alfred A. Knopf, 1980.

Weygand, Maxime. *Histoire de l'armee Française*. Paris: Larousse, 1938.

West Germany

William C. Rennagel

No army in history has been so condemned, so admired for its combat proficiency, and so analyzed as the German armies from the time of Frederick the Great through the Wehrmacht at the end of World War II. The German Army's prowess on the battlefield and the professional capabilities of its commanders and staff officers have been legendary. While there have been numerous shortcomings and shortsightedness in the areas of strategic analysis, in contrast with the army's theater and operational capabilities, the German Army has proven to be as resilient as the German nation and has of necessity risen back to power on several occasions—after Jena (1806), after World War I (1914–1918), and after World War II (1939–1945). Today, the German Army, tightly controlled and accountable to its political authorities, is once again the preeminent army in Western Europe in both size and expertise.

The history of the German Army can best be summarized as a continuing struggle between its relationship with the authoritarian powers of the state and its relationship with the German people. For far too long, the conservative (and Prussian) officer corps acted as opponents to political change, arguing that its powers flowed directly from the king. Even after the military reform movement, begun in response to the humiliating defeat by the French at Jena, when progressive officers such as Gerhard Scharnhorst and Karl von Clausewitz attempted to bring the army and the nation into an intimate union, the conservative defenders of the king were able to prevent the liberalizing elements of the French Revolution from gaining ascendancy— culminating in the Counterrevolution of 1848. This resistance to civil control of the military, or the sharing of political control by the king and his people, continued to be a source of tension through World War I. By the beginnings of World War II, the army, caught in the dilemma between

The views expressed in this article are those of the author and do not reflect the views of the U.S. government or the Department of State.

service to the "nation" and to its popularly elected leader, had abdicated its responsibilities, including its tactical and operational direction of the war, to the leader chosen by the people. In this latter context, perhaps as too much of a reaction to criticism of the military dictatorship of World War I, the army, to its professional embarrassment, even abdicated its responsibilities to the soldier.

Germany's earlier military reform did provide, however, a very instrumental contribution to the army's future battlefield success. By 1813, when the army again went to war against the French, the revitalization of the army provided officers who were willing to take the initiative in combat operations. As part of their new charter, they did not fear the responsibility of command and the necessity for taking independent action on the battlefield. This was the beginning of the concept, which has proven extremely valuable in the German Army, of mission-type orders. The second important reform was the establishment of a cadre of trained staff officers (the Prussian General Staff) who excelled in staff work and technical expertise and who shared a common philosophy about waging war. The Campaign of 1813 demonstrated the importance of staff support and coordination between the various elements of the army; in addition, it was the beginning of the crucial relationship between the commander and his Chief of Staff.[1] This latter tradition held constant throughout the army until at least 1945, with several notable exceptions.[2]

Nevertheless, the reformers did fail in their attempt to liberalize the army, arguing for civil reforms that would create an identity between the citizen-soldier and the state. In fact, during the Constitutional Reforms of 1848, when the emerging civil authorities attempted to force the officer corps to swear allegiance to the Constitution, the officers responded with anger and incredulity. The subsequent counterrevolution, supported by the army, left the army outside the Constitution, where it was to remain until the Weimar Republic, and subject only to the king.

The continued importance of the German Army was guaranteed by the geostrategic situation which faced the German nation in Central Europe. Surrounded at times by three potentially hostile powers, the geostrategic situation necessitated an army and nation strong enough to deter war and, equally important, to fight successfully should deterrence fail. In addition, steeped in the Clausewitzian dictum that war was an extension of politics, the army was continually called upon to support the consolidation of the German nation—which Bismarck so ably did through a combination of diplomacy and war. Thus, within its limited means, the German response to their security dilemma was threefold. First, they sought universal conscription, for which they were ultimately successful in building the German nation-in-arms. Associated with this change was a reserve obligation, with its mobilization potential, for those soldiers who completed their active service. Second was the army's professionalism, reflected in the prestige which the officer corps was accorded in the German nation. The army made a constant study of war and emphasized field training exercises designed to test the mettle of its commanders and troops. Third was the organization and functioning of the German General Staff.

The German General Staff perfectly embodied the spirit of the army, particularly in its role as adviser to the king, and was responsible for the war plans, mobilization and training, and the study of war. The General Staff was essentially organized into three major departments: the German Department, which was concerned with the "Home Army," mobilization plans, and training; the Eastern Department, which dealt with intelligence and war plans against the Slavic nations (and Austria); and the Western Department, which focused on intelligence and war plans directed primarily against the French, but also included the British and Americans. Strategic direction for planning and executing a war on two or three fronts was the proper dimension for the chief of the General Staff and his closest subordinates. Other sections of the staff, though no less important, were concerned with mobilization schedules and railways, armaments, and military history. To insure close integration between the General Staff in Berlin and the field armies, General Staff officers were rotated from the Berlin Staff to the Troop Staff in the particular theater with which the staff officer had had earlier responsibility.

The redeeming feature of the structure and focus of the General Staff was its excellent understanding of the operational and theater aspects of warfare. Its greatest failure was that its strategic vision was impaired; this failure ultimately produced the loss of both world wars. This impairment could, of course, be traced back to the narrow, technical education of the staff officer, Germany's threatened strategic position on the European Continent (which inhibited a world-view), and the staff officer's generally apolitical outlook in foreign affairs.

Relationship to Civil Order

To comprehend the current nature of civil-military relations as they affect the German officer corps requires understanding the evolutionary nature of civil-military relations in the German state and the ascendancy of the modern, post-World War II German state (defining the relationship of the army to the basic law of the nation), as well as understanding the military ethic of the professional officer corps. Samuel Huntington, in his seminal work *The Soldier and the State*, offers a useful model of competing types of civilian control of the military. He describes "subjective civilian control"[3] of the military as one means of maximizing civilian control by "civilianizing the military" to the denial of an independent military sphere in society. The civilian power structure attempts to coopt the military into the policy process—perhaps beyond the expertise of the military officer. "Objective civilian control,"[4] on the other hand, attempts to maximize the professionalism of the officer corps by developing an introspective military that is only bound to carry out the legal orders of the legitimately constituted authority in the state. This implies a nonpartisan officer corps which limits its political involvement while stressing its military values.

Huntington writes, "the simplest way of minimizing military power would appear to be the maximizing of the power of civilian groups in relation to the military."[5] However, this involves not only the power relationships between civilian groups competing for power, but also the competition between civilian groups and the military (or, potentially, partisan military groups). Hence, those political groups that control the military through like-minded attitudes and aspirations can use the power of the military to enhance its power over other groups in the state. This, of course, is a potential flaw in attempting to use subjective control in harnessing the military's power, for one group may use the military to displace the power of other social units as has happened in totalitarian states such as the Soviet Union.

In liberal, democratic societies, subjective control implies embodying liberal ideals in military institutions. Thus, in liberal societies, the military under the concept of subjective control is to have diverse opinions that tend to parallel and reinforce the diverse opinions (to an extent) prevalent in society. As such, the military will maintain an internal balance and be guided in its policymaking through appeals to the external sources of political power—usually the political parties of liberal society. The officer corps reflects the attitudes of the society that it is sworn to defend.

Subjective control, then, creates an officer corps that is affiliated with political parties. As a result, the officer corps is often partisan in its political outlook. Obviously, this method may have as many strengths as weaknesses. As long as the political system maintains its pluralism, the general distribution of politically affiliated officers, as well as their recourse to civilian power structures to balance military policy decisions, should remain proportional to the opinions extant in society. However, it also means that military assignments at the upper echelons of command and staff have increasing political power, and these positions must be negotiated between officers and civilian factions. Liberal and conservative elements must look over each other's shoulders to insure that an equilibrium is maintained. Obversely, it also means more civilian participation in military decisions (much more so than in the context of objective control). Such participation can adversely affect the development and maintenance of the military's professional capabilities since officers may prejudice their independent military judgments to the political expediency of the moment.

Today, the German Army is known for its political (partisan) generals, notwithstanding the professional military competence of the majority of its officers. This situation could create a split within the officer corps (replacing loyalty, sacrifice, and cohesion with careerism) and affect the "nonpartisan," introspective development of military strategy and defense planning. For example, one German Army major general (a member of the Social Democratic party and associated with its left-wing members), while a commander of the 12th Panzer Division, recently and publicly argued that the current programs for NATO's military modernization (which the federal government had agreed to implement) were nonsense. He made this comment on the basis that the Soviets and their Warsaw Pact allies were members of a defensive alliance that had no intention of either attacking or intimidating Western Europe. He made this observation in a public address, to the embarrassment of the Bonn government. Even though it was a political statement, no major disciplinary action was taken since the officer was operating within the principles of *Innere Führung*. Essentially, *Innere Führung* has created a German military more along the lines of subjective civilian control of the military. *Innere Führung* has two meanings. For the professional soldier, it signifies internal leadership, which requires accountability for actions and responsibility to the army and the state. For the conscript, it means that the military cannot suspend the majority of his rights which are guaranteed by the state.

The reaction to past abuses by the officer corps, the earlier reactionary nature of the officers to reform, the military dictatorship of World War I, and the abdication of responsibility in World War II—all are crucial in understanding the importance the Germans give to *Innere Führung*—the concept of the "citizen in uniform" with most of the rights and privileges of the citizen and soldier protected. Through the exercise of *Innere Führung* the members of the Bundeswehr "still enjoy the active and passive franchise and freedom of coalition."[6] Thus, "servicemen still. . .have considerable scope for the free expression of their political views."[7] That is, they have the free expression of opinion, free access to information, so that they can judge the objective political education (part of the soldier's training is centered on his civic responsibilities and rights) and the legal basis of orders within the military.

While this freedom is intended to "force" individuals to be accountable for their actions and to prevent the excuse of "just following orders," there have been unanticipated consequences. One example is the outspoken Panzer general cited above who embarrassed his government. A more important concern is to foster the conditions for "objective civilian control," allowing the army to maintain its professionalism and its traditions for excellence. To that end, the German Army seems to be achieving the desired results.

Social Conditions

Very few ethnic or religious differences have an impact on the combat capabilities of the German Army. The more important differences are between the political parties in Germany.

The Social Democratic party tends to be liberal, Protestant, northern, and urban. The leftist elements of the party are the most vocal opponents of specific military activities. In contrast, the Christian Democratic Union tends to be conservative, Roman Catholic, rural, and Bavarian, and it demonstrates the most support for both the German military and the NATO Alliance.

Of course, these differences are most importantly confined to the upper echelons of command and staff in the Bundeswehr. However, at the level of the draftee, the young Social Democratic party member is more likely to be antinuclear, anti-United States, anti-NATO, and antiwar. In addition, *Innere Führung* allows these young soldiers to participate in political rallies while in uniform.

Most Recent Combat Performance

The combat-effectiveness of the German Field Army in World War II was without peer; its exploits in France, North Africa, and Russia are legendary. Moreover, it fought equally well in victory and in defeat. Trevor Dupuy, in an analysis of the fighting quality of the German Army, has written:

[The] record shows that the Germans consistently outfought the far more numerous Allied armies that eventually defeated them...the German ground soldiers consistently inflicted casualties at about a 50 percent higher rate than they incurred from opposing British and American troops under all circumstances. This was true when they were attacking and when they were defending, when they had local superiority and when, as was usually the case, they were outnumbered, and when they had air superiority and when they did not, when they won and when they lost.[8]

Numerous commentators have attempted to explain the German battlefield success. Generally, it may be concluded that the effectiveness of the German military machine was based on organization, comprehensive staff work, and a combination of tactical and operational skills.

Martin van Creveld argues that the German success lay in the more effective use of its human resources. In his conclusion, he states:

Constructed on Clausewitzian principles (war as a clash between independent wills) and traditionally hemmed in by severe economic constraints and material constraints (both absolutely and in comparison with opponents it would have to face in a two-front war) the German Army responded by developing a single minded concentration on the operational aspects of war to the detriment, not to say neglect, of everything else. A fighting force first and foremost, the Army's doctrine, training and organization were all geared to fighting in the narrow sense. In striking a balance between "function related" and "output related" tasks it spent comparatively few resources—sometimes, perhaps, too few—on logistics, administration, or management. It systematically and consistently sent its best men forward to the front, consciously and deliberately weakening the rear. In matters of pay, promotion, decorations, *etc.* its organization was designed to produce and reward the fighting man. It went for quality and quality was what it got. In this sense, without doubt, lay the secret of its fighting power.[9]

The result was a German Army composed of men who understood human behavior on the battlefield and of units that possessed morale and cohesion. They thereby gained a most important battlefield commodity: resilience in the face of danger and adversity after suffering substantial combat losses. As van Creveld observes:

In the final account, the German Army's system of organization reflected a deliberate choice, a conscious determination to maintain at all costs that which was believed to be decisive to the conduct of war; mutual trust, a willingness to assume responsibility, the right and duty of subordinate commanders at all levels to make independent decisions and carry them out.[10]

The German Army leadership recognized that well-trained, socially cohesive units were the principal building block of successful combat operations, regardless of the style or philosophy of war selected by the high command or political leadership. Thus, the emphasis on buddy relationships in combat served to develop and maintain unit cohesion in battle. In stark contrast to the individual replacement system, the unit replacement system was more efficient in socializing new recruits to their organizations. This dividend paid off handsomely in sparing the life of the new soldier in his first combat action.

A second approach in analyzing German combat-effectiveness, which reinforces van Creveld's argument, can be found in German tactical and operational doctrine. By definition, such doctrine must include mission-type control with its decentralized execution. John Boyd is one of the better proponents of this analytic school.[11] In "Patterns of Conflict," a major study of the evolution of warfare (particularly the German *blitzkrieg*), Boyd argues that the unifying theme of German tactics and operational art was the concept of the *Schwerpunkt*. This concept literally means point of main effort and implies:

- An unequal distribution of effort to enable the commander to focus combat superiority in designated sectors by thinning out other sectors (and accepting momentary risk).
- A frame of reference used to focus combat and combat-support activities and to convey the intentions of combat operations at all levels from theater to platoon.
- A center or axis around which fire and movement of all arms and supporting elements are focused to maintain the tempo of opera-

tions and to exploit emerging opportunities; and, tactical initiative is meshed within the strategic intent.[12]

Thus, the *Schwerpunkt* is: "the unifying concept that provides a way to shape the focus and direction of effort as well as to harmonize support activities with combat operations, thereby permit a true decentralization of tactical command within the centralized strategic guidance—without losing cohesion of the overall effort."[13]

Everything in the German military tradition apparently has its *Schwerpunkt*—elements of the main attack over the secondary attack or feint; the field army over the home army; the best leaders over the staff officers; combat units over support units. The simplicity of the idea is compelling; it is a focus on the essentials. This approach is in contradistinction to the "engineering approach" to combat which divides a major problem into separate tasks and each task into separate components.

Within the context of John Boyd's analysis, he also demonstrates that the concept of the *blitzkrieg* was not a sudden phenomenon. Rather, it was the application of new technologies to older forms of traditional German combat philosophy.[14] Matthew Cooper makes the same observation; however, Cooper applies "negative logic" to show that the *blitzkrieg* was incorporated into the more traditional form of war—the *Vernichtungsgedanke*[15] (loosely, a battle of encirclement with combat on reversed fronts that led to annihilation of the opposing forces). According to Cooper: "The German Army was the prisoner of its heritage, both political and military, from which it never succeeded in breaking free...actions of mechanized forces were subordinated to the strategy of encirclement."[16] While Cooper clearly understands the evolutionary nature of the *blitzkrieg*, he fails to realize that it was the necessary operational form of German military doctrine and philosophy that led to success. As his model he uses the post-World War I British school of armored warfare (a model that continually failed in World War II), typified in the writings of Liddell Hart and "Boney" Fuller. The early British school emphasized command paralysis and not the physical destruction of the enemy's force. For instance, Cooper argues that:

The paralysis of command and the breakdown of morale were not made the ultimate aim of the operational employment of the German ground and airforces, and were only incidental by-products of the traditional manoevres of rapid encirclement and of the supporting activities of the flying artillery of the Luftwaffe, both of which had as their purpose the physical destruction of the enemy troops.[17]

This short analysis suggests that organization, command style, and tactical doctrine were all woven into a coherent philosophy and approach to war that was thorough—that focused one's attention and resources on a single idea, victory on the battlefield. As such, in their operations the German military became much more prone to worry over time rather than space. Command responsibility and initiative were continually decentralized, with the higher commanders intervening in operations only at critical junctures. Typically associated with this focus, the centerpiece of military operations, was that combat was the test of independent wills on the battlefield. To be successful required that the soldier impose his will over that of his adversary by using his initiative to carry out the intentions of the higher commanders. Helmuth von Moltke is said to have believed that an operational plan never survives the first encounter with the enemy. Thus, flexibility was an important cornerstone in German tactical doctrine. It was decentralized command and flexibility that reduced the time of decisions, giving the Germans a substantial advantage over their opponents who had a slower observation-decision-reaction time.[18]

As the history of German warfare demonstrates, this approach was a tactical and operational system within a larger philosophy that worked equally well with light infantry forces and heavy armored forces.[19] More importantly, this style and philosophy of warfare remains extant in the German Army of today. Only political considerations, which are the logic of war, govern the application of tactics (the grammar of war) on the battlefield.

Organization

The day-to-day administration of the Bundeswehr (the German armed forces) rests with the minister of defense who is appointed by the chancellor. The minister of defense is concerned principally with overall defense policy and with the procurement and integration of German defense policy into the NATO context. During crisis or commitment to combat, the command of the armed forces reverts to the chancellor and the Federal Security Council.

The Bundeswehr is itself unified under an inspector general (equivalent to the chairman of the Joint Chiefs of Staff in the United States) who is the military adviser to the minister of defense and the federal government. While the inspector general of the Bundeswehr is the premier officer in the German military, he usually acts in consultation with the inspectors general of the separate services. In fact, the inspector general of the Bundeswehr only has a small staff to assist him since the separate services maintain most of the military staff work.[20] Of course, the Ministry of Defense has numerous civilian and military analysts working to support the minister.

The service inspectors general are members of the Federal Armed Forces Defense Council. They are responsible to the minister of defense for the development of an overall concept of military defense in conformity with the political designs and constraints imposed on them by their civilian leadership.

As noted earlier, command within the German Army is based on mission-type control. Historically, this has been an essential principle of German military leadership. Mission-type control posits the necessary *will* to share the responsibility and to be accountable for one's decisions and actions. It has been a crucial ingredient in tactical success on the battlefield. In mission-type control, the commander's goals are defined by his superior within the larger context of the overall mission. (A company commander, for example, would not only know the goals and intentions of his battalion commander, but he would also be given the context of his brigade's mission.) Within these very liberal constraints, the company commander would have the freedom to work out the tactical details of his operation. Thus, in accordance with von Moltke's principle that a military plan never lasts past the first encounter (since one is reacting to an animate enemy who is also attempting to impose his will on the battle), mission-type orders and the responsibility given to the commander force him to react to unfolding events and unexpected situations and to respond within the context of the higher mission and the governing tactical situation.[21]

Within the German Army of today (now freeing itself of American concepts of war, which seem almost alien to the German approach), the officer corps is caught up in the dilemma of technology and communications. Modern technology, with its sophisticated communications systems and automatic data processing, lends itself to centralized control which is the antithesis of traditional German command and control techniques. Studies are now ongoing within the General Staff, and the Ministry of Defense is investigating ways and means of decentralizing command, control, and communications (C3). The aim is to parallel and reinforce the older methods of command and control that were prevalent throughout the history of the modern German Army, perhaps before Clausewitz, but certainly in existence by the time of the Franco-Prussian War of 1870.[22]

Structure

The German Army is divided into its Field Army (the active component) and Territorial Army (its reserve). This division is historical—the Field Army is the cutting edge in combat, while the Territorial Army is responsible for rear (home land) security, training, and replacements as well as logistics.

The German Army has recently undergone a reorganization—the Structure (or Model) IV Organization. In this new organization, the battalions of the combat brigades are smaller in configuration, while the number of battalions in the brigade has been increased from three to four. There are several tactical and philosophical reasons for this change.

First, under the older organizational concept (modeled along U.S. lines with U.S. equipment), company commanders had only limited flexibility, which was contrary to the decentralized tactical doctrine prevalent in the German approach to war. When the new HDv 100/100, *Command and Control in Battle*, was issued, the German Army had to face the fact that rigidities in the lower command echelons did not generate the flexible state of mind that their tactical repertoires required. Moreover, the junior officers could not easily make the transition from the rigidities of the platoon and company structure and tactical style to the more flexible style required at the battalion, brigade, and division levels. This difficulty further influenced the development of responsibility and authority in the junior officers. The transition to Model IV has sought to eliminate these problems.

Second, smaller battalion organizations are thought to increase the effectiveness of combat power by allowing more personal intervention by commanders at critical junctures in combat—for example, during the commitment of the reserve. For example, General Herman Balck, a general of Panzers in World War II, observed that, after combat losses were taken, a typical German combat unit did not suffer substantial losses in its combat power.[23] As he explained it, a regimental commander, who had significant experience in the German operational style, would be commanding a unit that was just a bit larger than a battalion. Additional expertise at lower levels enhanced control over individual weapons and small units. More importantly, the authority, responsibility, and tactical knowledge were embedded at a lower level—a level that was a key to the successful operation of the German tactical and operational system.

Third, the new organization increases the wartime size of the Field Army by using ready reservists to fill out the combat organizations of the fourth battalion which, on mobilization, receives the line/training companies of the other line battalions in the brigade. This mobilized battalion can be used in combat roles, or, more likely, each of the line/training companies can provide replacements to their parent battalion. Hence, the cohesion of the combat battalions is maintained since fillers are trained and commanded by the officers and men of the parent battalion.

The final rationale for the selection of the Structure IV Organization proceeds from this analysis and the high costs associated with the additional infrastructure necessary to support other organizational alternatives. Today, the German Field Army, under NATO wartime control, has been able to maintain its existing manning levels and existing *kaserns* (barracks) while adding new equipment and fielding additional units, with only some additional increase in costs.

The Field Army consists of three corps headquarters and twelve divisions controlling thirty-six brigades (Table 12). The new order of battle will be composed of sixteen Panzer brigades, seventeen Panzer Grenadier brigades, and three airborne brigades (with only three light infantry battalions and "up-gunned" with anti-tank guided missiles for use as an anti-tank blocking force in each corps sector). Each division has also received a Gepard anti-

Table 12
Structure of the West German Army, 1980-1981

	Number
Active personnel	335,200 (225,000 conscripts)
Field Army	272,000 (reorganization completed late 1981)

Corps headquarters	3
Divisions	
Panzer	6
Panzer Grenadier	4
Airborne	1
Mountain	1
Total	12
Maneuver battalions	
Pz battalions	69
PzGd battalions	64
Parachute battalions	12
Total	145
Panzer brigades	17
(with 3 Pz, 1 PzGd, and 1 self-propelled artillery battalions)	
Panzer Grenadier brigades	15
(with 1 Pz, 3 PzGd, and 1 self-propelled artillery battalions)	
Mountain brigade	1
Airborne brigades	3
(with 1 Pz and 4 parachute battalions)	
SAM regiment (36 Roland) (2 more forming)	1
Anti-aircraft regiments (36 Gepards)	11
Lance missile battalions (with 26 Lance missile launchers per battalion)	4
Territorial Army	
Territorial Commands	3
Military Districts	6
Home Defense Panzer Grenadier brigades	
(with 2 Pz, 2 PzGd, and 1 artillery battalions)	6
Security troops	
Home Defense regiments (composed of 45 motorized infantry battalions)	45

Source: *The Military Balance, 1980-1981*, London: International Institute for Strategic Studies, 1980, pp. 26-27.

aircraft artillery regiment (thirty-six dual 35mm guns) and a second reconnaissance battalion (mostly technical intelligence units). To each of the corps
a Roland regiment (thirty-six launchers) for air defense has been added, and
an anti-tank helicopter regiment is being formed. Additional corps support
troops (mostly combat service support) are in the reserve structure, while
the units are in equipment-holding status.

To complement the Field Army, the Germans maintain the Territorial
Army (which remains under national control in wartime). The Territorial
Army is composed of the Territorial Command—three Territorial Command headquarters which control six Military Districts. These Military
Districts (usually associated with a *Länder*) coordinate wartime support
with local civilian agencies and control Military Region Commands and a
Home Defense Group. Within the Military District, the commander has
responsibility for rear area security (area and point defense), communications and communications lines, engineering and damage control, and medical services. The Home Defense Force of the Territorial Army is currently
composed of six motorized, light infantry regiments. In response to NATO
initiatives, the German government, within Model IV reforms, has agreed
to form six heavy regiments that will deploy with second-line equipment
and will be committed to the Field Army. Thus, they will be under NATO
wartime control.

There are approximately 600,000 men in the reserves. After their required
term of active service of fifteen months, these men undergo four training
periods of one to two weeks during their six-year reserve obligation. The
ready reserve (about 25,000 men) are assigned to fill out the line/training
companies in the combat battalions of the brigades at mobilization. Most
reservists have unit designations in their mobilization orders, usually as
either replacements or, more likely, the manning strength for the combat
service support units at corps and army level. The latter type of unit must be
fully mobilized within seventy-two hours of warning.

Thus, following full mobilization, the German Army, counting the Field
and Territorial armies, will field almost 1 million men who are well equipped
and well led. The only potential problem of increasing concern to many
professional German officers is the lack of sufficient light infantry forces.
Budget planners are continually sacrificing such forces to heavy force and
armor formations.

Strategy, Tactics, and Deployment

Strategic Doctrine

The Central Region of NATO, comprising the totality of the Federal
Republic of Germany, is the principal region for NATO's defense. Strategic
planning for the Ministry of Defense, the Bundeswehr, and the army is to

be subsumed under the planning of NATO, with specific strategic/theater guidance coming from the Supreme Allied Commander, Europe (SACEUR). This strategic guidance is implemented in Germany by the Commander, Allied Forces Central Europe (COMAFCENT). In wartime, this German general would have operational control of all Allied ground and air units committed to battle in the Central Region.

NATO's military strategy is defined as the Strategy of Flexible Response, which seeks to avoid war through deterrence. Deterrence is predicated on Allied unity, a demonstrated ability to defend (warfighting), and the potential for nuclear escalation which presents the attacking nation with incalculable costs and risks. The operational requirements for Flexible Response involve direct defense, forward defense, and deliberate escalation. Direct defense is the capability to meet the level of violence initially chosen by the aggressor, be it conventional, chemical, or nuclear. Forward defense is a coherent defense that seeks to yield as little of Allied (German) territory as possible. Finally, deliberate escalation is the capability to geographically extend the conflict at the times and places of the Alliance's choosing and/or to initiate the use of nuclear weapons—from battlefield use of tactical nuclear weapons delivered by artillery or aircraft through the decision to go to general nuclear war.

Flexible Response aims to insure that the prospects for an enemy's success are disproportionate to the risks (including the potential destruction of his homeland) he will encounter in taking aggressive action.

The implementing mechanisms for Flexible Response are the weapons systems that comprise the NATO triad. This triad consists of conventional, theater nuclear, and strategic nuclear forces, each of which must be individually credible to the potential adversary. That is, each element must achieve the military requirements established by NATO's strategy. In the face of the growing capabilities of the Warsaw Pact, the credibility of each element of the triad continues to remain under stress.

To understand German strategic doctrine and the current composition and deployments of the German Army, one must understand the relationship between the German Army and the Alliance of which it is a part. Conventional forces of the Alliance (where the Germans make the largest contribution on the ground) are required to implement the concept of forward defense. These conventional forces are, in reality, precursors in that they provide two necessary and critical requirements in implementing the NATO strategy. First, these conventional elements force the aggressor to increase the size of his conventional attack—allowing unmistaken signs of enemy force buildup. Second, a coherent defense allows NATO's political authorities sufficient time to weigh the gravity of the situation, including the degree of initial success of the defense which is a necessary input to other necessary political-military decisions, including the decision to escalate the conflict to nuclear war.

In fulfilling the requirements for the forward defense, the Germans occupy three corps-sized sectors in the Federal Republic of Germany, sharing the potential frontline with the U.S. Army's V and VII Corps, the Belgian Corps, the Netherlands 1st Corps, and the British Army of the Rhine (BAOR). These deployments are depicted in Map 2.

The importance of the conventional and nuclear means of defense in German military planning and operations cannot be overemphasized. The Germans share both the conventional and nuclear roles necessary to insure that the elements of Flexible Response are present. For the remainder of this analysis, since medium and longer range nuclear roles are the mission of the Luftwaffe and since shorter range nuclear weapons are essentially a means for direct defense, we shall concentrate upon the German Army's role in conventional war.

Tactical Doctrine

The German Army today is caught in a doctrinal and strategic dilemma. Its operational model has historically been a defense in depth; the timing of decisions was critical, while space was not. When faced with numerically superior opponents, the Germans have traditionally gained a tactical or operational advantage by sidestepping (vetting) heavy attacks, drawing in and overextending the enemy's forces before vigorously counterattacking against an unsecured, vulnerable flank of an adversary. The intent was to fragment the enemy's organizational integrity by forcing him to react to an unexpected situation. Each of the enemy's subelements could then be attacked by massed German forces at overwhelming odds (in numerous, sequential pitched battles), or the enemy could be forced to throw unsupported, piecemeal attacks against German units that were in their rear area, defending (with the inherent advantages of local defense), and astride the enemy's line of communication (the classical *Vernichtungsgedanke*). To execute this type of defense-offense requires space and time to maneuver throughout the depths of the theater. Today, the German Army, as part of NATO, does not have the space to retire and subsequently stretch out an opponent's thrusts. Thus, the German Army, as well as the rest of the Allied Army corps, is wed to a doctrine of a strong forward defense that protects the German nation, its people and its industry.

German military planning must operate from the strategic defensive and, within an agreed NATO context, from the tactical defensive. However, the requirement to defend forward does not mean a linear defense in-place. Historically, a cordon defense is known to fail. Within the context of HDv 100/100, there is room to believe that the Germans are again looking toward a form of maneuver warfare that could "vet" the strength of an armored thrust from Warsaw Pact nations. The Germans would trap the leading echelons of a Warsaw Pact attack by driving flank counterattacks between the initial and follow-on echelons of the standard Warsaw Pact operation.

Map 2.
German Corps Composition

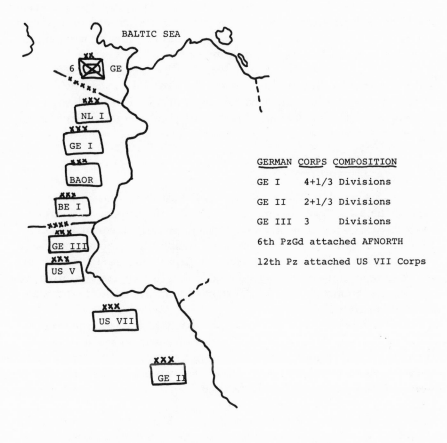

BALTIC SEA

6 GE

NL I

GE I

BAOR

BE I

GE III

US V

US VII

GE II

GERMAN CORPS COMPOSITION

GE I   4+1/3 Divisions

GE II   2+1/3 Divisions

GE III   3   Divisions

6th PzGd attached AFNORTH

12th Pz attached US VII Corps

Numerous division and corps level operations on the Eastern Front were carried out using a similar scheme.

The implementation of these defensive-offensive concepts requires well-trained and well-led troops. Evidence of this capability remains contradictory. For example, one U.S. Army colonel, when he commanded a tank battalion in Germany, participated in field exercises with a German Panzer brigade. It was his impression that the Germans practiced their traditional mobile defensive form of combat. He vividly recalled an 80-kilometer night movement to contact against an adversary's flank, followed by an attack deep into the enemy's rear. However, other U.S. Army officers, in observing German Panzer companies practice the defense, viewed the German approach to defense as very static and as exhibiting little initiative on the part of the platoon leaders and company commanders.

As can be gleaned from reading accounts of battles on the Eastern Front and in the current HDv 100/100, both views could be correct within the German concept of combat. Nevertheless, it may have been this inactivity in company defensive doctrine that the Model IV reorganization was designed to prevent.

Combat Capabilities

The German industrial complex remains as capable of producing sophisticated, rugged military equipment today as it did in the past. Currently, German Army procurement is bringing indigenously designed and manufactured equipment to the field, replacing equipment previously purchased from the United States. Newer German Army equipment has been designed to support the mobile, flexible, and high tempo operations envisaged by their operational philosophy. Current equipment inventories for major items are listed in Table 13.

Recent cutbacks in the defense budget may have dramatic effects on the force size of the German Army. The earlier inventory objective of Leopard II tanks was 1,800 units; today, that objective may be lowered to 1,500 units. In addition, the formation of the anti-tank helicopter regiments as well as Roland purchases may be delayed.

Sustainability

That the Germans prefer and rely on deterrence is nowhere more evident than in their logistical sustainability. Under the current budget crunch, ammunition and spare parts have been sacrificed to the "out years" in budgetary planning. Today, the German Army has several weeks' worth of sustaining items. However, to qualify the ammunition situation, the projected rates of expenditures are driven upwards by U.S. planning factors which are based on high firepower, attrition-driven models (as well as by heavy use of Harassing and Interdiction fires which consumed over 50

Table 13
West German Army Equipment Inventory

Type of Equipment	Number
Armored Fighting Vehicles	
M-48A2/A4 tanks (being phased into Territorial Army or removed from inventory)	1,289
Leopard I	2,437
Leopard II	100
	(1,800 to be procured)
Marder (infantry fighting vehicle)	2,136
M-113 (armored personnel carrier)	4,030
Artillery	
FH-70 howitzer (towed 155mm)	164
M-109 howitzer (self-propelled 155mm)	586
M-107 gun (self-propelled 175mm)	149
M-110 howitzer (self-propelled 203mm)	77
120mm mortars	1,062
Multiple rocker launchers (self-propelled 140mm)	208

Source: *The Military Balance, 1980-1981*, London: International Institute for Strategic Studies, 1980, pp. 26-27.

percent of ammunition tonnage in Vietnam). The German Army, with its focus on mobile operations, will not be nearly as dedicated to continuously high rates of fire. High rates of fire are usually associated only with the *Schwerpunkt*. Thus, while the German supply of ammunition may not meet the requirements of NATO/U.S. planning standards, it may be sufficient for the operations and strategy that the Germans envisage. Nevertheless, additional supply sustainability would be comforting to NATO strategists.

Ability to Fight

The quality of officers in the German Army remains high, with a small percentage attending the General Staff Academy for approximately two years. In order to insure that high quality, company and battalion commanders serve long tours (up to four years) as commanders, sufficient time to cycle two sets of fifteen-month conscripts through the units. In addition, company commanders are usually very senior captains (a tradition in most European armies). This policy, of course, allows a well-experienced officer to command troops.

The quality of the German troops also remains high. The fifteen-month draftee is given sufficient tactical and technical training to perform his specific duties within the requirements of German tactical doctrine. One critical problem—retaining senior noncommissioned officers—is being studied by the Ministry of Defense.

The German Army has elected to retain locally recruited, trained, and based regiments. This tradition of high unit cohesion and its impact on battlefield effectiveness would be impossible to replace. The German Army, within the political constraints in which it must operate, remains focused on the essential ingredients of combat-effectiveness—unit cohesion, training, and tactical doctrine.

Scenarios

The German Army was created to fight one particular enemy—the Russians or Soviets. It is the only Western army that has fought against the East in this century and fought both for and against the Russians in Napoleonic times. These combat experiences have defined the German national armies. The result is a German Army oriented against a single, traditional threat. Much of its doctrine and the tactical case studies used to train German officers have derived from this experience.

Regardless of its orientation and specific operational capabilities, any assessment of the German Army's contribution to the outcome of any conflict in Central Europe must contain numerous uncertainties. Many of these uncertainties are "scenario dependent." For example, since NATO is a defensive alliance, it has surrendered the strategic initiative to the Warsaw Pact, including the timing of mobilization and attack and the weighting and location of the adversary's main effort. Tactically, NATO and the German Army have also surrendered many important local initiatives.

In addition, since the German Army must fight as a member of a coalition, there are the problems of assessing the performance of other national army forces which occupy the flanks of each German corps sector. (See Map 2.) The lack of sufficient Dutch and Belgian forces stationed in their respective corps sectors in peacetime would create serious tactical deployment problems for German forces which would have to screen these sectors during a mobilization until the Dutch and Belgian reinforcements arrived.

Finally, NATO's strategic aims must be incorporated in any assessment for the constraints they would place on operations. For purposes of this analysis, NATO's strategic aims, once deterrence failed, would be to defeat any attack and to eject the attacking forces from German territory. Only recently have certain political and military leaders begun to discuss "cross-border" operations to gain territory that would be politically useful in negotiations for terminating a war.

The most severe constraint in any scenario is the problem of combat operations within the context of the forward defense. The lack of depth would force the German Army to accept some risks along the inter-German border. Disposition of the three German corps would also forbid major strategic undertakings. Within these constraints, the German Army could only conduct combat operations at the corps level and below—essentially at the operational and tactical level.

The dispositions of two of the German Army corps (the Ist and IIIrd Corps) are to provide defense along the Northern German Plain. The German Army's IInd Corps is less strategically located; it protects Bavaria and Warsaw Pact operations from Czechoslovakia.

Across the Northern German Plain, the Netherlands Army Corps occupies the northernmost defensive sector of Allied Forces, Central Europe (AFCENT). This Dutch corps links its left flank with the German 6th Panzer Grenadier Division, the largest of the German divisions. (This division protects Landjut.) To the south of the Dutch corps is the German Army Ist Corps, the largest of the German Army corps. It occupies the central position in the defense of the North European Plain.

The German Army IIIrd Corps protects the southern part of the North European Plain and sits astride the Gottinger Corridor which ends in the heavily industrial Ruhr Valley. Between the Ist and IIIrd Corps lie the British Army of the Rhine and the Belgian corps. This center is AFCENT's most strategic area, for this avenue of approach leads to the Channel ports and their southward lines of communication. Unfortunately, this center—actually on both sides of the Ist Corps—is the weakest link, where the terrain supports high mobility to attacking Warsaw Pact forces.

Neither the Dutch nor the Belgians deploy many combat forces forward in peacetime. And while the BAOR is manned in some strength, occupational duties in Northern Ireland sap it of some strength. For all of these three corps to reach full combat manning requires a declaration of mobilization, followed by reinforcement. With a short warning attack by the Warsaw Pact, many of the Dutch and Belgian forces would be moving toward their general defense positions. This reinforcement might have to travel under intensive enemy air interdiction.

Finally, neither the Dutch, Belgian, nor British corps is fully modernized. They all have deficiencies in mobile, medium artillery firepower, tanks, anti-tank weapons (guns and guided missiles), and armored personnel carriers. The weaknesses of these national army corps create major vulnerabilities across the breadth of the Northern European Plain.

The threat scenarios are usually divided by a time division, with an attack starting after a specified number of days. Typically, the short warning scenario (often referred to as the "standing start") would allow about forty-eight hours of Warsaw Pact mobilization—with a very short NATO response time. The long warning scenario assumes that the Warsaw Pact nations would attack ten to fourteen days after mobilization. This scenario usually suggests that NATO would begin mobilizing approximately seven days after the Pact's mobilization began.

In the short warning scenario, NATO assumes that approximately fifty Category I Pact Divisions would be available for immediate combat. They are disposed as shown in the accompanying tabulation.

	Forces Deployed in		
	East Germany	Czechoslovakia	Poland
Soviet divisions	20	4	3
East German divisions	6	—	—
Czech divisions	—	7	—
Polish divisions	—	—	10

These dispositions suggest that the combined Warsaw Pact attack would initially have twenty-six divisions to allocate across three major avenues of approach—the North European Plain, the Fulda Gap, and the Hot Corridor. Elements of the U.S. VIIth Corps (those not defending in the Hot Corridor), along with the German IInd Corps, would be defending against eleven Pact divisions attacking out of Czechoslovakia. While it is not political to discuss, these forces in southern Germany have some opportunity to trade space for time. This is not so in Northern Europe where strategic lines of communication are easily threatened.

Thus, we should expect that the Pact's major effort would be placed along the Northern European Plain. With minimum allocations of Pact forces in the Landjut area, Fulda and Hof, one could expect some ten to twelve Pact divisions to attack into the areas occupied by the Dutch, Belgian, British, and German IIIrd Corps areas. Immediate follow-on, second forces would consist of some eight to thirteen Pact divisions aimed at NATO's strategic center.

To counter this situation, numerous Dutch, Belgian, and BAOR units would still be marching to their general defensive positions along the inter-German border. Only single Dutch and Belgian brigades, reinforced with German covering force units from the German Ist and IIIrd Corps, could offer initial resistance. Few U.S. reinforcing units, both tactical aviation or ground combat units, would be available for combat operations.

Nevertheless, while a short warning scenario maximizes the Pact's quest for strategic and tactical surprise, it does not maximize the Pact's desire for most favorable force ratios.

The long warning scenario (ten to fourteen days of mobilization) would allow the Pact to maximize force ratios—approximately a 2.4 to 1 ratio in division equivalents. While this scenario would substantially inhibit the Pact's ability to achieve strategic surprise, allowing the necessary mobilization and deployment of Belgian and Dutch corps-sized units plus British reinforcements to the BAOR, it would still permit tactical surprise—selecting the final time for the attack and allocation of forces to the critical avenues of approach. Finally, by M + 30 the Pact could field from 85 to 125 divisions, all of them tank or motorized infantry, excluding several Soviet airborne divisions.

In response to either of these scenarios, one should expect the Germans to fight a vigorous covering force action along the inter-German border in accordance with the accepted NATO strategy of the forward defense. In the short warning scenario, the German Army would be conducting numerous meeting engagements with Pact forces. These types of mobile, independent operations fit well into established German tactical doctrine.

In the initial stages of the battle, stemming from the "standing start" scenario, German forces would be "strung out" across five corps sectors along the Northern European Plain. With the arrival of the Dutch and Belgian reinforcements, these heavy German units would probably retire behind Home Defense brigades, preparing to launch major, divisional-sized counter-attacks behind the Pact's first echelon forces, which would now be fully engaged with the Dutch, Belgian, and British corps. Thus, the Home Defense brigades (not under NATO control) would protect the flanks of the German corps as well as the heavy, mobile striking power of the German Corps in the Field Army as they reorganized for offensive operations.

While this type of operation would not be a pure *Vernichtungsgedanke* since there would be a major second echelon force arriving near the battlefield, it would offer a best chance of destroying the Pact's first echelon army(ies). Within this context of operations, tactical airpower could contribute by providing battlefield interdiction for the Germans' counterattack force and by delaying the arrival of a second echelon force through deep interdiction.

This form of manpower, classic of German operations on the Eastern Front (1941-1943), is well established in HDv 100/100. It is a major topic of conversation of German officers. One can only suggest this operational style, however, since it has not been developed in published form. If this is the case, which much evidence supports, then there remains an immense gulf between operations envisaged in FM 100-5 and HDv 100/100.

In the long warning scenario, the situation facing the German forces changes appreciably. First, the Dutch, British, and Belgian corps would be deployed at their general defensive position. German Army units would be concentrated in their respective corps sectors, having been relieved of their covering force responsibilities in the Dutch and Belgian sectors.

As the attack commenced, one would expect the Germans to fight a vigorous action along the inter-German border—terrain in the Ist and IIIrd Corps sectors is favorable for this forward defense. However, good defensive terrain for the Dutch, British, and Belgian corps would start some 30 to 50 kilometers from the border. As the Warsaw Pact main effort might well be diverted into this area of the North European Plain, a salient would develop on the southern flank of the Ist Corps and the northern flank of the IIIrd Corps. This situation would create vulnerable flanks for these corps to exploit. The attempt would be made to move from less mobile, terrain-oriented defense along the inter-German border to more mobile, force-oriented combat against the flanks and rear of Pact first echelon armies. Again, the Home Defense brigades contribute to this operational concept by relieving the heavy armored striking power of the Bundeswehr. This is the style of war for which the German Army is structured, even to the extent that the Panzer Grenadiers would conduct their operations by remaining inside their mechanized infantry fighting vehicles.

In either scenario, the Germans would initially conduct major combat operations to support the forward defense, giving them the time to evacuate their civilians from combat areas. This forward defense would also give the German political authorities time to gauge NATO's intent to escalate the conflict by employing theater nuclear weapons. By protecting German territory through forward defense, the German authorities hope that any initial use of nuclear weapons will not be on German soil.

If for some reason nuclear escalation were to cease being viable policy, then one should expect the Germans to commit their Territorial Army, relieving as much of the Field Army as possible. With this concentrated, armored striking force, the Germans could be expected to launch major operational-level counteroffensives. These counteroffensives would be designed to destroy the operational cohesion of the first echelon Pact armies. The Pact's entire operational scheme would thereby be placed in jeopardy since the Pact's detailed military plans would be overtaken by these sudden events and the rapidly changing situation.

In conclusion, however, projecting the current situation into the future only reinforces the negative factors in any assessment. Budgetary limits on German defense spending will slow the modernization of the German Army, cut into its training program, and limit sustainability (ammunition; petroleum, oil, and lubricants [POL]; and spare parts) to less than the NATO requirement of thirty days on-hand. Cast against this future, the contribution of the German Army to NATO's defense, while remaining impressive, will diminish.

Notes

1. Gordon A. Craig, *The Politics of the Prussian Army, 1640-1945* (New York: Oxford University Press, 1955), pp. 62-63. See also Walter Goerlitz, *The German*

General Staff, 1657-1945 (New York: Frederick A. Praeger, Inc., 1959), pp. 27-28 and 41.

2. For example, Gneisenau was Chief of Staff to Blucher in the 1814 Waterloo Campaign; Ludendorff to Hindenberg; Mackenses to Seeckt; Manstein to Rundstedt. One failure in this system of creative tension between commander and his Chief of Staff was at Stalingrad when von Paulus and his Chief of Staff were too like-minded to debate the significant aspects of the operational requirements imposed by Hitler.

3. Samuel Huntington, *The Soldier and the State* (Cambridge, Mass.: Harvard University Press, 1967), pp. 80-85.

4. Ibid. Huntington observes that the Bismarck-Moltke era was the height of objective civilian control of the German Army.

5. Ibid.

6. *The German White Paper on Defense, 1979* (Bonn: Government Printing House, 1979), p. 190.

7. Ibid.

8. Trevor N. Dupuy, *A Genius for War: The German Army and General Staff, 1807-1945* (Oxford: Oxford University Press, 1977), pp. 253-54.

9. Martin van Creveld, *Fighting Power: German Military Performance, 1919-1945* (Westport, Conn.: Greenwood Press, 1980), pp. 187-88.

10. Ibid., p. 189.

11. John Boyd, "Patterns of Conflict," unpublished paper, 1980. p-E-4.

12. Ibid.

13. Ibid.

14. During the time of von Schlieffen, however, the strategic and operational direction of the "swing through Belgium" in 1914 was overly centralized. Without the ability to decentralize operations to army and corps commanders, the temporary setback at the Marne was allowed to freeze all initiative. Operational mobility and flexibility were not regained in the West until the decentralized tactics of von Hutier were incorporated in 1918.

15. Matthew Cooper, *The German Army, 1933-1945* (New York: Zebra Books, 1978), p. 4.

16. Ibid.

17. Ibid., p. 21.

18. This is a major point made by Boyd, "Patterns of Conflict," p. 26.

19. Boyd and Steven L. Canby in his *German Army Reorganization* (Potomac, Md.: C&L Associates, 1978) observe that many of the most successful German Panzer commanders often had a light infantry background.

20. This is perhaps a continuing example of the traditional German emphasis on decentralized planning by subordinate headquarters.

21. It is reputed that a German corps commander was relieved during an operation in the Franco-Prussian War for following orders. The rationale was that he had failed to react to an unexpected opportunity—and that the king had entrusted him to think. This approach to command and control remains embodied in German philosophy in the dictum that "commanders who merely wait for orders cannot exploit the opportunity of the moment."

22. Actually, the strategic direction of the Schlieffen Plan required little of the traditional flexibility demonstrated earlier by the German Army.

23. *Generals Balck and Von Mellenthin on Tactics: Implications for NATO Military Doctrine* (McClean, Va.: BDM Corporation, 1980), pp. 37-43.

Bibliography

Boyd, John. "Patterns of Conflict." Unpublished manuscript. 1980.

Canby, Steven L. *A Comparative Assessment of the NATO Corps Battle*. Potomac, Md.: C&L Associates, 1978.

————. *German Army Reorganization*. Potomac, Md.: C&L Associates, 1978.

Conversations with General Hermann Balck. Columbus, Ohio: Battelle Laboratories, 1979.

Cooper, Matthew. *The German Army, 1933-1945*. New York: Zebra Books, 1978.

Craig, Gordon A. *The Politics of the Prussian Army, 1640-1945*. New York: Oxford University Press, 1955.

Dupuy, Trevor N. *A Genius for War: The German Army and General Staff, 1807-1945* Oxford: Oxford University Press, 1977.

FM 100-5: Operations. Department of the Army, Headquarters, 1976.

Generals Balck and Von Mellenthin on Tactics: Implications for NATO Military Doctrine. McLean, Va.: BDM Corporation, 1980.

The German White Paper on Defense, 1979. Bonn: Federal Ministry of Defense, 1979.

Goerlitz, Walter. *The German General Staff, 1657-1945*. New York: Frederick A. Praeger, Inc., 1959.

Huntington, Samuel. *The Soldier and the State*. Cambridge, Mass.: Harvard University Press, 1967.

Lupfer, Timothy T. *The Dynamics of Doctrine: Changes to German Tactical Doctrine During the First World War*. Fort Leavenworth, Kans.: U.S. Army Command and Staff College, 1981.

The Military Balance, 1980-1981. London: International Institute for Strategic Studies, 1980.

Van Creveld, Martin. *Fighting Power: German Military Performance, 1919-1945*. Potomac, Md.: C&L Associates, 1980.

Greece

James M. Dunn

Responsibility for protecting the territorial integrity of Greece falls to the Hellenic Army. This mission entails two areas of operations: mainland Greece and the Aegean with its multitude of islands. On the mainland Greece shares a common border with Albania in the northwest, Yugoslavia in the north central region, Bulgaria above the Macedonia/Thrace panhandle, and Turkey adjoining eastern Thrace. Bulgaria, the only Warsaw Pact state contiguous to Greece, represents the source of a potential threat to Greek security. It will be recalled that during World War II Bulgaria pushed its frontier through Greek territory to the Aegean, occupying the area between Salonika and a German-held buffer zone on the Turkish border. While the notion of Bulgaria and its Soviet ally having designs on direct access to the Aegean at the expense of Greek territorial integrity is plausible, it is more likely that Bulgarian forces would be employed in an assault to seize the Turkish Straits. Nevertheless, a Warsaw Pact attack on Greece could be launched as part of a main attack on the Straits to deny Greek and other NATO reinforcements to the Turkish defenders.

The Aegean area of operations includes all the Greek islands in the Aegean Sea from the mouth of the Dardanelles to the island of Crete. The area has three major subcomponents: the chain of islands off the Turkish coast; the Cyclades in the central Aegean; and Crete in the south. The strategic value of these islands to support naval and air operations in the Aegean and the surrounding area is self-evident, as Allied (mainly British) and German battles for their control during World War II historically attest. More because of a threat perceived from Turkey than in recognition of the role of the Aegean in East-West global competition, Greece has remilitarized the islands opposite the Turkish mainland. This contravenes the Lausanne Treaty, but Greece uses Turkey's creation of a so-called Fourth (or Aegean) Army as a pretext for its actions.[1]

The views and opinions expressed in this article are exclusively those of the author and are not indicative of support from any institutional affiliation which the author may have.

The tensions between Athens and Ankara are a particular annoyance to NATO. Both Greece and Turkey have been members of the Alliance since 1952. Greek Prime Minister Andreas Papandreou has spoken frequently of a "threat from Turkey" and of his desire that the Alliance guarantee Greece's territorial integrity. Greece withdrew from the military wing of NATO in 1974, claiming that NATO and the United States should have prevented the Turkish invasion of Cyprus. The outlook is that eventually Greece will move away from its present "neither in nor out" position and return to serious participation in the Alliance, but only after it has secured favorable concessions in base rights and defense and economic aid agreements from the United States.

Greece and Southern Flank Strategy

In view of the unprecedented buildup of Soviet ground forces, increased Soviet naval activities in the Mediterranean, and the continued modernization of Warsaw Pact armies, Greece plays a key role in NATO's strategy for the protection of its southern flank. NATO strategy depends on Greek and Turkish cooperation in defense of the Turkish straits and in maintaining the security of the Aegean. Issues of sea power notwithstanding, the Hellenic Army is the guarantor of Greek territorial integrity. Without the Greek land link in the NATO defensive chain, Turkey would be isolated in the east and NATO sea and land lines of communication and supply through which vital Middle Eastern oil supplies would have to pass would be more vulnerable to attack and interdiction. On the other hand, it has been suggested that the Soviet military buildup and increased naval presence in the Mediterranean do not constitute the basis of a serious attempt to challenge NATO militarily on its southern flank. Rather, another interpretation of Soviet objectives appears to be as follows:

- to weaken and undermine the Mediterranean component of NATO;
- to induce Greece and Turkey to opt for a foreign policy that tilts toward de facto nonalignment;
- to demonstrate (Soviet) credibility as a patron and protector to present and prospective regional clients;
- to ensure that Soviet preferences and interests enter into the considerations of regional actors.[2]

Therefore, ensuring the political stability and military effectiveness of NATO's southeastern flank is an important countermeasure to take in order to constrain the political effectiveness of Soviet naval deployments and Warsaw Pact efforts in force modernization.

The contributions of Greece and Turkey of ready combat forces are "obvious and visible contributions" to the collective defense of the alliance; but these countries have other potentially more significant advantages: "their geographic/strategic locations blocking the line of advance of Soviet influence to the Mediterranean and the Middle East, the tying down of Soviet reserves in southern Russia, and the facilities whereby the United States is able to project its power into the area and further counter or exclude Soviet influence."[3]

The Greek military art and tradition began before most other cultures had evolved beyond the hunting and gathering stage. School children everywhere still read of the Spartan military regimen, of Leonidas's stand at Thermopylae, and of the conquering exploits of Alexander. Even in those days of antiquity significant military and political behavioral patterns were established whose consequences have been felt in the modern era. Except for rare periods during which city states entered into convenient alliances, loyalties were fiercely sectional. Hellenism in its full fruition represented more an expression of esthetic and philosophical ideals rather than a force for political regimentation like the Pax Romana.

Unlike Rome, an imperial Greece never emerged and custody of Greece passed from the Romans to the Byzantines to the Ottomans. Thus, while there were always Greeks bearing arms and Greeks renowned for their soldierly and technological skills, they were in the service of successive imperial governments and not contributing to the development of a Greek military that served exclusively Greek interests.

The modern Greeks look back on the fall of Constantinople to the Turks as the beginning of a long dark age for their country. The Ottoman occupation that was to last 400 years severed the tenuous connections that bound fifteenth-century Greece to its classical heritage. The Ottoman millet system of administration allowed the Greeks to govern themselves as a separate nation within the empire. This autonomy was exercised through the Orthodox Church. The Patriarch of Constantinople was the leader of the Christian millet, which made him both spiritual and temporal leader of the Greek nation. At the lower community level the governing authorities were the local clergy and landowners. Their obligation was to render taxes to the Turkish overlords, who otherwise left them free to conduct their own business and provide for their own education. The Turks provided for their defense. Furthermore, under the Ottoman rule one out of every five Greek Christian males was surrendered every four years for induction into the Corps of Janissaries.[4]

The description of the millet system leaves a misleading impression of Ottoman benevolence. Such was not the case. The Greeks in general held the status of *rayas*, that is, vassals or slaves. Some took advantage of the Turks' eagerness to ensure the smooth operation of their empire by assimilating educated Greeks into their bureaucratic and financial structure. These "collaborators" not only gained comfortable social and ecomomic status, but also succeeded eventually in dominating the Greek economy. Most prominent among these were the Phanariots, named from the Phanar district of Constantinople where the Patriarch's seat of power was located.

The Phanariots were entrenched in the very heart of the empire, while in the provinces, where the Turkish overseers were but a minority, a very different type of Greek grew up. Known as klephts they were part brigand, part hero, part partisan in a protracted battle for national liberation. The klepht was "unlettered, but straightforward; uncouth, but jealous of his honor; ignorant of fine phrases, but an expert marksman."[5]

Between the two extreme stereotype figures, the Phanariot and the klepht, fell the majority of Greeks. They were "organized in semiautonomous communities (and) lived as best they could, sometimes in the servility that befitted the *raya*, sometimes in revolt after the example of the klepht. They were torn between prudence and bravery. They detested and at the same time submitted to the backward Ottoman administration which was so oppressive that it was inefficient."[6]

When the Greeks struck their blow for independence in 1821, it was natural that their leaders should come from the lower clergy, the klephts, pirates and merchant captains, and from organizers of locally recruited guerrilla bands.[7] But it was also natural that the battle for independence should degenerate into a struggle among the Greeks: islanders vs. mountain dwellers; Peloponnesians vs. Roumeliots, and among divided supporters of the big three "Protecting Powers," Great Britain, France, and Russia.[8] It was not until the Protecting Powers imposed a monarchy on Greece with Otho (son of the king of Bavaria) on the throne that something resembling an independent and sovereign state emerged. Otho's monarchy was scarcely an improvement over the Turkish rule. The Greek army at that time was predominantly a body of irregulars which Otho disbanded and replaced with a corp of Bavarian mercenaries. "As a result many Greek soldiers returned to their old habits of brigandage in the mountains, increasing a problem that would plague Greece for decades. Brigandage remained an accepted method of political intimidation, and the countryside showed greater loyalty to the klephts than to the representatives of the national government."[9]

It was not long after the birth of the Greek nation-state that the military began playing an assertive role in politics. A small uprising staged in 1843 by Greek officers commanding the Athens garrison forced Otho to establish a constitutional monarchy and form a parliament. Additionally, he was obliged to dismiss his Bavarian advisers and allow Greek officers to assume command positions within their own army. Because of the lingering Bavarian influence, the regular army of Greece initially was organized and trained on a German model.

Two points are worth noting. First, even from the beginning there were at various times two armed forces within Greece: the irregular guerrilla (klepht) bands that kept mainly to the provinces, and the regular army whose officers were intimately involved with the intrigues of the central government in Athens. Second, these two forces represented two aspects of the Greek national persona: one sectionally oriented, fractious, jealously independent; the other nationally oriented, corporate, and Westernized. In the century and a half of modern Greek nationhood these forces have had occasion to clash—most recently during the aftermath of the Axis occupation and in the course of the Greek Civil War, 1944–1949.

In their turbulent history the Greeks have developed survival skills that have run contrary to what has evolved as the modern Greek military professionals' notion of appropriate social behavior. Some of these characteristics are:[10] narrow local patriotism; naive faith in the great powers; a tendency to circumvent civic obligations by means of deception and bakhshish; an alternation of heroic gestures with a fatalistic submission to the powers that be; an inability to cooperate, and a trust in good connections and personal favors rather than abstract principles. The Greek Army professional's disdain for these characteristics has not necessarily liberated him from acting quite naturally—and in many cases pragmatically—in response to them. But the ideals that motivate him are in good measure based on a rejection of these factors as detrimental to the achievement of national goals.

Hence, to discuss the evolution of the Hellenic Army from the War of Independence to the present is not so much to account for the development of military science and technology in Greece as it is to account for the evolution of a military "counterculture" opposed to the persistent and negatively perceived traits of Phanariot and klepht as they are seen in the social environment.

The Modern Greek Army

The Hellenic Army entered the modern era in a succession of four wars: Balkan Wars (1912–1913), World War I, the Greek-Turkish War (1921–1922), and World War II. Greek intervention in the First World War on the side of the Allies was urged by Prime Minister Venezelos as a means to realizing the *Megali Idea* (The Great Idea)—a dream of returning Greece to the greatness of antiquity by uniting Constantinople, Ionia, and the Aegean coast of Asia Minor with the mainland. It seemed for a while as if Venezelos would accomplish his goal: Greek forces—part of the ten divisions Greece committed to Macedonia—were among the Allied contingents that entered Constantinople in 1918. The Greeks occupied Smyrna (Izmir) in 1920. Hoping to consolidate their control over Asia Minor, the Greeks attacked into the Anatolian heartland in 1921. The Turks under Mustafa Kemal (Ataturk) allowed them to overextend themselves and then counterattacked, inflicting a humiliating defeat on the Greeks. Equally demoralizing as the tragic military defeat was the collapse of the *Megali Idea*. The dream had been a unifying factor among the Greeks, and with an external enemy no longer the primary concern they turned against themselves.

In the years between 1923 and 1935 rival factions struggled for control of the government. The military attempted to assert itself but failed in several coup attempts. Finally, in 1935 King George II was returned to his throne by a plebiscite, but because of a parliamentary deadlock among the royalists, republican, and (the smaller) Communist parties, he requested General Ioannis Metaxas to step in as prime minister and form a government. General Metaxas, a former Chief of Staff of the Hellenic Army and respected soldier, dissolved the Parliament in 1936 and commenced to rule as a dictator on the pretext that the Communists were conspiring to strike a coup from within the armed forces.

General Metaxas "rejected Western liberalism as alien to Greek traditions and spoke in terms of creating a 'Third Civilization' in Greece based on order and discipline."[11] At the same time he eschewed the ideological and physical trappings of contemporary Fascist states. Above all, his regime was "authoritarian and oppressive—and, like its leader, puritanical."[12] The government of General Metaxas reflected the perceptions of the professional military counterculuture—disdainful of the elitist "Phanariots" and undisciplined "klephts." (The same counterculture asserted itself later during the "Colonels' Regime," 1967-1974.)

One of Metaxas's main undertakings was to improve the armed forces. After their defeat in the Greco-Turkish War and as a consequence of the political dissension and coup plotting that had preceded Metaxas's assumption of control, the armed forces' morale was low. He purged the officer corps of over 2,000 known or suspected republicans and Communists.[13]

The strength of the Hellenic Army in 1939 was approximately 5,000 officers and 65,000 men. It was a conscript force in which men served for two years. The corp of officers was professional. The force structure consisted of fifteen infantry divisions, one cavalry division, and additional infantry brigades. On mobilization these units would be filled out by reservists. The infantry had mainly small arms, most of which were antiquated; the artillery consisted of a few French and German mountain and field guns; anti-aircraft artillery consisted of some 140 guns; and there were no anti-tank weapons. There were no tanks in the inventory. Motor transport was scarce to nonexistent, and logistical support was delivered mainly by ox-drawn vehicles.[14]

The army was ill equipped and short on supplies, but because of the reforms and improvements in training Metaxas had introduced, morale was high. Metaxas had foreseen the inevitable confrontation that was to take place with the Axis powers and had been quietly mobilizing after the Italian invasion of Albania in 1939. On October 28, 1940, Mussolini delivered an ultimatum to Metaxas, demanding that Greece allow Italian units to occupy portions of its territory to guarantee Italian security. Metaxas replied with one word: "no." At the same moment Italian units were already crossing from Albania into Greece.

The Greek resistance was unexpectedly strong, and within a few days the Greeks were on the offensive. They drove the Italians back into Albania as far as Koritsa and Argyrocastron before the end of the year. However, "the Italian forces recovered courageously from the criminal follies of Mussolini and his contemptible entourage. After the first shock of defeat, they succeeded in holding a line in the wintry mountains of Albania, and prevented the Greeks from capturing Valona, the principal port in the south, which would have enabled the Greek forces to be supplied by sea. The Albanian War was thus reduced to deadlock, from which neither side could break out."[15] Hitler, poised in the Balkans, and intent on securing his southern flank in anticipation of his attack on Russia, intervened to break the stalemate on April 6, 1941.

Most of the Greek strength—some fourteen divisions—was committed to the Albanian front. British reinforcements (including Australian, New Zealand, and Polish units) had been deployed to beef up the thinly spread Greek units in Macedonia, Thrace, and northcentral Greece. The German Twelfth Army attacked through the Struma and Vardar valleys. Again, the Greeks offered stiff resistance: the Greek soldiers holding the Rupel gap fought to the last man. Other German columns hit through the Monastir gap in the west, cutting off the Greek forces on the Albanian border. The Greek and British forces remaining withdrew southward, fighting in successive stages from the Aliakmon line to Mt. Olympus to the pass of Thermopylae. The British were able to avoid encirclement and withdrew 50,600 men to Crete. The Greek forces, their main strength cut off in the northwest, were forced to surrender on April 22.[16]

The battle for Crete began on May 20. King George II of Greece and his government had evacuated to the island where 10,000 Greek and 32,000 British soldiers were defending. After twelve days of fierce fighting, Crete fell and the king narrowly escaped to Egypt.

At this point the history of the modern Greek Army takes an unfortunate turn. With Greece under Axis occupation it was natural to expect that a resistance movement would begin. The occupying forces essentially ignored the provinces where armed bands of guerrillas began to emerge. The first of these were the National Popular Liberation Army (ELAS) under control of the National Liberation Front (EAM), a Communist organization, and the National Republican Greek League (EDES), as well as other smaller organizations. As these resistance movements grew in strength, the legitimate military authorities sat helpless and ignored, exiled in the Middle East.

Woodhouse explains the removal of the regular army from a major role in the resistance in this way:

The armed forces in the Albanian war were largely under officers loyal to the King. While they were occupied at the front, their left wing or Venzelist predecessors were unemployed in Athens, where they were readily available for recruitment and preparation for post-occupational activities. When the collapse came in April 1941, some senior officers on active service escaped with the king; others returned home, demoralized by the surrender and discredited by failure, however undeservedly. The absence of the king left them without a rallying-point or political guidance, and their association with the Metaxist regime damaged their prestige. A small group of monarchist officers, known as the Six Colonels, established a link by wireless with the government in exile and acted as a liaison with the officer corps in Athens. But their instructions were not to engage in premature activities of a provocative character, and few officers above the rank of captain disobeyed them.[17]

It became evident that the EAM and its military wing, ELAS, were not singly motivated by sentiments of patriotic resistance, but rather were determined to fight for the establishment of a Soviet-aligned Greek Communist state. Not all who served EAM-ELAS were so motivated: some were duped, some were eager to join a resistance unit—regardless of its politics—in order to fight a common enemy, and some fought out of crass opportunism. But what was beginning to unfold was the first stage of the Greek Civil War. Without going into an extensive account of the events of the occupation, suffice it to say that the Greek partisans fought each other with equal, if not greater zeal than the Axis enemy. ELAS emerged as the strongest of all the factions but was unable to assert complete control of the country.

The first round of the Civil War began in earnest after the withdrawal of Axis forces in 1944. With the restoration of the legitimate government the regular army returned from exile, led by the Rimini Brigade, which had distinguished itself on the Albanian front, and the Sacred Company, a commando-type unit manned only by officers, the predecessor of the present-day Greek Special Forces.

Two armed forces of Greeks now confronted each other in their newly liberated country: ELAS and the regular army backed by the British. ELAS was reluctant to demobilize since without the force of arms, it could not maintain control of the areas it held. The shaky truce erupted into the Battle of Athens—otherwise known as the second round of the Civil War—which, after thirty days of street-fighting left the city in ruins. Under terms of an armistice ELAS agreed to turn in its arms (mostly old, prewar equipment). Because the Communists lost the opportunity to win representation in the new government (they boycotted the election), it was just a matter of time before they would seek other means to take control.

On December 15, 1945, at a meeting in Bulgaria of the Moscow-oriented Greek Communist party (KKE) central committee, and delegates from the Yugoslav and Bulgarian general staffs, it was decided to reorganize ELAS into an insurgent army to fight against the newly restored Greek government. Originally dubbed the "Republican Army," its official title became the "Democratic Army." Bulgaria, Yugoslavia, and Albania, all under Communist governments, promised material assistance and safe havens for the Democratic Army.

At that time the regular army—also known as the Greek National Army (GNA)—was at a strength of around 100,000 and poorly equipped.[18] After some desultory operations against the Democratic Army, two things became clear: one, that Communist expansionism was a serious threat to Greece, and two, that the GNA was not equal to the task of stopping it. In 1947, the United States, under the Truman Doctrine, initiated a flow of defense and economic aid to start the reconstruction of Greece and stop the spread of Communism.

The Joint U.S. Military Advisory and Planning Group (JUSMAPG) "was formed to coordinate operations and to give logistic advice. U.S. tactical experts were brought in, and battle plans were hammered out by the Americans, although it was done in the name of the Joint Staff. JUSMAPG took a tough line and insisted that all recommendations be carried into effect, at once and in full. This attitude of urgency was something new to Greece, its government, its General Staff and its politicians."[19] Some of the American advisers were attached to units in the field (ordinarily at division level or higher) but held no leadership positions.

There was no standard system of individual or unit training in the GNA. The Americans observed that large numbers of units would be withdrawn from operations for retraining. To correct the inefficiency in GNA training and operations, the United States instructed the Greeks in American doctrine and tactics. Instruction included commando tactics, mountain warfare, communications, and logistical support techniques. The roles of the National Guard and the GNA became more sharply defined: the former assuming rear area security responsibilities, the latter, combat operations.[20]

During the year 1948 the American efforts began to pay off. Equipment was flowing in at adequate levels—the Greeks acquired modern artillery, tanks, transport vehicles and mules, and aircraft to support ground operations. The efficiency of the GNA improved, and with it, the morale and self-confidence of the Greek soldiers.

The Democratic Army had been reasonably successful in keeping the larger and better equipped GNA at bay through the effective use of hit-and-run tactics, but two things happened that brought the war to an end. First, Yugoslavia closed its border with Greece, cutting off the flow of supplies to the Communist guerrillas—an action Yugoslavia took to improve relations with the West following Tito's break with Stalin. Second, the Democratic Army began to engage the GNA in conventional warfare. After suffering a succession of defeats the Communists called for a "temporary cessation" of hostilities—an admission of defeat.

The Hellenic Army today is the direct descendant of the victorious GNA. Because of the massive U.S. support the GNA received during the Civil

War, a lingering American imprint has been left in its doctrine, tactics, and equipment. The civil war left other imprints as well. The army professionals, with some exceptions, are by and large strongly anti-Communist.

Internal Political Role

The Greek Army—as the previous section has outlined—has always been intimately involved with politics. Since 1922 there have been five separate governments headed by active or retired military people. Since Greek politics is historically notorious for its fractious instability, the military has been regarded in different contexts as a guardian or a threat to the government in power. Accusations of praetorianism are inappropriate, as evidence shows the military is more likely to be the object of manipulation by senior government officials (themselves often former military people) than the other way around.[21]

An aspect of this interaction is the system of clientage. An officer often stakes the success of his career (to include promotion, transfer, and choice assignments) on the influence wielded by his political friends with the Ministry of National Defense. The driving principle behind this system is the exchange of favors, which—though sometimes offensive to the idealistic sensibilities of those professionals who reflect the aspiration of the military counterculture—is accepted as a fact of life.[22]

Role in Nation-building

The Hellenic Army has contributed in various ways to nation-building and modernization. Obviously, in the post-Civil War period it played a significant role in the reconstruction of Greece. In the contemporary setting its technical training of conscripts and preparation of young officers for national service are noteworthy. Furthermore, the value of developing defense-related industries to stimulate the Greek economy is self-evident.

The most recent experience of a dominant military role in Greek national politics was the period of the Colonels' junta, 1967-1974. Their agenda for nation-building was predicated upon a perception of the civilian government's inability to halt the spread of Communist influence and failure to promote the growth of the Greek economy. When the Colonels were finally ousted, by all accounts the military left Greece in worse shape than it was before they had assumed power. Their poor performance in four significant areas explains their failure to realize their goals:[23]

(1) The military regime was unable to "create a basis for legitimacy and allegiance to its rule."[24] The military alienated large segments of the population and the majority of government civil servants. In the eyes of the general population the junta kept to themselves, serving their own

interests and those of their friends, while disregarding the Constitution and Greek law.

(2) The military was ineffective in resolving and managing conflicts between itself and the civilian sector. To a great extent this was based on widely differing perceptions of procedures to follow to coordinate action between superiors (mostly military) and subordinates (mostly civilian) and among agencies of the government. The resulting conflicts only became worse as time passed.

(3) The military was unable to "make and implement prompt and relevant decisions in response to internal demands and external challenges."[25] The Danopoulos and Patel survey showed that the military governors were unwilling to "allow subordinate bodies to make and implement independent decisions,"[26] and were unresponsive to the professional concerns and responsibilities of their subordinates. The damage done by these shortcomings was reflected in botched attempts at educational and economic reform, and disastrous management of foreign policy. The latter, culminating in the Cyprus debacle, contributed directly to the Colonels' fall from power.

(4) The military regime "had unclear goals or no goals at all. Policy directions were very ambiguous and confusing in comparison to those of the civilian regime."[27]

The policies implemented by the military government succeeded in retarding agricultural production (brought about by the exclusion of some Greek agricultural products from European markets), caused a decline in industrial investment, and raised the cost of living.[28] Military notions of social reform remained fixated on creating a "Helleno-Christian civilization" that "protected Greek youth from Western neo-anarchism."[29] Defense expenditures increased to nearly three times the rate of spending for public health and education.[30]

Hence, in its most recent attempt at nation-building the Greek military was a failure. (The army bears the heaviest burden.) But the failure must be put in perspective:

The source of the failure of the Greek military as political governors is rooted in their professionalization. For military professionalism contains both modern managerial qualities and traditional values such as bravery, discipline, and obedience. The existence of these traditional values alongside the managerial serves the military well in their mission as managers of violence. But the political arena—which is slow and deliberate—due to the myriad of economic, political and social variables—presents military governors with diametrically different problems. Attempting to transplant military perceptions—norms, standards and decision methods—to politics leads to inconsistencies and failures.[31]

Social Aspects of the Hellenic Army

Greece has no aristocracy. Social differentiations are based mainly on an individual's educational background, his profession, and what he can personally accomplish through talent, ambition, and good connections. Prestige is often related to professional and material indications of success. It is no surprise, then, that "socioeconomic considerations and careerism were generally more important factors for entering professional military service than, for instance, service to the nation."[32] A family tradition of army service does not play an important role as an incentive.[33]

A survey (1971) taken among candidates for admission to each of the Greek service academies showed that the army aspirants came mostly from rural areas or small towns. About 50 percent of the population resides in urban areas. Additionally, 77 percent of the candidates had grown up in families that were defined as lower class.[34]

Greek society is ethnically homogeneous. It is estimated that of the over 9 million inhabitants of Greece nearly 98 percent identify themselves as ethnic Greek. The remaining 2 percent of the population is composed of Turks (about 1 percent), Vlachs or Aromani (ethnically related to Rumanians), Slavs, Albanians, and Jews.[35] The religious composition of the society follows roughly the same proportions, the dominant group belonging to the Eastern Orthodox Church of Christ. Because of this strong ethno–religious congruence, the Greeks tend to regard adherence to the Orthodox faith as a prerequisite quality of "Greekness."

The most important social value to a Greek is his sense of self-esteem or, put another way, his sense of honor. The word for this concept is *philotimo* and to understand what this entails is to understand what it means to be Greek. "The essence of *philotimo* is inviolability and freedom ('to be Greek means to be free')." Out of a sense of shame, modesty, propriety, a Greek "avoids saying things and doing things which would reflect on the *philotimo* of himself, his family, his country." Greek nationalism derives naturally from the *philotimo*. "A man may be ignorant and poor, but when his country is threatened, it is his right and privilege to shed his blood on the altar of Greek freedom." The *philotimo* does not imply pride—that suggests arrogance. "A Greek mother is not proud of her son, she is honored by him. The *philotimo* is enhanced through honor, not pride."[36]

An aspect of the *philotimo* is the high value Greeks place on the qualities of manliness. This emphasizes bravery and daring, defiant independence, and contempt for authority. This, of course, recalls the virtues of the klepht and fits naturally with the historical Greek sense of provincial loyalty, self-determinacy and suspicion of authority figures. These virtues combine favorably to make the Greek an excellent and reliable soldier. Most important, it seems, to maintaining cohesion of a Greek fighting force is to ensure understanding of a clear objective in which the nation's honor, the unit's honor, and the individual's honor have a common identity.

Recent Combat Experience

The Hellenic Army has had no recent combat experience, except for those few that may have been drawn into the fighting in Cyprus against the Turks in 1974. Before that a brigade of the Hellenic Army was committed to Korea in 1951 where it remained until 1955. The combat experiences of the regular and guerrilla forces during World War II and the Civil War that followed have been discussed in previous sections.

Although the Turkish invasion of Cyprus did not provide the Hellenic Army with much combat experience, its impact on Greece was profound. In the years that followed defense spending skyrocketed. The army began to reevaluate its training, its operational readiness, its deployments (by remilitarizing the Aegean Islands and creating a new corps in Thrace, opposite Turkey), and its sources of supply (seeking to diversify and remove itself from nearly total dependence on the United States for defense and economic assistance).

Organization

According to the Greek Constitution, the president of the republic is the commander-in-chief of the armed forces. Actual control of the armed forces is exercised by the government through the prime minister. The government formulates national defense policy in consultation with the Supreme National Defense Council. The prime minister is the chairman of the council whose members also include the minister of national defense, representatives of other appropriate ministries, and representatives of the armed forces. The minister of national defense directs implementation of policy through the National Defense General Staff. This is composed of the general staffs of the army, navy, and air force and is headed by a Chief of Staff who answers to the minister of national defense.

Major Combat Units

The Hellenic Army is a conscript force with a strength of around 145,000 (123,000 conscripts) and a service obligation of twenty-four to thirty-two months.[37] There are four training cycles per year, but recently because of a static birth rate the government has had difficulty making its quota of recruits.[38] Major combat units of the Hellenic Army are as follows:[39]

- 1 armored division
- 11 infantry divisions (some of which are being mechanized)

- 2 armored brigades
- 1 paracommando brigade
- 1 marine infantry brigade
- 12 artillery battalions
- 2 surface-to-surface missile battalions (with 8 Honest John launchers)
- 1 surface-to-air missile battalion (with 12 Improved Hawk launchers)
- 14 aviation companies

Tactical Deployments

The Hellenic Army is tactically deployed in four corps:[40]

- I Corps, headquartered at Larissa, disposes of four infantry divisions;
- II Corps, at Kozani, also fields four divisions;
- III Corps, based at Thessaloniki, consists of one armored division and three infantry divisons;
- IV Corps, at Xanthi, is the most recently formed. Two infantry divisions (12th and 16th) are in the process of formation here. (Whether these are new formations or units created out of existing assets cannot be determined.)

Many of the units are kept at cadre strength. In the event of a mobilization, over 200,000 reservists would be activated to fill out the force structure.[41]

Augmenting the regular army is the territorial army, or National Guard, with a strength of around 90,000. The National Guard is organized into 17 subcommands and disposes of 100 battalions, whose mission is mainly coastal defense and—as in the Civil War era—rear area security. Additionally, in time of war the 29,000-man national Gendarmerie will revert to control of the minister of national defense.[42]

A Greek infantry division is organized on a triangular pattern: three brigades to a division, three battalions to a brigade, three companies to a battalion, and three platoons to a company. Organic to an infantry division are additional combat and combat-support elements: an armored battalion, an artillery battalion, engineer and signal units, and combat service support units.[43] A Greek infantry division can attain a strength of 14,300 men with 62 tanks, 80 armored personnel carriers, 1,800 vehicles, 10 aircraft, 76 howitzers (8-inch, 155mm, 105mm), 114 mortars, 50 106mm recoilless rifles, and up to 450 anti-tank weapons.[44] The armored division is organized into three brigades: six tank battalions (55 tanks each); four mechanized infantry battalions (750 men, 60 armored personnel carriers), reconnaissance battalions, three self-propelled artillery battalions (18 105mm), and one mixed artillery battalion (10 self-propelled howitzers, 155mm and 8-inch); engineer, signal, and aviation company, and combat service support units. The total strength is 13,000 men and 360 tanks.[45] A separate armored brigade has two armored battalions, one motorized infantry battalion, one self-propelled artillery battalion and combat service support units, totaling in strength at 3,600 men, 119 tanks.[46]

Equipment

The Hellenic Army has the following equipment:[47]

Armor
   (Medium tanks)
   M47   350
   M48   800
   AMX-30   170
   (Light tanks)
   M-24   190

Armored personnel carriers
   M113   520
   M59   460
   AMX-10P   Unk
   Mowag   Unk
   M8 armored car   180

Artillery
   75mm pack   100
   105mm howitzer   80
   155mm howitzer   Unk
   105mm SP M52   Unk
   155mm SP M44   Unk
   8-inch SP M110   Unk
   Honest John SSM   8 launchers

Anti-tank weapons
   106mm recoilless rifle   550
   SS-11 anti-tank guided missile
      launchers   Unk
   Cobra anti-tank guided missile
      launchers   Unk
   MILAN anti-tank guided missile
      launchers   Unk

TOW anti-tank guided missile
    launchers   Unk

Air Defense
    Guns (40mm, 75mm, 90mm)   Unk
    Redeye surface-to-air missile   Unk
    Improved HAWK surface-to-air
       missile   12 launchers

Army Aviation assets include 1 Super King Air, 2 Aero Commander, 20 U-17A, 15 L-21 fixed wing aircraft, and 5 Bell 47G, 20 UH-1D, 42 AB-204B/205 helicopters.[48]

A cursory examination of this weapons inventory shows that it consists predominantly of U.S.-made equipment. Since the time of the Greek Civil War, the United States has been the major arms supplier to Greece (more than $2 billion in grant aid, exclusive of credits between 1947 and 1977). After the 1967 Colonels' coup, the United States embargoed shipment of military equipment to Greece. The deliveries resumed in 1968 on the faulty assumption that a plebiscite held that year indicated a return to democratic government. Because of the Soviet invasion of Czechoslovakia, the United States continued to deliver military equipment for fear of letting a NATO ally's defensive capability deteriorate. Since 1974 Greece has sought to diversify its sources of armaments among European suppliers. West Germany and France have been the most active in selling equipment to Greece, and Germany has also extended grant aid and credits.[49]

The United States still remains the major source of military assistance to Greece. For fiscal year 1978 the United States pledged $140 million of credits. An additional $700 million in grant aid and credits to be spread over a period of years was in the process of negotiation in 1977.[50] Greece and the United States are seeking to resume negotiations on a firm defense and economic aid agreement, part of the bargain being continuation of American access to military bases in Greece.

Some of the new equipment acquisitions projected for the Hellenic Army will leave it with an odd mix of United States- and European-made major weapons. From Germany Greece plans to acquire 160 Leopard 1 main battle tanks.[51] Already on hand are French AMX-30 tanks and AMX-10P armored personnel carriers. Added to this is a fleet of old U.S. M47 and M48 tanks which Greece plans to modernize by upgrading 600 M48s to the M48A3 (diesel) model.[52] Additional U.S.-made artillery is scheduled for acquisition: 144 M101A1 105-mm towed howitzers and 11 M109 155mm self-propelled howitzers.[53] Greece is also in the market for improved air defense assets. Under consideration is a purchase of 37 M48 Improved Chaparral tactical air defense systems.[54]

Tactical Doctrine

The Hellenic Army, up to the time of the Greek Civil War, followed a British model of organization, doctrine, and tactics. Under the influence and training of American advisers during the Civil War and in the period of reconstruction that followed, the Hellenic Army adopted U.S. organizational patterns and tactical doctrine. Reinforced by NATO, the American doctrinal influence remains today.

Scenarios

What kinds of war can the Hellenic Army fight?

The Hellenic Army is well equipped to fight a conventional war of limited scale. In keeping with NATO policy, it is a defensive force, and except for staging counterattacks against an aggressor, it is not intended for offensive operations outside of Greek territory. It goes without saying that Greek soldiers are well disposed to fight unconventional or guerrilla war. As indicated in previous sections, because of their traditions and historical experience, the Greeks are "naturals" for this kind of combat. The only potential drawback to their effectiveness in this environment is their historical tendency to divide into hostile factions.

The neighboring countries include two neutral (i.e., non-Warsaw Pact) Communist states (Albania and Yugoslavia), a member of the Warsaw Pact (Bulgaria) and a NATO ally, Turkey. Unfortunately in recent years, it is with Turkey that Greece has had the most strained relations. The most likely setting for a Greek-Turkish confrontation would be in the Aegean, starting with one violating the other's airspace or intruding into territorial waters. It must be assumed that despite the often heated rhetoric from both sides of the Aegean reason counsels against any rash acts, the outcome of which would only be disastrous for both sides. The prospects for the restoration of amicable Greek-Turkish relations in the spirit of Venezelos and Ataturk are not excellent in the near term, but Greece and Turkey's NATO partners are striving to promote an Aegean detente.

The potential enemy Greece and Turkey face in common as members of NATO is the Warsaw Pact. Bulgaria fields a ground force smaller than the Hellenic Army (115,000)[55] but has nearly twice the number of tanks—a fleet it has been modernizing with T-62 and T-72 models. Rumania, which also has been modernizing its ground force (strength: 140,000),[56] would possibly augment Bulgarian units in operations against Greece or Turkey. The Soviet Union would foreseeably reinforce a major Warsaw Pact operation to seize the Turkish Straits and pin down Greek units in western Thrace.

The German invasion of Greece during World War II and the Greek (and Allied) defensive actions provide a model from which to surmise a scenario for the defense of Greece. The aggressor would attempt to penetrate the mountainous northern frontier through the few gaps, passes, or river valleys that allow passage of mechanized columns south. The Greeks would take advantage of the terrain to delay and canalize the aggressor forces. Where the terrain permitted, the Hellenic Army would counterattack. Against an equal or slightly larger aggressor force the Greeks would probably prevail.

Quality of the Troops

The Greek soldier is tough, reliable, and resourceful. The literacy rate in Greece is high (90 percent), and the average conscript enters the army with a secondary school education. Most Greeks are raised in an urban environment and therefore not unacquainted with modern technology. Instruction includes basic and advanced individual training—similar to the U.S. Army system in which individuals are designated for education in special skills as the needs of the army dictate and as their aptitude allows. Unit training rounds out the individual's abilities to function in coordination with the other members of the combat team.

Quality of the Officers

Most of the regular army officers are graduates of the Greek Military Academy in Athens, which grants commissions to approximately 200 officers per year. Greek law also allows for a number of noncommissioned officers (equivalent to 10 percent of the graduating class of the Military Academy) to be commissioned annually. Sometimes draft boards will identify a conscript as "officer material," but few of these designees actually become officers. Those who are designated "candidate reserve officers" will serve as platoon leaders for the duration of their service, receiving a commission shortly before they leave active duty. As reservists they are promoted at established intervals.[57]

The professional officer corps forms a distinct corporate entity within Greek society. Its political orientation tends to be populist, which includes an abiding suspicion of the goals and motivations of the ruling social and economic elite. Because of a self-perceived identity with the interests and aspirations of the average Greek, the professional military has not hesitated in the past to intrude into politics on the assumption that its actions reflected the best interests of the nation. For the most part, however, Greek Army officers are concerned with issues of professional development: their careers and the day-to-day management of Greek national security.[58]

Since the formation of a regular army (back in the time of King Otho I), the Greek officer corps has been "drawn extensively from relatively humble socioeconomic backgrounds."[59] This would appear to explain their populist orientation. Many Greek civil servants in high positions, in criticizing the management and leadership style of the junta (1967-1974), complained about the highhandedness and unwillingness or inability to communicate shown by top-level military executives. This conflict may very well have sprung from a fundamental class antagonism, not to mention the cultural differences that existed between the two sectors of Greek society.

As leaders of the largest corporate entity in Greece, the army officers are commonly motivated by a sense of professionalism, striving to build the army into a model of efficiency and discipline—in contrast to the near chaos of competing interests and patronage systems they perceive as dominating the society around them.

Experience

The Turkish invasion of Cyprus forced the Hellenic Army seriously to evaluate its training and readiness, as major increases in defense spending in the years that followed would seem to attest. Although constrained by the escalating cost of training and equipment that is being felt throughout NATO, Greece is trying to compensate by maintaining high performance standards in basic combat skills.

Cohesion

Cultural, linguistic, and ethnic homogeneity contribute significantly to promoting unit cohesion within the Hellenic Army. Greeks pride themselves as direct descendants of the ancient Hellenic and see their military service as a reflection of the glory of Greek antiquity. They are rugged individualists, but have an amazing ability to set aside personal and factional differences when threatened by a foreign invader. Greek tradition considers it a sacred right and privilege to be chosen to sacrifice one's life for his country.

Individuals usually remain with the same unit for the duration of their conscript service. In the event of a national mobilization, reservists are returned whenever possible to the major unit with which they performed active duty.

Sustainability

Most writings on the Hellenic Army portray the support system as modest and the soldiers as accustomed to living frugally. The Greeks do not emphasize creature comforts in the field. The most important elements of the sustainability formula are ammunition for the weapons, petroleum, oil and lubricants (POL) for the mechanized equipment, and food for the men. Above all it is necessary to have an effective transport system to ensure delivery of the materiel, fresh troops, and evacuation of the wounded.

Because of the galvanizing effect of Cyprus, Greece has doubtless marshaled its resources to implement this formula in combat against an aggressor of comparable strength. Under conditions of intense mechanized warfare against a numerically superior enemy, the Hellenic Army's support system would be strained to the limits. This, of course, is a problem often cited as common to all the NATO partners. Greece has a domestic defense industry that manufactures conventional ammunition and small arms, but for supply of precision munitions (such as ATGMs), and major weapon systems it depends on Allied support. Greece also depends on Middle Eastern suppliers for POL. Hence, the sustainability of the ground forces during a period of prolonged combat would depend in large measure on the ability of the Greek and Allied naval and air forces to keep the sea and land lines of supply open and free from interdiction.

Strengths and Weaknesses

The Hellenic Army is basically an infantry force. It can fight well in the rough terrain of northern Greece, and on the more trafficable plains it can call on armored and mechanized units to support a counterattack. The Greek soldier is well led by a professional officer corps. He is respected for his toughness, resourcefulness, and ability to withstand deprivation of comfort. As commandos or guerrilla fighters Greeks are in their natural element. Likewise, the Greek soldier is capable of asserting individual leadership and can function imaginatively in an atmosphere of mutual trust and confidence with his peers. These are the Hellenic Army's obvious strengths.

Its weaknesses are more in the realm of foreseeable technical problems. For example, since the army has a mixed force of main battle tanks (M47, M48, AMX-30, and eventually the Leopard 1), it must contend with the problems of maintaining a rather complex support system to keep these vehicles operational. As already mentioned, Greek lines of supply through which parts, munitions, and replacement equipment from foreign suppliers will have to flow may be vulnerable to interdiction.

Trends

The major trend within the Hellenic Army today is toward modernization. This includes not only replacing old equipment acquired from the United States during the Korean War era, but also applying modern technology to improving techniques of logistical management and communications, command and control. Part of this modernization effort is a serious attempt to diversify sources of supply to avoid dependence on single suppliers. Additionally, there is an effort underway to expand the domestic defense production capabilities.

Foreseeable Crises

Within the realm of possibility are three crises: continued tension with Turkey, primarily over the Aegean, secondarily over Cyprus; Greek withdrawal from NATO; and a military coup. These crises could occur as a succession of related events, singly, or not at all. The dispute with Turkey may linger for some time to come, alternately heating up after provocative acts or rhetoric, and cooling down as compromises are sought. The withdrawal from NATO could be forced by any number of issues. Two prominent factors are, sufficient domestic (leftist) pressures on the government to pull out and pursue a course of neutrality, or a perception of Alliance support for Turkey against Greece in some context (or both). The possibility of a military coup is raised out of historical necessity. A military view that a government in power was seriously jeopardizing Greek national security may impel some officers to act. Whether a military coup succeeded or failed would be immaterial. The damage done would be profound. Bad memories of the junta period have not faded.

Notes

1. James Brown and Gwen Dyer, "Greece," in John Keegan, ed., *World Armies* (New York: Time-Life Books, 1980), p. 263.

2. Alvin Z. Rubinstein, "The Soviet Union and the Eastern Mediterranean: 1968-1978," *Orbis* 23, No. 2 (Summer 1979): 302.

3. Ibid.

4. *Area Handbook for Greece* (Washington, D.C.: U.S. Government Printing Office, 1977), pp. 17-18.

5. This paragraph is paraphrased and quoted directly from "Athenian" (pseud.), *Inside the Colonels' Greece* (New York: W. W. Norton & Co., 1978), p. 18.

6. Ibid.

7. *Area Handbook for Greece*, p. 18.

8. "Athenian," *Inside the Colonels' Greece*, p. 18.

9. *Area Handbook for Greece*, p. 21.

10. "Athenian," *Inside the Colonels' Greece*, p. 19.

11. *Area Handbook for Greece*, p. 27.

12. Ibid.

13. Edgar O'Ballance, *The Greek Civil War, 1944-1949* (New York: Frederick A. Praeger, 1966), p. 33.

14. Ibid., p. 34.

15. C. M. Woodhouse, *Modern Greece: A Short History* (London: Faber and Faber, Ltd., 1968), p. 237.

16. O'Ballance, *The Greek Civil War*, pp. 41-44.

17. Woodhouse, *Modern Greece*, p. 245.

18. O'Ballance, *The Greek Civil War*, p. 41.

19. Ibid., p. 156.

20. Ibid., pp. 173-74.

21. *Area Handbook for Greece*, pp. 208-209.

22. Ibid.

23. G. Danopoulos and K. Patel, "Military Professionals As Political Governors: A Case Study of Contemporary Greece," *West European Politics* 3, No. 2 (May 1980): 191-200.

24. Ibid., p. 191.

25. Ibid., p. 194.

26. Ibid.

27. Ibid., p. 196.

28. Ibid., pp. 197-98.

29. Ibid.

30. Ibid.

31. Ibid., p. 199.

32. *Area Handbook for Greece*, p. 208.

33. Ibid.

34. Ibid., p. 207.

35. Ibid., pp. 67-70.

36. Margaret Mead, "Greece," in Margaret Mead, ed., *Cultural Patterns And Technical Change* (New York: New American Library of World Literature, Inc., 1955), pp. 60-61.

37. *The Military Balance, 1979-1980* (London: International Institute for Strategic Studies, 1979), p. 27.

38. Brown and Dyer, "Greece," p. 265.

39. *The Military Balance, 1979-1980*, p. 27.

40. Egbert Thomer, "Greece's Defense Economy Industry and Defense Planning," *Military Technology and Economics* 4, Issue 18 (1980): 45.

41. *Area Handbook for Greece*, p. 216.

42. Thomer, "Greece's Defense Economy Industry and Defense Planning," p. 45.

43. *Area Handbook for Greece*, p. 214.

44. Brown and Dyer, "Greece," p. 264.

45. Ibid.

46. Ibid.

47. *The Military Balance, 1979-1980*, p. 26.

48. Ibid.

49. *Area Handbook for Greece*, pp. 224-25.

50. Ibid., p. 225.

51. "Major Defense Contracts—Value Over $1 Million," *International Defense Review* 14, No. 6 (1981): 799.

52. Ibid., p. 440.

53. *The Military Balance, 1979-1980*, p. 26.

54. "Major Defense Contracts—Value Over $1 Million," *International Defense Review* 14, No. 6 (1981): 126.

55. *The Military Balance, 1979-1980*, p. 14.

56. Ibid., p. 16.

57. *Area Handbook for Greece*, p. 212.

58. Ibid., p. 206.
59. Ibid., p. 207.

Bibliography

Area Handbook for Greece. Washington, D.C.: U.S. Government Printing Office, 1977.

"Athenian" (pseudonym). *Inside the Colonels' Greece*. New York: W. W. Norton & Co., 1978.

Brown, James, and Dyer, Gwen. "Greece." In John Keegan, ed. *World Armies*. New York: Time-Life Books, 1980.

Danopoulos, G., and Patel, K. "Military Professionals As Political Governors: A Case Study of Contemporary Greece." *West European Politics* 3, No. 2 (May 1980): 191-200.

"Major Defense Contracts—Value Over 1 $million." *International Defense Review* 12, 13, 14, (1981): 440-799.

Mead, Margaret. "Greece." In Margaret Mead, ed. *Cultural Patterns and Technical Change*. New York: New American Library of World Literature, Inc., 1955.

The Military Balance: 1979-1980. London: International Institute for Strategic Studies, 1979.

O'Ballance, Edgar. *The Greek Civil War, 1944-1949*. New York: Frederick A. Praeger, 1966.

Rubinstein, Alvin Z. "The Soviet Union and the Eastern Mediterranean: 1968-1978." *Orbis* 23, No. 2 (Summer 1979).

Thomer, Egbert. "Greece's Defense Economy Industry and Defense Planning." *Military Technology and Economics* 4, Issue 18 (1980): 14-26.

Woodhouse, C. M. *Modern Greece: A Short History*. London: Faber and Faber, Ltd., 1968.

Turkey

James M. Dunn

Turkey holds the anchor position in the defense of NATO's southeastern flank. The Turkish Army is the largest standing armed force in NATO besides that of the United States. Modern Turkey is the custodian of an ancient martial tradition. The reputation of the Turkish fighting man as a tough, reliable soldier is undisputed. However, the Turkish Army is facing increasing difficulties in meeting its commitment to national defense and to the NATO alliance. The most serious problem is equipment obsolescence. Turkey is in a severe economic crisis which sharply limits its ability to modernize the army. In an effort to replace its aging equipment and to maintain a ground force that is a credible deterrent to the Soviet Union and Warsaw Pact, Turkey is seeking help from its Western allies.

Turkey's relationship to its NATO partners is suffering some strain. Western Europe has been critical of Turkey's management of its internal affairs and, aside from the United States and West Germany, few of the allies have been forthcoming with significant military and economic assistance. The Soviet Union, and tsarist Russia before it, historically has sought to extend its influence to Turkey. Most coveted by the USSR are the Turkish Straits— the water route from the Soviet-dominated Black Sea to the Mediterranean.

Although control of the Turkish Straits figures prominently in global naval strategy, it is ultimately the Turkish Army that will insure the security of this key terrain. But what kind of a combat force is the Turkish Army? Can it accomplish its mission to protect the Straits and the security of Turkey? To answer these questions, this chapter presents a look at the phenomenon of Turkey itself: at Turkish society, its military traditions and experiences as a way of introducing the reader to the forces that have molded the Turkish army today.

This easternmost member of the Atlantic Alliance forms a natural bridge between two continents. On its European frontier Turkey's neighbors are

The views and opinions expressed in this article are exclusively those of the author and are not indicative of support from any institutional affiliation which the author may have.

Greece, also a NATO partner, and Bulgaria, a member of the Warsaw Pact. On the Asian side, beyond Turkey's mountainous eastern border, lie the Soviet Union and Iran. To the south are Iraq and Syria. This great land link between the European Balkan states and the oil fields of the Middle East is bordered on the north by the Black Sea, which, except for the Turkish presence, would be a Soviet lake. On the west Turkey is flanked by the Aegean, and on the southwest by the eastern Mediterranean. Turkey, then, not only physically connects Europe and Asia, but finds itself in a position to exert control of strategically important waterways. The most crucial of these are the Turkish Straits and the Sea of Marmara between them. The Turkish Straits constitute the only passageways between the Black Sea and the Aegean. Their importance to Turkish national security and to military operations in global power projections therefore is crucial.

Turkey falls within the so-called "crescent of crisis," an arc of political instability described across the Islamic world from Afghanistan to the Horn of Africa. Turkey is the only Moslem country in NATO. In addition to its physical bonds to the Middle East, and its common religion with its Arab and Iranian neighbors, Turkey shares several deep historical links with the region. At the zenith of its conquests the Ottoman Empire spread Turkish influence from the Barbary States to the Persian Gulf; from the Caspian Sea to the gates of Vienna. Another subtle aspect to the geography of Turkish influence is the distribution of Turkic people in the world. Kinsmen to the Turks of Anatolia inhabit parts of the Soviet Union from the Black Sea to the Altai Mountains. The Turks, therefore, have religious, historical, and ethnic ties to people and countries far beyond the borders of the Turkish Republic. Most of these people and nations are found in the heartland of one of the most explosive parts of the world today.

With the foundation of the Turkish Republic in 1922, Turkey turned inward to concentrate on nation-building, abandoning its historical role as a world power. Yet, while Turkey chose to confine its national interests essentially to what transpired within its own boundaries, events following World War II cast Turkey as an important player in the Cold War and, more recently, as a key element in the East-West competition for influence in the Eastern Mediterranean and Middle East.

Turkey applied for NATO membership in 1950 to counteract a renewed threat to its security from Stalinist Russia. This alliance with the West against a traditional enemy was actually a step away from a course of neutrality Turkey had hoped to steer. The Turks had, after all, successfully maintained neutrality during World War II. But the Turkish Republic had been founded and nurtured in a spirit of Westernization and modernization. The Turks reasoned that to realize the nation-building goals set by Mustafa Kemal (Ataturk), the founder of the republic, and to protect Turkey against Soviet expansionism, an alliance with the Atlantic states seemed to be a prudent course of action.

Not a people to do anything in half measures, the Turks eagerly sought to

demonstrate their solidarity with the West against the threat of Communism. They contributed a brigade to the U.N. forces in Korea, but were
disappointed when that gesture of commitment did not hasten their admission to NATO. Membership was not formally granted until 1952. Mainly
with the help of the United States, the Turks proceeded to raise and equip
the largest standing army in European NATO as the tensions of the Cold
War era increased. The infusion of equipment, training, and financial aid
that began in 1947 was prodigious. In 1959 Ankara became headquarters of
the Central Treaty Organization (CENTO), an alliance of the "Northern
Tier" that included Iran and Pakistan, with the United States and United
Kingdom as peripheral participants. Turkey formed the lynchpin between
NATO and CENTO, a bridge between alliances extending from the North
Cape of Norway to the Himalayan frontier of China.

This extensive chain of mutual defense agreements was not to endure.
The CENTO alliance disbanded in 1979, leaving Turkey as the only Western-
aligned state in the region. But that was only one event of many that
reflected a trend uncongenial to Western interests. The Turkish economy
had been deteriorating steadily, leaving Turkey with little or no money to
keep pace with military modernization. So, as the frontiers of pro-Western
alignment receded to the Turkish border, the obsolescence of the Turkish
Army became a focus of concern.

The Soviet Union, meanwhile, had been working to improve its relations—
and its leverage—with Turkey. Post-Stalinist Soviet strategy was to re-
nounce bellicose claims to Turkish territory and to develop a more accom-
modating relationship with Ankara. Soviet diplomacy has not been without
success. On one hand, Turkey has been the largest recipient outside the
Communist world of nonmilitary aid from the USSR. Additionally, as the
atmosphere of detente with the Soviet Union began to evolve in the 1960s,
the Turks regarded the development with mixed feelings. They approved
of a relaxation of tensions with the USSR, but were dismayed by what they
deemed to be a diminished Allied interest in Turkish defense requirements.
Turkish perceptions of diminishing support from their NATO allies grew
most acute following the negative Western reaction to the 1974 occupation
of northern Cyprus. The U.S. arms embargo from 1975 to 1978 only
sharpened the Turks' sense of estrangement.

In 1976 Turkey, applying a loose construction to the Montreux Conven-
tion (that regulates naval passages through the Straits), allowed the Soviet
aircraft carrier, Kiev, to transit the Straits, passing from the Black Sea into
the Mediterranean. The naval balance in the Mediterranean was undergoing
a permanent change. By 1979 the Soviets had deployed forty-two ships in
the Mediterranean (as compared with none in 1963), half of which were
combat vessels.[1]

On the other hand, while the Turks have joined in the spirit of detente,
they have in no way allowed themselves to be reduced to a status of compli-
ant neutrality. The Soviet invasion of Afghanistan, the modernization of

Soviet forces in the Caucasus (opposite eastern Turkey), as well as Soviet deployment of SS20 IRBMs within range of Turkey and other targets in NATO's southern flank,[2] have served as discomforting reminders that the Soviet olive branch is clutched in a mailed glove.

"To Safeguard Democracy against Anarchy"

In September 1980, in a bloodless "coup," the Turkish armed forces assumed control of the government. Violence generated by rivalries among political factions had been escalating to an unacceptable level, and it appeared the civilian government was powerless to contain it. Claire Sterling asserts that much of the violence was orchestrated by the KGB whose objective was "to mount a brutal campaign of urban terrorism, kidnapping, and assassination against Turkey" in order to destabilize the "sole remaining Moslem state to have authentic elections and multiple parties."[3] The Terror claimed the lives of 2,000 people in the first half of 1980 alone.[4] Turkey was vulnerable to the onslaught of terrorism and to the provocation of factional combat because of staggering economic problems that created widespread unemployment and social disruption. Organized groups of terrorists were able to exploit these conditions to precipitate the country toward anarchy. The danger appeared even more imminent when seen in the light of events in neighboring Iran and more distant Afghanistan.

The Turkish military considered the measures it followed necessary to preserve, rather than to abrogate, the country's democratic institutions. Important to note is that the action of 1980 was not the first time the military ejected a civilian government. The military's self-perception as protectors of the Turkish Republic from the abuses of ambitious politicians is shared by the majority of Turks. When the military took charge in 1980 the national sigh of relief was almost audible.

The general pattern of military intervention has been reiterated in almost ten-year cycles: first in 1960, then in 1971, and most recently in 1980. Although in each instance the combination of variables that motivated the military to step in differed somewhat, there has been a common denominator to all. That is, the military interpreted the developing events as threatening to undermine the principles of Kemalism, the fundamental guidelines for modern Turkey set down by Mustafa Kemal Ataturk.

Keepers of the Flame

The military occupies a central role in Turkish society. This is as true of modern Turkey as it was of ancient Turkish polities. The warrior Turk has been a well-known figure in the West. Turkish historians assert that the armies of Jenghis Kahn and Atilla were armies of Turks. The English word "horde" would seem to attest to that—it derives from the Turkish word *ordu*, "army."

Yet these warriors were gifted diplomats as well. Their skill was sufficient to hold together the crumbling Ottoman Empire until it finally succumbed in 1918. The transition from a multinational empire to an independent nation state of Turks was led by the military (meaning, of course, the army as the dominant service). It was the military that rallied the nation to the nationalist cause. At the head of the Turkish armies that scored a series of decisive victories over the invading Greeks was Mustafa Kemal and his second in command, Ismet Pasha. These were later to be honored, respectively, with the names Ataturk, "Father of the Turks," and Inonu (after his famous victory). These military successes gave them the diplomatic leverage they needed to win recognition from the Soviet Union and to negotiate the withdrawal of French, Italian, and subsequently English forces of occupation. The Turkish Republic emerged under the leadership of a small group of *ghazis*, a title that means "victorious warrior." It originally denoted a Moslem who waged holy war against the infidel, but in Turkey it is a distinction conferred on veterans of all wars, to include, for example, the Korean War.[5]

In those early days of the Turkish Republic the army assumed a seemingly paradoxical role. It was simultaneously the instrument of modernization, Westernization, and reform, as well as a guarantor of an authoritarian political system. The ghazi spirit of the nationalist movement was doubly effective. Its intrinsic authoritarianism provided the impetus for the revolution while preserving the fundamental operational principle of the Ottoman Empire. In other words, the revolution led by Mustafa Kemal Ataturk came from the top down to the people. It concentrated political power and authority in the elite circles of Turkish society and above all, in the head of state.[6]

Ataturk was the genius that would oversee the transformation of the new Turkish Republic into a modern, Westernized, secular society. The popular perception of Ataturk was as a general, a ghazi, even though he shed his uniform and donned the clothes of the Western diplomat. Ataturk required all military officers who sought public office to resign their commissions. Although de facto the military was in charge of Turkey during the early days of the Republic, Ataturk worked to separate it from the centers of power by diverting it to nation-building projects in the provinces. He frequently warned against the politicization of the military.

As the advanced guard of the nationalist revolution, the military has always been radical and reformist, a fierce opponent of reactionism— particularly of the sort that seized Iran under the Ayatollah Khomeini. In Turkish society the tension between the secular reformists and the Islamic reactionaries has occasionally turned violent. The overwhelming majority of Turks is devoutly Moslem. However, it is important to note that with the exception of some active extremist groups, this great majority is essentially passive. The elite minority subscribes to the principles of Westernization and secular reform. The bond that keeps all this together is the army. Its leadership is Kemalist. Its ranks are filled with conscripts from the Moslem peasantry. Yet, the soldiers in the ranks commonly regard their military service as an opportunity to prove their manhood and as a chance to rise above the illiteracy and economic deprivation of the backwards village. The army, then, is the instrument of Kemalism. It simultaneously steers Turkey in the direction envisioned by Ataturk and keeps the reactionaries and political extremists of every stripe at bay. Enough of the warrior ethic or courage culture still endures in Turkish society to make military service desirable. Enough of the ghazi reputation of Ataturk and his lieutenants persists to ensure compliance with achievements sought in his name. And the army still retains its popular image among the majority of Turks as an institution for personal fulfillment, for national improvement and as a preserver of national stability. Hence, although the army is the cutting edge of Kemalism, it is also the great reconciler of widely diverse interests.

Turkish Society

Ethnic Composition

It has been observed that twenty empires, ten religions, and countless heresies have left their impressions in Anatolia. The bearers of these diverse cultural manifestations have sprung from a multitude of ethnic origins. Relative newcomers to that peninsula of Asia Minor are the Turks. The population of modern Turkey numbers some 45 million and between 80 and 85 percent of these are ethnic Turks.[7] Within this group there are differences—mainly found on the basis of geographic origin: central Asia, the Anatolian plateau, or Rumelia (former European provinces of the Ottoman Empire).

The next most numerous ethnic group in Turkey is the Kurds. Their exact number has never been established. Some estimates put them between 3 and 5 million;[8] other more recent guesses say there are 6 to 8 million.[9] The Kurds are concentrated mostly—although not exclusively—in the southeastern mountains of Turkey. International attention has been focused on the Kurds mainly because of their insurgencies against the central governments in Iran and Iraq. There is evidence of Kurdish nationalism in Turkey, but it appears to be isolated and sporadic, and certainly not expressed as armed insurgencies as seen in neighboring countries. Nevertheless, the Turkish government is very watchful of events in the Kurdish parts of the country and is extremely suspicious of subversion and interference from foreign powers.

The Turks have been reluctant to even recognize the existence of the Kurds. They refer to them euphemistically as "mountain Turks." Since the southeast is one of the poorest sections of the country, it is likely that some of the friction between Turks and Kurds is attributable to economic problems, leading to complaints that the Kurds have received short shrift from Ankara. The Turkish government is not eager to provoke the Kurds, but is also quick to suppress manifestations of Kurdish nationalism. There is no policy of excluding Kurds from public service—they are conscripted for the military along with every other Turkish (male) citizen, and several Kurds have held high government positions (although their ethnic origin is never discussed).

Kurds are ethnically different from Turks (their linguistic and tribal origins are Indo-European), but they are overwhelmingly Moslem. At least two-thirds of the Kurds are Sunni, the same sect as the majority of Turks. The other third is mostly Alevi, or adherents to the Shiite sect, which also contributes to occasional conflict betwen the two groups.

After the Kurds the Arabs are the most numerous minority. There are an estimated 600,000 to 900,000 Arabs in the Turkish Republic. They are concentrated mainly in the southeast near the Syrian border. Other minorities in Turkey include Caucasians, Jews, Greeks, and Armenians.

Social Structure

Andre Falk suggested that a graphic representation of the composition of Turkish society would look like this:

First you draw the figure of a huge peasant, and there you have the main feature. After that you draw an artisan reaching up to the peasant's knees. Finally, reaching the calves or even just up to the ankles draw three tiny little figures: The intellectual, the worker, the middle-class man.[10]

But in a depiction of the power structure of Turkish society, the image would have to be shown with completely opposite proportions. The heirs to power when the Ottoman Empire collapsed were the same people who kept it running for so long—the educated bureaucrats and the military elite. Surveys taken in the 1970s showed that Turks still regard government service and a career in the "traditional professions" as more prestigious than technical or commercial work, which accounts for the continuing shortage of professional technicians.[11]

Challengers to this elite power structure have emerged from a new class of businessmen and entrepreneurs. This group arose after many of the ethnic groups (such as the Greeks, Armenians, and Jews) which in Ottoman times traditionally ran trade and commerce in the Empire were either ejected or emigrated. The vacuum they left was filled by Turks. It is suggested that as a class apart from the established military-bureaucratic elite, this entrepreneurial class is somewhat antagonistic to the Kemalist-reformists.[12] What the outcome of a still-evolving social structure will be is uncertain, but two observations are worth noting. First, although the relatively new business and commerce-oriented class is diversifying Turkish social structure, it is still perpetuating a stratified society where the power remains concentrated in the hands of a few. Second, survival in international competition imposes demands for a class that can rise to the occasion with the required commercial and industrial skills. While these talents are in short supply in Turkish society, the opportunity for their application is creating a new kind of upward mobility. In an almost Darwinian model, the old elite is being forced to share power with those who can provide entrepreneurial leadership. "Share" is, of course, the word. The military-bureaucratic leadership is still in control, and standing behind this power structure is the strongest Kemalist institution in Turkey, the army.

Self-Perceptions

The Turkish Army is an institution of tremendous influence in Turkey. Although from time to time it shares this power, it still appears to be the ultimate fulcrum of control. The leadership is seen to be progressive and reformist, yet authoritarian and elitist. The preponderance of the conscripts is Turkish (80 to 85 percent); virtually all of these are Sunni Moslems, and the overwhelming majority comes from a peasant background.

In addition to being the most important political and social institution in Turkey, the army is, and has been, a source of ethical leadership. Hotham points out that "Turkish armies were linked from the earliest times with high moral and spiritual conduct."[13] A 900-year old military manual sets forth the desired qualities of a Turkish military commander: he must be "strong to stand against evil, and must have love and respect for good."[14] The manual states that the four most important attributes of a general are: "honesty, generosity, courage, and sound military knowledge."[15]

It is significant that among the enlisted men there is a very clear perception of the moral value of military service. Hotham recalls an interview with a young soldier, a peasant's son from eastern Turkey. His attitude toward military life was, "It brings you in touch with three important things: discipline, humanity, and civilization."[16]

The word "civilization" is particularly evocative when used by Turks. It reflects, on one hand, an ethnocentrism in which the Turks see themselves as the bearers of civilization: "Europe is not fit for much more than destroying its civilization. But we will bring it to life again and carry it on."[17] An aspect of this ethnocentrism is xenophobia. Turks tolerate, but are suspicious of, all foreigners. A correspondent writing about Turkish-American relations observed that the high esteem in which the Turks held the United States was indicated by the fact that after Germany, America was the least hated foreign power.[18]

"Civilization" spoken by a Turk is also a rallying cry of the nationalist revolution. The expression is often mistakenly equated with "Westernization." While it is true that Westernization of technology was, and is, a goal of the Kemalist reformers, it represented something to be accomplished on Turkish terms, in a Turkish idiom. It meant bringing Turkey up to par with the rest of the world and out of the grip of Islamic theocracy. Above all, where "civilization" and "Westernization" converge in meaning the word is "secular."

Ataturk used the word in the ghazi spirit in many of his speeches:

We shall follow the road to civilization and get there. Those who halt on the road...will be drowned by the roaring flood of civilization.

Civilization is so strong a fire that he who ignores it is burnt and destroyed.

We must prove that we are capable of becoming active members of the society of civilized peoples.

Our great struggle is to lift ourselves to the level of the most civilized and prosperous nations.[19]

While striving mightily to haul Turkey out of the Middle Ages and onto the road to civilization, Ataturk also worked hard to raise the Turk's self-esteem. During the Ottoman era an individual identified himself as an "Ottoman," not as a "Turk." "Turk" was a term of contempt, indicating an unrefined person of low birth. One of Ataturk's aphorisms commonly seen on banners all over Turkey to this day proclaims: "Lucky is he who can say 'I am a Turk.' "

The young man who serves in the Turkish Army today is therefore instilled with a perception of the army as a humanizing and civilizing institution. What these concepts of "humanity" and "civilization" translate into are expressions of the Kemalist aspiration to compete on equal terms with the rest of the world. The army is the crucible in which the new Kemalist man is forged. The army reinforces sense of national identity and reminds the young man of pride in his martial traditions—Turkish—not Ottoman traditions. And finally the army becomes a moral and ethnical shelter for the young man, a substitute for the influence of the *hodja*, the Islamic holy man, by offering a tradition, an ethos, and a mystique more ancient than his professed religion.

Military Experiences, 1912-1918

"He went off to Yemen with his regiment and has not come back again."[20] Even today the words of a song remembering the tragic squander of Turkish soldiers' lives in a futile effort to hold on to a colonial possession (ca. 1912) are recalled with some sad fatalistic reflection. That was the beginning of the end of the Ottoman Empire. World War I was to place the final crushing burden on the Empire and more proximately on the army. The period 1914-1918 was the last time Turkey waged war on any large scale. But the magnitude of the Ottoman contribution to the Central Powers' effort was impressive. Not only did the Turkish soldiers fight well and their government hold together, but they lasted a year longer than imperial Russia. The Turkish Army expanded to 52 divisions or 800,000 men, fought a multi-front war, and successfully pinned down over 1 million Allied troops for most of the war.[21]

Perhaps the most famous engagement of World War I (involving Turks) was the battle at Gallipoli. The campaign began with the Allied landing on April 26, 1915, in an attempt to seize the Gallipoli Peninsula, win control of the Dardanelles, and capture Constantinople. Initially, the Turkish forces were under the command of a German general, Liman von Sanders, who was senior adviser and inspector general of the Turkish Army. For all intents and purposes, von Sanders had operational control of the entire army. Later, command of the five Turkish divisions at Gallipoli passed to a hitherto unknown colonel, Mustafa Kemal. The Allies outnumbered the Turks, but their plan was ill-conceived and the operation was badly organized. The main advantage to the Turks was that they were defending the high ground. In fact, it is speculated that had the Allies known how desperately undermanned and short of ammunition the Turkish defenders were, they would have pressed their attack with greater resolve. That is, of course, speculative. What it ignores are several factors among which is the fact that the Allies were up against a force that had received the following command from Mustafa Kemal: "I do not order you to attack. I order you to die!" The Allies withdrew finally in February 1916 after suffering 150,000 casualties.

The Central Powers finally collapsed and Turkey signed an armistice on October 30, 1918, at Mudros. Between 1914 and the end of the war the Ottoman Empire had mobilized 2.8 million men. Of these, 325,000 died in battle.[22] The Ottoman Turks' ability to offer an effective resistance to the attacks on every quarter had become exhausted. It is interesting to note that they had successfully defended the Straits, and subsequently—again under Mustafa Kemal—had mounted a successful counteroffensive against the Russians who had penetrated as far west as Erzincan. The Bolshevik Revolution of 1917 ended Russian involvement in the war. Kemal appeared again on the southern front to mastermind a successful withdrawal from Syria back into Turkey in 1918. The story, it seems, was essentially the same from front to front: the Turks held on tenaciously, but were underequipped and were spread too thinly. The First World War left Turkey stripped of its colonial possessions but concentrated Turkish strength in the Anatolian heartland.

The new Turkish Republic under Mustafa Kemal Ataturk emerged after a fight against occupation by the Greeks and other Allied powers (as mentioned earlier). Aside from some domestic actions to stabilize the Republic, the army was not involved in military operations against foreign powers until the Korean War. Turkey adhered to Ataturk's dictum, "Peace at home, peace abroad" during the foundational years that included World War II.

The Korean War

The Turkish infantry brigade sent to Korea in 1950 to serve under the United Nations Command was a gesture of gratitude for assistance from the United States. One popular Turkish conception of their display of solidarity was expressed in a political cartoon published in an Istanbul newspaper. There the reader saw "America as a terrified maiden who would have been violated by a North Korean brute, but for the prompt arrival of a Turkish soldier."[23]

The infantry brigade had a personnel strength of around 4,500 and served three years in combat. The Turkish brigade earned an outstanding reputation for its combat effectiveness and for the soldiers' courage and ferocious tenacity. Notable engagements in which the Turks fought were the battles at Wamon, Simnimni, Kaechon, and Kunuri. The brigade sustained the highest casualty rate of all the U.N. forces that engaged in combat. A system of rotational assignments allowed a total of 29,882 men to serve in Korea. Brigade losses were 717 killed and 2,246 wounded.[24]

Cyprus, 1974

The next significant military action took place in 1974 when a coup supported by the Greek military junta removed Cypriot President Makarios from office. The Turks were alarmed by what appeared to be a major step toward *enosis*, or unification of Cyprus with Greece. Since the Cyprus independence agreements of 1960 guaranteed protection of the rights of the Turkish Cypriots, Ankara interpreted the move toward *enosis* as a clear threat to their lives and property.

On July 20 to "save the Turkish community from a massacre" approximately 6,000 Turkish troops landed near Kyrenia. In the two days that followed an additional 25,000 reinforcements were landed. The ground forces consisted of two infantry divisions and a mix of armored, mechanized infantry, self-propelled artillery, and airborne units.[25] Additional combat support was provided by the Turkish Navy and Air Force. In heavy fighting against the Greek Cypriots the Turks advanced some 20 kilometers from Kyrenia to Nicosia until a cease-fire was called.

While preliminary negotiations began in Geneva on July 30, the Turks continued landing reinforcements to consolidate their bridgehead, which included in some places up to 30 kilometers of territory east and west of the Kyrenia-Nicosia road. The Geneva talks began on August 8. A week later they broke down.

On August 14 Turkey launched a major attack toward Lefka in the west and Famagusta in the east. The objectives were taken by the evening of August 15. This two-directional assault succeeded in cutting off the northern third of the island. The Turkish advance continued through August 18 by which time the army had secured nearly 40 percent of the country and had surrounded Nicosia. By August 20, 40,000 Turkish soldiers controlled 45 percent of the island nation.[26]

A critique of this Cyprus incursion is difficult in the absence of published reports by trained military observers. The operation was impressive in scale—the Turks were able to deploy roughly a corps-sized force, seize and hold their objective within forty-eight hours. Since the political events that precipitated the Turkish intervention had transpired rather abruptly, it would appear that the units committed to combat had been standing at a high state of operational readiness. The Turks applied an economy of force by confining the scope of the operation only to the predominantly Turkish sectors on the island, leaving the impression they could have taken more, had they desired. On the other hand, they were fighting against a poorly equipped and numerically inferior force. The Greek Cypriots clearly compensated for their own materiel weakness with an intense courage and a grim determination to make the Turks pay dearly for every inch they advanced.

Army Organization

The commander-in-chief of the Turkish armed forces is the president of the republic. His office is "integrated in the moral existence of the Turkish Grand National Assembly,"[27] meaning that the function of the president is linked to the will of the people as represented in the national Parliament. The Council of Ministers and the prime minister—appointed by the president but subject to a legislative vote of confidence—are responsible for "national security and preparing the armed forces for war."[28]

The Chief of the Turkish General Staff (TGS) is the commander of the armed forces. He is appointed to this office by the president upon nomination by the Council of Ministers. The Chief of the TGS is responsible to the prime minister. The General Staff itself is organized into five major divisions: personnel (J-1); intelligence (J-2); operations (J-3); logistics (J-4); and communications (J-5). It is a multi-service staff, but most of its officers are drawn from the army. The army is commanded by the chief of Land Forces Command (LFC). Headquarters of LFC is in Ankara.

Most of the Turkish ground forces are committed to NATO. The NATO command to which they would be assigned in time of war is LAND-SOUTHEAST, headquartered in Izmir. This command is subordinate to the Commander-in-Chief Allied Forces Southern Europe, CINCSOUTH.

Tactical Deployments

The mission of the Turkish Land Forces is to deter an enemy ground attack, to render such an attack ineffective, and to destroy enemy forces. To accomplish this mission the Turkish Land Forces are organized into four field armies. These are supported by four communication and logistical zone commands and a training command. Army aviation support consisting of helicopters and light observation aircraft is provided at division and higher levels.[29] A more detailed breakdown of unit types is shown in Table 14.

The First Army, with headquarters in Istanbul, defends European Turkey or Turkish Thrace. Because the gentle terrain is optimal for mobile operations, First Army units are reportedly heavy in armor.[30] This is the first line of defense for Turkey, since Thrace is bordered on the north by Bulgaria and constitutes the land approach to the Straits (the Bosporus and the Dardanelles). The NATO concept of defense for this key terrain requires cooperation between Turkish and Greek units deployed in the region.

The Second Army has its headquarters in Konya. Its area of responsibility is defense of the south and southeastern parts of the country. The Third Army defends the Transcaucasus border with the Soviet Union.[31] The severe mountainous terrain in eastern Turkey would appear to favor the defenders. Armored and mechanized operations would be extremely difficult, and enemy movements would be easier to canalize. In the past, however, invading forces have fought through this area. It will be recalled that in recent history Mustafa Kemal Ataturk himself commanded the counterattack to halt the Russian advance to Erzincan, which is west of Erzurum, current headquarters of the Third Army.[32]

The fourth field army has been designated the Aegean Army, to circumvent the negative association with a Turkish figure of speech. "Transferred to the fourth army" is a Turkish euphemism meaning to be killed in combat. Headquarters of the Aegean Army is in Izmir. Its defensive area is the Aegean coastline opposite the Greek islands. The Aegean Army is hardly an army. It was organized as the result of heightened tensions with Greece but is believed to consist mostly of training brigades.[33]

The Turkish units on Cyrus are referred to as the Cyprus Turkish Peace Force.[34] The strength and composition of this force is not known. *The Military Balance* (1979-1980) reports two divisions there.[35]

Equipment

The Turkish Army is equipped with weapons obtained primarily from the United States. A quick glance at Table 15 will reveal—where it is possible to determine from the nomenclature—that the bulk of this equipment is obsolescent or obsolete. Turkey is, in fact, primarily armed with weapons that are of the Korean War vintage or earlier. With the assistance of the U.S. government, Turkey has recently begun to modernize its armed forces. More modern weapon types are being incorporated into the inventory (such as the TOW or the MILAN anti-tank guided missiles). Additionally, Turkey has begun to purchase the Leopard main battle tank.

Table 14
Turkish Land Forces Command, Major Unit Types[36]

Strength: 470,000 (210,000 conscripts)

	Armored	Mech Infantry	Infantry	Parachute	Commando
Divisions	1	2	14	—	—
Brigades	5	4	5	1	1

(additionally, 4 SSM battalions with Honest John)

Prepared by the author.

Table 15
Turkish Land Forces Command Equipment

Armor	
Medium tanks (M47, M48)*	3,500
Armored personnel carriers (M113, M59, Commando)	1,600
Artillery	
Howitzers (75mm, 105mm, 155mm, 203mm)	1,500
Guns	
144mm	190
175mm self-propelled	36
Mortars (60mm, 81mm, 4.2-in)	1,750
SSM Launcher (Honest John)	18
Anti-tank	
Recoilless rifles	
57mm	1,200
75mm	390
106mm	800
Anti-tank guided missiles (cobra, SS-11, TOW)**	85
Air Defense Artillery (40mm guns)	900

* On order: Leopard medium tanks
** On order: Additional TOW and MILAN ATGM Systems

Source: *The Military Balance, 1979-1980*, London: International Institute for Strategic Studies, 1979, p. 30.

Sources of Supply

The primary source of military materiel and training assistance to Turkey has been the United States. Between 1950 and 1978 the United States provided Turkey with more than $3.2 billion in military assistance.[37] Most of the weapons provided were excess items of U.S. military equipment.

U.S. Secretary of Defense Caspar Weinberger announced in December 1981 at the conclusion of a visit to Turkey the establishment of a high-level joint defense group to "enlarge and improve defense cooperation" between Washington and Ankara. Mr. Weinberger described Turkey's need for arms as "very real." He also observed that the badly needed equipment modernization would be "an expensive undertaking." The United States is scheduled to provide $703 million for military assistance. Turkey reportedly requested $900 million for fiscal year 1983.[38]

The West German government has been another major supporter of Turkish defensive needs. The annual contributions from Bonn to Ankara have amounted to some $20 million between 1964 and the late 1970s, after which time the figure has risen. An agreement concluded in 1979 provided $104 million worth of assistance. For the land forces, an unspecified number of Leopard tanks was a significant feature of the aid package.[39]

Turkey's other NATO allies have contributed relatively little to its defensive requirements. Norway agreed in 1979 to deliver some military equipment through credits for commercial sales. The land force may have gained some M-72 light anti-tank weapons from this agreement.[40] Otherwise, what minimal assistance some of the Western European allies were previously motivated to commit to Turkey has been suspended in an expression of protest over alleged human rights infractions by the military government.

Tactical Doctrine

Little specific is known about Turkish tactical doctrine. Much will have to be reconstructed from inference. For example, it is known that many Turks have received training in the United States and that the preponderance of Turkish military equipment is U.S.-provided. To a significant extent doctrine follows equipment. (For example, where the Soviets have been the major supplier of equipment, their tactical and logistical doctrine has followed. So, too, with the United States.)

Additionally, although not too much can or should be concluded from this, the Turkish Army has since 1945 patterned the structure of its major combat formations (divisions and brigades) after the U.S. system. Hence, the main maneuver elements of a division are three regiments (which compare to present-day U.S. divisional brigades); of a regiment, three battalions; of a battalion, three companies. There are, of course, additional combat (armor, anti-armor, recon), combat support (artillery, air defense), and combat service support (transport, medical, and supply) units organic to each major formation.[41] Hence, to the extent that tactical doctrine patterns alter combat formations, the model is American.

What Kinds of War Can Turkey Fight?

Potential threats to Turkey from the Soviet Union and Warsaw Pact could assume any or all of these scenarios:[42]

- a combined arms (tank and motorized infantry) attack out of Bulgaria toward Istanbul, the Straits, and the Aegean;
- a combined arms attack out of the Soviet Transcaucasus area into eastern Turkey and Central Anatolia;
- maritime and strategic air attacks over the Black Sea.

The USSR and its allies have reportedly been modernizing the land, sea, and air forces that are deployed opposite Turkey. The Soviet forces in the Transcaucasus have until recently lagged behind other military regions in the USSR in military modernization. However, since the destabilization of Iran and the Soviet invasion of Afghanistan, these units, too, are undergoing upgrading.[43] This threat becomes even more serious in view of the often publicly stated need for Turkish modernization.

In a conventional war against an opponent of comparable strength, Turkish performance would be exceptional. Where doubts about Turkish military capabilities arise is with respect to numerically superior opposing forces equipped with state-of-the art weaponry. This, of course, is a concern not unique to Turkey and the southern flank.[44] The NATO Alliance is generally concerned about the Soviet conventional forces buildup that appears far out of proportion to the requirements of a peacetime defensive force structure. Additionally, there is concern about the apparent ability of the Soviet and Warsaw Pact forces to function in a chemically or radiologically contaminated environment. In conclusion, Turkey is not lacking in manpower, nor is it lacking in national willpower to defend its territorial integrity. But its equipment is growing older, while potential adversaries are replacing their obsolescent equipment with newer and more effective systems. In imagining the "worst case," where conventional Turkish forces were overrun or forced to withdraw by enemy forces, that would by no means signal the end of Turkish resistance to an invading force. There is also the Home Guard.

Home Guard units (sometimes called "Hunter" units) may be formed in important regions at the discretion of the Turkish General Staff. These units are formed by male citizens between sixteen and sixty years old and female citizens between twenty and forty-five. The missions of these units are as follows:[45]

1. Units near the borders and seacoast carry out observation of their regions, resist enemy raids, cooperate with army units as needed, protect important installations, and conduct guerrilla operations behind the enemy lines in the event that the main forces withdraw.
2. Prevent enemy activities at airports and other areas suitable for landing. Destroy enemy landing aircraft and gliders.
3. Protect road and rail networks against enemy attacks from land, sea, and air.
4. Protect the mining areas and industrial installations against sabotage.
5. Protect installations and depots that are a potential public hazard. Prevent activities of enemy agents. Protect the operations of administrative organizations.

If there is any doubt from where the Turks perceive a historical enmity, Andre Falk proposes this analysis (paraphrased here):

It is not Communist ideology which is so repugnant to the Turks. It is for Holy Russia in its successive manifestations that the Turk cherishes a hatred based on very solid reasons that long memory can provide. Between *Moskov* and Turk hostility is the constant rule. There is a history of fourteen wars and ninety-seven less important conflicts between Turks and Russians. The conflict dates from a time when Slavic archers loosed their arrows at the horseman of the Sultan of Kazan. Sometimes when they speak their thoughts aloud, the Turks will remind you that the Volga is a Turkish river called the Idil and they will show you maps of the Caucasus on which Novotcherkask is still written Yeni Tcherkess and whisper in your ear that in the USSR there are thirty million of their lost brethren.[46]

Quality of Troops

The Turkish Army is a conscript force. All physically fit male citizens are required to enter military service at age twenty. The term of service is twenty months. Because of Turkey's growing population, the army usually exceeds the required conscript quota. In that event surplus candidates are then trained and assigned to other defense-related jobs or to nation-building projects.

Training of enlisted men proceeds through several stages before they begin functioning as a member of a regular unit:

Arrival and preparation (1 week)—this is the period during which the new conscripts process in and are allocated to training units;

Basic training (4 weeks)—conscripts for all services are given basic infantry training. The program emphasizes teaching fundamental military skills, close order drill, combat training, and battlefield survival techniques;

Specialization training (9 weeks)—here the individual undergoes training for the branch of the army to which he has been assigned (e.g., armor, artillery, etc.).

In the fourteenth week of training, the new conscripts undergo testing to evaluate the progress they have made during the first thirteen weeks. Upon successful completion of their tests, the conscripts are dispatched to units where they receive further instruction in a variety of general and special military subjects. Once in a unit the new privates begin intensive training with the rest of the unit to bring them up to the performance levels demanded by the Turkish Army. Conscripts may be promoted to temporary grades of corporal or sergeant but rarely serve longer than the required twenty months.

Professional noncommissioned officers are graduates of the NCO preparatory school. Upon completion of secondary school, NCO candidates must take three years of academic and military education, after which they are assigned to a branch school for an additional year of training in their specialized area. Upon graduation they enter the army with the rank of sergeant for a long tour of duty.

The Turkish soldier is well known for his toughness and tenacity in combat. The training is demanding, and Turkish army life prepares soldiers well for the hardships of warfare. Although the discipline is reportedly rigorous, most conscripts recall their tours of duty with pride, seeing it as an opportunity for self-improvement, and as a passage into manhood. Although it is not known how many young men leave the service with training in a useful trade, many of the conscripts are taught to read and write. This is especially true of those drawn from remote rural areas, where even elementary educational opportunities are few. (The literacy rate in Turkey is estimated to be between 50 and 60 percent.)

The NCOs, backbone of the army, provide the small unit leadership and technical skills that keep the army stable during the constant turnover of conscripts. The Turkish Army relies heavily on the technical expertise of its NCOs. During their fourth year of preparatory education, NCOs acquire specialized training in such areas as combat unit operations (armor, infantry, commando, or artillery and missiles); combat support (communications, engineering); and combat service support (administrative, logistic, quartermaster, transport, or health and veterinary). NCOs with "positive records" are promoted at intervals set by regulation. Those with exemplary records who pass a special examination may become officers, attaining a rank as high as captain during their careers.

Quality of the Officers

The Turkish Army is led by a select group of well-educated professional officers. Preparation for a career as an officer begins in a military high school or in a public high school (provided the student has been enrolled in the science curriculum). The Land Forces Military Academy (established in 1834) offers a four-year program of instruction to those cadets passing the entrance examination. Cadets receive thirty-two weeks of academic education and six to seven weeks of applied training in their first three years (five weeks of practical training in the fourth year). They are grouped into science and social science curricula within which individuals are identified for further specialized development according to their capabilities and academic success. Upon graduation the cadets are commissioned as second lieutenants and sent to a branch school for an additional year of training before they take up duties with a regular unit.

Alternative programs exist whereby graduates of military or public high schools enter a university as military students to study in "required fields" such as education, law, medicine, or engineering. For the duration of their academic program they are attached to a Military Student Command, which provides for lodging and other administrative services. Military training takes place during school vacation periods. The civilian universities provide the major input of reserve officers for the Turkish Army. Normally a reservist has a twenty-month tour of duty, but it is possible to "contract for additional service of up to 26 years, subject to some limitations."[47]

At various junctions in their career, officers will attend branch advanced courses and possibly go to the United States or Western Europe for additional training. A select few among the officers are chosen to attend the General Staff College at Istanbul. Graduates of this college are designated as members of the General Staff Corps. Membership in this elite group is a prerequisite for selection for higher command positions and an assignment to the Turkish General Staff.[48]

Experience

The most recent combat experience was the incursion into Cyprus in 1974. Many of the officers and NCOs who took part in that corps-sized action are still on active duty. The duration of the fighting was relatively brief, but the task of moving, deploying, and supplying a source of that size no doubt taught the Turks some valuable lessons. Unfortunately, the cost in international consequences was high. Two divisions are reported to be still in garrison on the island.

Cohesion

Between 80 and 85 percent of the population consists of ethnic Turks and nearly 98 percent is Moslem. These factors alone help to promote cohesion in the Turkish Army. The army also cultivates the warrior ethic, still present in Turkish society, reminding the soldiers of the glorious history of Turkish men in the profession of arms.

Since it is a conscript force, there are two levels at which cohesion functions. First, among the troops, conscripts are generally assigned to the same unit for the duration of their tour of duty. The soldiers are adequately clothed and fed—in fact often far better in the army than in civilian life where they face economic deprivation and unemployment. There is little evidence of draft dodging or petitions for deferment. The soldiers, it seems, regard their active duty as "an all too brief respite from the problems they faced as civilians."[49]

Among the officers there is the cohesion of professionalism. The Turkish Army is an elitist organization, and its officers are well aware of their special status in society. It is a status that sets them apart and, in so doing, brings them together. The army and the government work hard to promote programs that improve morale through pay increases and other fringe benefits.

Sustainability

Turkey's sustainability problems are scenario-dependent. In combat actions of brief duration the Turks would be able to ensure the continued flow of men, ammunition, and fuel to their combat units. In intense prolonged combat against an enemy of equal or greater strength, the Turkish Army's support system would be subjected to severe strain. In defending the Turkish Straits, the units on the European side (Thrace) would have to rely on resupply from the Asian side, once they exhausted their stockpiles. These lines of communication and supply would be highly vulnerable to interdiction from enemy aircraft. In the east the mountainous terrain would aid the defenders in delaying the enemy, but it would work in the same way against the rapid movement of support to the units in combat. These lines of communication and supply would also be vulnerable to interdiction.

The Turkish defense industry provides some materiel support to the army through a government-owned cartel of military factories and maintenance facilities. The domestic industry is capable of producing ammunition, cartridges, small arms, gun powder, caps and charges, and batteries. Attached to the Land Forces Command are also factories for tank overhaul, depot level maintenance and repair, and spare parts production.[50] For high-technology equipment and major weapons systems Turkey is dependent on foreign suppliers, such as the United States and West Germany.

Conclusions

Strengths and Weaknesses

One of the greatest strengths of the Turkish Army is the quality of its fighting men. They are tough, fatalistic, and willing to endure severe hardships. Manpower is no problem for Turkey—annually there are more available men than the force structure of the army and the paramilitary Gendarmerie can absorb. Although Turkey does not have a system of organized reserve units, it is estimated that at any given time there is a pool of more than 800,000 trained veterans available for recall to active duty.[51]

A significant weakness of the Turkish Army is the obsolescence of its equipment. This would be a tolerable condition were it not for the unabated modernization and military buildup taking place within the Warsaw Pact. The army is predominantly a foot infantry force. Its older mechanized equipment is not likely to stand up to the rigors of intense combat. The weaponry is generally below state-of-the-art technology which, again, leaves the army vulnerable to an enemy with advanced high-tech equipment. Additionally, its defensive capabilities against chemical-biological-radiological (CBR) and electronic warfare are probably commensurate with the capabilities and age of its major weapons systems.

Trends

Unfortunately, the current trend in the Turkish Army is toward advanced obsolescence. The army is painfully aware of this shortcoming and is striving to reverse the trend. The main obstacle is money. The Turkish Army began a Reorganization and Modernization (REMO) program in 1977, but the economic recession that hit so hard delayed indefinitely the full implementation of the plan. Since the military government imposed domestic stability, the Turkish economy has begun to show signs of improvement. If and when more funding for modernization materializes, the army will probably place highest priority on acquisition of new or modernized armored vehicles, anti-armor, and air defense weapons. Additionally, it will want to modernize communications, command and control, and battlefield intelligence (C^3I) capabilities, as well as invest in upgrading its technique of personnel and supply management. However, even a dramatic recovery of the Turkish economy would not diminish the need for foreign assistance in getting modernization underway. The trend Turkey would like to see implemented is a steady transition from a low-technology Korean War-era army to a force at least marginally competitive in the rapidly changing high-technology environment of the 1980s.

Foreseeable Crises

The spectre stalking Turkey at this point in its history is terrorism. After the return of civilian government to Turkey, the question will be, whether terrorism and factional violence will again reduce the country to a state of anarchy, necessitating another military takeover. This may be a cynical appraisal, but it is grimly realistic. The Soviet Union stands to gain much from a destabilized Turkey, and evidence abounds that the Soviets have aided either directly or indirectly a multitude of terrorist groups whose purpose is to spread anarchy in Turkey. Successful combat against this assault will depend on the will of the Turkish people to resist and to persuade their political representatives to look beyond the short-range gains sought in factional in-fighting to which the common good is often sacrificed.

A crisis with Greece is possible, as well as a crises with the Western European community. In the aftermath of its crackdown on terror, Turkey has been irritated by complaints about abuse of human rights from its allies. Given the proper circumstances, the Soviet Union could succeed in driving a permanent wedge between Turkey and Western Europe by exploiting terrorist groups to cause Ankara to overreact to the threat in a way that would incur European condemnation.

Notes

1. "Instability and Change on NATO's Southern Flank," in Derek Leebaert, ed., *European Security: Prospects for the 1980's* (Lexington, Mass.: D. C. Heath & Co., 1979), p. 108.

2. Ibid.

3. Claire Sterling, *The Terror Network*, 1981, pp. 228-46.

4. Ibid.

5. Metin Tamkoc, *The Warrior Diplomats* (Salt Lake City: University of Utah Press, 1976), p. 2.

6. Ibid., p. 3.

7. Richard Nyrop, ed., *Turkey: A Country Study* (Washington, D.C.: U.S. Government Printing Office, 1980), p. 86.

8. David Hotham, *The Turks* (London: John Murray, Ltd., 1972), p. 178.

9. Nyrop, *Turkey*, p. 65.

10. Andre Falk, *Turkey* (London: Vista Books, 1963), p. 115.

11. Nyrop, *Turkey*, p. 104.

12. Ibid., p. 106.

13. Hotham, *The Turks*, p. 53.

14. Ibid., pp. 53-54.

15. Ibid.

16. Ibid., p. 64.

17. Falk, *Turkey*, p. 59.

18. Ibid., p. 60.

19. Hotham, *The Turks*, pp. 23-24.

20. Falk, *Turkey*, p. 128.

21. *Area Handbook for the Republic of Turkey* (Washington, D.C.: U.S. Government Printing Office, 1973), p. 33.

22. Nyrop, *Turkey*, p. 43.

23. Falk, *Turkey*, p. 53.

24. Nyrop, *Turkey*, p. 252.

25. "Der Zypernkonflikt," *Osterreichische militarische Zeitschrift*, Heft 6 (1974): 487.

26. Ibid., p. 487.

27. Nyrop, *Turkey*, p. 260.

28. Ibid.

29. Ibid., p. 266.

30. Ibid.

31. *The Military Balance, 1979-1980* (London: International Institute for Strategic Studies, 1979), p. 30.

32. Nyrop, *Turkey*, p. 267.

33. Ibid.

34. Ibid, p. 266.

35. *The Military Balance*, p. 30.

36. Ibid.

37. Nyrop, *Turkey*, p. 275.

38. Marvin Howe, "US and Turks Agree to Create a Joint Defense Unit," *The New York Times*, December 6, 1981, pp. 1-21.

39. Nyrop, *Turkey*, p. 280.

40. Ibid.

41. Otto von Pivka, *The Armies of Europe Today* (New York: Beekman, 1974), pp. 80-81.

42. Fritz Ermarth, "The Strategic Importance of Turkey," *Advertising Supplement to the New York Times*, December 4, 1981, p. 15.

43. Ibid.
44. Ibid.
45. "Facts and Figures on Defense: Turkey," *Military Technology* 26 (1980): 72.
46. Falk, *Turkey*, p. 50.
47. Nyrop, *Turkey*, p. 268.
48. Ibid., pp. 268–69.
49. Ibid., p. 274.
50. *The Turkish Armed Forces* is a Turkish government publication which cites no office or agency and no publication date but first appeared in 1980. This magazine is circulated in English presumably as part of an effort on the part of the Turkish government to improve the image of its armed forces.
51. Nyrop, *Turkey*, p. 258.

Bibliography

Area Handbook for the Republic of Turkey. Washington, D.C.: U.S. Government Printing Office, 1973.

"Der Zypernkonflikt," *Osterreichische militarische Zeitschrift*, Heft 6 (1974): 486–490.

Ermarth, Fritz W. "The Strategic Importance of Turkey." *New York Times*, December 6, 1981, p. 15.

"Facts and Figures on Defense: Turkey." *Military Technology* 26 (1980): 62–72.

Falk, Andre. *Turkey*. London: Vista Books, 1963.

Hotham, David. *The Turks*. London: John Murray, Ltd., 1972.

Howe, Marvin. "US and Turks Agree to Create a Joint Defense Unit." *The New York Times*, December 6, 1981, pp. 1–21.

"Instability and Change on NATO's Southern Flank." In Derek Leebaert, ed. *European Security: Prospects for the 1980s*. Lexington, Mass: D. C. Heath & Co., 1979.

The Military Balance, 1979-1980. London: International Institute for Strategic Studies, 1979.

Nyrop, Richard F., ed. *Turkey: A Country Study*. Washington, D.C.: U.S. Government Printing Office, 1980.

Pivka, Otto von. *The Armies of Europe Today*. New York: Beekman, 1974.

Tamkoc, Metin. *The Warrior Diplomats*. Salt Lake City: University of Utah Press, 1976.

"The Turkish Armed Forces." Turkish Government Publication, 1980.

THE WARSAW PACT

Soviet Union

Richard A. Gabriel and William C. Martel

The Soviet Army is among the largest standing armies in the world and probably the best equipped. The term "army" as understood in the Soviet context implies a somewhat different type of military institution than in the West. The Soviet Army includes within it five separate components: strategic rocket forces, ground forces, airborne forces, air defense forces, and special troops. All components are operationally unified under a general staff and are administered and commanded at the national level by a cabinet-level official, the minister of defense. Within the Soviet military system large numbers of additional component MVD and KGB troops could be made available in time of crisis.

That the Soviet Union maintains a very large ground army is not particularly noteworthy, for historically Russia has always had one of the largest standing military forces in Europe. The size of Russian ground forces today is more explicable in terms of history and tradition than in terms of the rise of Communism in the Soviet Union.

The Soviet Army is a classic European army modeled after the armies typical of Europe around the turn of the century and persisting throughout World War II. This European army is predicated upon maintaining professional officer and NCO corps constituting a cadre of military professionals and expected to provide central direction for the country's large conscript and reserve forces. In the event of mobilization, this cadre would provide a corp of leaders to command and direct the large mobilized force in the field.

Today the Soviet Army continually conducts reserve mobilization exercises in the classic tradition to demonstrate that at any time it could mobilize literally millions of trained reserves for war. As in other classic armies, military service in the Soviet Union is also closely linked to the rights and privileges of citizenship. It is understood that as a condition of citizenship every individual in Soviet society has a basic obligation to serve in the military.

There are several major points of difference between the military structures of the West and the Soviet Union. First, the size of the standing armies in the West, both absolutely and relatively, is small compared to that of the Soviet Army. This is true not only in terms of the percentage of the gross national product each army consumes but more so in terms of the importance of the military as a social institution within its host society. Second, Western armies are less dependent upon conscription to fill their military ranks. The Soviet army, in the mainstream of the nineteenth-century European army, continues to rely almost exclusively upon conscription to furnish its military manpower. Many of its officers as well as almost the entire noncommissioned officer corps started as conscripts. Perhaps as much as 95 percent of all NCOs serving at any time are still drawn directly from the conscript ranks.[1]

Yet another difference between the two armies is that in the West the tendency is to develop modern organization forms and to utilize modern motivational techniques. By contrast, the Soviets have adopted few modern forms and even fewer modern techniques. One reason is that many organizational forms characteristic of Soviet *society* have been adopted from those found in traditional *military* organizations. Moreover, a totalitarian society is prone to emphasize those mechanisms of control and organization that have already proven effective. In the Soviet case, this means the use of traditional bureaucratic methods of control. As a consequence, there is a noticeable lack of modern approaches to industrial organization within the larger society that could be transferred to the military. When a military experiment proves effective it is often transferred to and adopted by the civilian society. Thus, Soviet military structures remain highly traditional in organizational form and operation.

With regard to motivational techniques, the Soviets have been reluctant to deviate from proven methods. Thus, all the traditional forms of organization and motivation associated with classic European armies continue largely unchanged in the Soviet Army today.

The Soviet Army serves wider functions as a social institution than do the armies of the democratic West. It performs at least four such additional functions.[2] First is the role the army plays in nation-building. Nearly one-half of the Soviet population consists of nationality groups that are ethnically, linguistically, racially, and religiously distinct from the Slavic minority. As a result, the Soviet Union has a major problem in trying to build a national consciousness. A primary mechanism for accomplishing this goal is universal conscription and military service. What Frederick the Great said of the German Army, that it was a "school of the nation," is also true of the Soviet Army. Accordingly, the Soviet Army acts as a giant socialization mechanism for disparate peoples.

The military in the Soviet Union also serves an education function.[3] The party quite openly views the army as a giant educational mechanism, especially for teaching various nationality groups the Russian language. The

Soviet Army issues all orders and commands in Russian only. The regime considers linguistic assimilation important to building a common sense of national identity.

Universal conscription also fosters habits of obedience and acquiescence to authority that are critical to maintaining social control in a totalitarian society. The Soviets contend that two years of military service get one acclimated to the commands, lack of individuality, physical hardships, and ways of dealing with bureaucracy that are normal in a totalitarian social system.

Still another task of the Soviet Army is to suppress and control the younger elements of Soviet society during their crucial period of adolescent restiveness. Military service provides close control of adolescents until they have passed through their "dangerous" age, until they have seen there are no real alternatives to conformity or, if nothing else, until they are two years older and somewhat wiser. The Soviet Army is actually a shock absorber for dissent: it absorbs groups that are most likely to create social trouble and places them in an environment where indiscipline and dissent are permitted expression only at great risk. At the same time, it reinforces habits and practices that erode any propensity for social deviance. The circle of control is tightly closed.

Manpower

The number of men in the Soviet ground forces exceeds the total for all four U.S. services by almost a half million men. Indeed, total Soviet ground force manpower (some 4,832,000) is more than twice that of the United States. In addition, active Soviet military regulars, even excluding their security forces, exceed the size of the entire U.S. military establishment, including its civilian and reserve forces. If Soviet paramilitary and reserve forces are counted, the amount of Soviet military manpower available to pursue military objectives is more than four times the total forces available to the United States.[4] In the decade since 1970, the ground forces available to the Soviet Union increased from 1,420,000 to approximately 1,680,000.[5]

Military manpower by itself does not tell the whole story. The organization and equipping of that manpower are crucial elements in fighting ability. Since 1970, counting only Category 1 and 2 divisions, the Soviets increased the number of available divisions by almost 10 percent. In 1970, it had seventy-three Category 1 and 2 divisions, and by 1980 it had eighty of these divisions. Twenty-six of the divisions were armored, forty-seven motorized rifle, and seven airborne. Moreover, the Soviets have increased the number of Category 3 and 4 divisions from eighty-six to ninety-three, or an increase of seven divisions since 1970. Of these divisions, twenty are armored, seventy-two motorized rifle, and one airborne.[6] The Soviets began with 159 deployable divisions in 1970 which have now increased to 173.[7] By any standard it is clear that in a short period of time, say within thirty days of the outbreak of war, the Soviet Union could bring to bear a substantial manpower advantage in terms of deployable divisions.

Weaponry

The Soviet Army also enjoys a considerable advantage in certain types of weaponry, and here the Soviet emphasis on mobile and heavily armored forces is evident. The Soviet Army currently has over 49,000 tank vehicles in its inventory, 47,000 of which are heavy and medium tanks accompanied by 2,000 light tanks. Equally impressive is the fact that in the period between 1965 and 1980 the Soviets were able to deploy and bring into production three new prototype tanks: the T-62, T-72, and, the most recent prototype, the T-80 which is already undergoing tests. Their ability to field massive tank armies is sustained by their tank production, which is roughly ten times that of the United States. The Soviets can produce and deploy about 4,000 tanks a year compared to only 400 for the United States. The Soviet emphasis on armor (which is discussed in detail later in this chapter) is readily apparent, as is its advantage of almost four to one in armored vehicles that would have to be engaged on the battlefield.

The Soviets also have a numerical advantage in the deployment of armored personnel carriers. Because the Soviet Army is configured to move large masses of armor in a high tempo rapid attack, large stocks of APCs are vital if infantry forces are to keep pace. Since 1967, no Soviet infantryman has been required to walk into battle; since then, all ground forces have been fully mechanized, and troops move through the battle area in their APCs accompanied by tanks. So thorough and complete has the mechanization of the Soviet Army been that all eight airborne divisions are now equipped with the new BRD light air droppable armored personnel carrier.[8]

The Soviet Army has 60,000 armored carriers, an increase of 30,000 since 1970.[9] By most intelligence estimates, the quality of Soviet armored vehicles is very high. The Soviet versions are more heavily armored and less susceptible to breakdown than the Western, and provide full capability for movement through and survival on nuclear and chemical battlefields. The deployment of large numbers of these vehicles is fully consistent with the Soviet emphasis on mobile mass armored warfare that has typified its employment doctrine over the last twenty-five years.

The Soviets' massive casualties in World Wars I and II suffered from artillery are too well known to warrant elaboration here. It is a canon of Soviet thought that artillery is truly the "king of battle," and rightly so when it is recalled that fully 60 percent of all battle casualties occurring in warfare since the invention of gunpowder have been inflicted by artillery. The introduction of nuclear battlefield munitions may well increase this number. Soviet doctrine reflects this concern for deliverable artillery munitions. The Soviet Army can deploy 24,000 pieces of artillery, up almost 8,000 from the 1970 figure.[10] The Soviet Army clearly views the integration of armored and artillery forces as vital to conducting successful operations on the modern battlefield. Another reason why the Soviet advantage in artillery tubes is important is that long-range artillery is absolutely vital to the ability to deliver both nuclear and chemical munitions. Soviet doctrine presumes that both types of munitions are a normal part of the tactical deployment of the Soviet Army at war.

The Soviet Army has outpaced all other countries in another area: from 5,000 launchers in 1970, it had over 22,000 precision-guided munitions (PGMs) as of 1980.[11] Such weapons are simple to operate, very reliable, accurate, and very deadly. When firing from a defensive position, the probability of achieving a first-round hit against an armored vehicle exceeds 90 percent. In addition, PGMs are relatively cheap, costing in most instances under $3,000 per missile. Whether examined from a defensive or offensive posture, the Soviet Army's ability to wage anti-tank warfare with PGMs is substantially greater than that of its potential adversaries. (For an itemized list of Soviet Army equipment, see Table 16.)

Augmenting the awesome Soviet artillery force are those tubes available to it in the heavy mortar range capable of delivering a wide range of special munitions. The Soviet Army has approximately 8,000 mortars. With regard to surface-to-surface missiles, it has 1,330.[12] More important, the army has functionally integrated SCUD and FROG rocket battalions into its forward combat formations for the combat application of surface-to-surface missile power. This element is functionally integrated into the entire frontal area battle plan. Moreover, in terms of numbers, the Soviet Army has 3,300 air defense missile launchers and 8,700 anti-aircraft guns.[13] Soviet anti-aircraft artillery is normally self-propelled, mounted on a self-propelled chassis, or at least can be rapidly towed into battle. Most Soviet guns have a radar direction and multifire capability, and are expected to deploy rapidly alongside advancing armored armies and armored personnel carriers. Thus, the Soviet air defense forces have an awesome capability to provide effective security in the battle area for deploying ground and armored forces.

Doctrine

The Soviet Army's primary combat doctrine is the *offensive*: the army will attack in order to defeat the enemy with overwhelming material and firepower. The Soviets view the offensive as the optimum tactic because it gives the attacker both momentum and advantage over the defender who cannot so control the course of the war.[14] A successful offensive is very dependent on an army's ability to fight high-intensity operations, thereby pushing the attacker farther into enemy territory. Hence, the defender is subjected to tremendous psychological and physical pressures. The disinte-

Table 16
Soviet Army Equipment

	Total
Tanks	50,000
IS-2/-3, T-10, T-10M, T-54, T-55, T-62, T-64, T-72, and PT-76	
Armored Personnel (or Fighting) Vehicles	55,000
BRDM scout cars	
BMP motorized infantry combat vehicles	
BTR-40, BTR-50, BTR-60, and BTR-152	
OT-64	
MT-LB	
BMD armored personnel carriers	
Artillery	
100mm, 122mm, 130mm, 152mm, 180mm, and 203mm guns,	
122mm, 152mm self-propelled guns	20,000
82mm, 120mm, 160mm, and 240mm mortars	7,200
122mm, 140mm, 140mm, and 240mm multiple rocket launchers	2,700
76mm, 85mm, and 100mm towed and ASU-57/85 self-propelled anti-tank guns	10,800
Swatter, Sagger, Spigot, Sprandrel, and Sprial anti-tank guided weapons	n.a.
Anti-Aircraft Artillery	9,000
23mm and 57mm towed	
ZSU-23-4	
ZSU-57-2 self-propelled	
Surface-to-Air Missiles	10,000
SA-4, SA-6, SA-7, SA-8, SA-9, and SA-11	
Surface-to-Surface Missiles	1,300
FROG, SS-21, SCUD A/B, and SS-12 (nuclear capable)	

Source: *The Military Balance: 1979-1980* (London: International Institute for Strategic Studies, 1979).

gration of the defense may result as much from the quality of the attacking force as from the stressful character of modern warfare.

The Soviets have tended to emphasize the doctrinal use of armor. Historically, they have fought most of their wars on their own soil. Battlefields in the Soviet Union are marked by great distances and plenty of room for maneuver. These elements require highly mobile armored or rail forces in order to move military forces in significant numbers. Furthermore, during the early development of the Soviet Army, the impact of Marshal Frunze as minister of defense in 1927 cannot be understated. Frunze was very impressed with the power of the tank and saw clearly the need to modernize the Soviet Army along armored lines. This stress on modernization, coupled with the desire to construct a first-rate heavy industrial plant, led to the Soviet dependence on armor. By World War II, the Soviet Union had become accustomed to fielding large armored formations along with its infantry. These were capable of rapid movement through the wide expanses of the Soviet Union. Russia is ill-fit geographically to be defended by infantry. This historical reality has also played its part in the development of doctrines that stress the deployment of large armored and mechanized infantry units.

Under Stalin, throughout World War II and immediately after, Soviet ground forces were regarded as essentially defensive in nature. The shortcomings of this approach revealed themselves in the Cuban Missile Crisis of 1962. Today, the Soviet Army is positioned to take the offensive, as is reflected in their military doctrines. Soviet doctrines stress offensive action and increasing the tempo of battle even to the point of not replacing units that have been badly damaged. Soviet units are not replaced in battle but are simply augmented by fresh units which absorb the remnants of the battered unit and continue the attack. Despite the fact that modern war will be accompanied by high rates of attrition in men and materiel, the Soviet "push" supply system will constantly fuel the army with the equipment necessary for the offensive.

The Soviets make little distinction in battle tactics among nuclear, nonnuclear, chemical, and nonchemical battle environments. Regardless of how a war may begin, the Soviets have configured their forces to achieve absolute victory at all levels of combat. If a war begins in Central Europe, at least at the tactical level, the Soviets will probably deliver a first strike, using both nuclear and conventional weapons. They would utilize surprise and always carry the battle to the enemy, never relinquishing the offensive.

In addition to numerical and perhaps qualitative superiority, Soviet doctrine also espouses the integration of all capabilities into a coordinated operation. First the Soviet Army is given constant preparation for war; for example, the troops are given extensive night training. A second factor is the level of artillery support for attacking ground forces, both the armored and infantry units. The Soviet Army would likely coordinate extensive artillery bombardment with nuclear and conventional munitions against enemy frontline and rear echelon command and staging areas.

Prominent in Soviet doctrine is the use of nuclear, chemical, and biological weapons during all phases of war. The Soviets quite clearly state that nuclear weapons would be used in the earliest phase of war in order to destroy enemy units, thereby weakening the defense. This nuclear doctrine is radically different from that of NATO, which views the use of nuclear weapons as a last resort, a move of desperation. If the Soviets were to destroy critical enemy supply, command, and combat groups at the outset of the war with preemptive strikes, the enemy would probably collapse.

Of course, the Soviet Army would have to maintain battle momentum and sustain their forces. Western intelligence analysts contend that the Soviets would not be able to sustain their forces for sufficiently long periods. Proof for this claim is ostensibly reflected in the Soviet objective of finishing a war in Europe in thirty to ninety days. Apparently, the Soviets are *not* interested in sustainability in the sense that they are prepared to maintain ground forces in battle for a period of years. The Soviets believe that the ability to win rests on factors such as the tempo of battle, momentum, shock action, and massive firepower, all aimed to bring a war to a rapid conclusion. In one sense, Soviet doctrine is similar to the general European military thinking prior to World War I in which it was held that the nation that mobilized the fastest and delivered the quickest and heaviest blow would carry the day in a relatively short period of time. Regardless of the accuracy of this view, and it proved to be disastrously inaccurate in 1914, there is no doubt that the Soviets cling to it.

Soviet Army operations have an element of the German Wehrmacht's *blitzkrieg* in which the enemy attacks with numerical superiority with massed armor, infantry, and artillery units. By focusing this firepower on the enemy at selected points, the Soviet Army seems to think that this force, together with the effects of nuclear and chemical attacks, will cause the enemy to collapse quite rapidly. Thus, the Soviet Union has deployed large numbers of armored systems in armed forces and trains for a brief, yet intense, war.

Reserves

The Soviet Union with its history of conscription has a long tradition of sustaining large reserve forces. The Soviet Army has even exceeded the Tzarists' considerable ability in this area. Its awesome reserve manpower pool can be deployed on short notice.

Approximately 2 million men reach draft age in the Soviet Union each year. Of these, all but about 12 percent serve on active military duty for two years, and all are assigned to reserve units until age fifty.[15] Although there is a question of how good reserve training is once the soldier leaves active service, periodically individual soldiers in these units are called to active service for training, sometimes for periods as long as two years. The manpower reserve system is enormous. If one counts only those soldiers who have been released from active service in the last five years, the ready reserve force of the Soviet Army exceeds 10 million trained men on rapid call.

Every soldier in the reserve has his age, draft status, and medical records computerized and stored at the local draft commissariat. Hence, reserve manpower can be quickly located and notified. Estimates suggest that within twenty-four hours the Soviets could mobilize and move almost 3 million reservists into their active ranks. Moreover, they could double that number in forty-eight hours.[16] Hence, at D (battle date) plus thirty days, the Soviets could deploy over 400 Category 1 and 2 divisions in the field ready to fight.[17] Along with these troops, the Soviets would be able to deploy their civilianized support facilities in the form of domestic transportation and civilian air transport. Very clearly the Soviet Army's ability to double its active ground forces within such a short period of time represents a significant military advantage in its own right. This capability has been demonstrated in the invasions of Hungary, Czechoslovakia, Poland, and, most recently, Afghanistan. In all of these instances, reserve units were used alongside regular units. Afghanistan provides an interesting case study. Of the eight divisions initially deployed in Afghanistan, only two were regular divisions while six were reserve divisions. In the invasion, the Soviets brought up their reserve divisions in less than ten days, mobilized their equipment, placed them in the field, and kept them there for at least ninety days before replacing them in normal rotation. The army's ability in this area is probably the best in the world.

Experience

The combat experience of the Russian soldier cannot be examined simply because since the end of World War II Soviet ground forces have not seen significant action against a formidable enemy. With the Soviets' firepower, mobility, and reserves, however, they would be an impressive force in battle. To be sure, Soviet ground forces have been used several times to suppress unrest in the satellites, most recently in the 1968 invasion of Czechoslovakia. In all instances, troops have been used effectively and in mass, and have demonstrated a capability for rapid deployment. In addition, in all Soviet military actions since World War II Soviet units have shown a capability to mobilize selective reserve units and to deploy them. Only in Afghanistan have large numbers of Soviet troops been committeed against an even moderately tenacious enemy. The available data again demonstrate their ability to mobilize, deploy, and sustain reserve forces for sufficient periods.

The Soviet Soldier

The Soviet Army relies almost exclusively upon conscripts. In 1967, the General Law of Universal Military Service was promulgated, requiring military service of all eighteen-year-old males. The conscription cycle operated on a semiannual basis with two-year tours of duty made mandatory.

Upon completion of active service, soldiers are required to remain in reserve units until age fifty. While in these units, soldiers are subject to training and periodic call to active service as circumstances warrant.[18]

Training for the armed services begins before entry on active duty. The 1967 General Law established a compulsory system of premilitary training for all men and women between the ages of sixteen and eighteen. This training is controlled by an organization directly under the Ministry of Defense called the Voluntary Society for Cooperation with the Army, Aviation, and Navy (more commonly referred to by its Cyrillic initials, DOSAAF). DOSAAF designs, manages, and conducts all premilitary training and is a system of military commissariats parallelling governmental jurisdictions from the Republic level through the *rayon* (a governmental unit equivalent to the county level). Premilitary training begins in high school but is also provided to working youths in factories. It is designed to provide future soldiers with the equivalent of basic training and has reduced the training time required for new recruits once they enter active service.

There are about 60 million males between the ages of seventeen and forty-nine in the Soviet Union, about 80 percent of whom are fit for military service. As cited earlier each year approximately 2.5 million young men reach the age of military registration, that is, the year in which they turn seventeen. At the very least three-quarters of them are inducted when they reach eighteen. If deferred, they are assigned to reserve units where they are required to participate in reserve drills, exercises, and training. If they are deferred beyond their twenty-seventh birthday, the last point at which they may be conscripted, they must remain assigned to reserve units and are subject to periodic training and even extended recall until age fifty. The number of individuals who actually succeed in escaping military service in one form or another is very small, probably not more than 12 percent.[19]

A universal conscription system produces a relatively high-quality recruit inasmuch as the Soviet population has a rather high literacy rate and general educational level. Unlike his American counterpart, the Soviet soldier does not have critical deficiencies in aptitude skills, verbal and math skills, and reading skills.[20] The conscription system ensures that a proportionate mix of aptitudes and skills is projected into the military.

In general, the conscript system works rather well in the Soviet Union insofar as it provides the military with a sufficient supply of good quality manpower on a regular basis. The two-year term of service is generally shorter than is found in other armies. With the massive size of the Soviet Army, at least twice a year the personnel structure undergoes extreme turbulence as new soldiers move in and old soldiers depart.[21] As a result, the time and effort that would normally be used for training must be devoted to integrating large numbers of conscripts into main forces while simultaneously discharging large numbers of others. The problem is exacerbated by a very low retention rate for Soviet conscripts beyond their required tour of duty.

Yet, there is no doubt that the conscript system is able to marshal large manpower pools of high-quality conscripts for use by the Soviet Army.

The Soviet NCO

Soviet authorities have attempted to build a career NCO corps as part of the army's traditional structure. Their goal was to establish a corps of NCOs that would constitute a highly stable and professional element within the authority structure of the army. On balance, Soviet efforts to create such a corps have failed.

The Soviets' failure to develop a professional NCO corps marks one of the major differences between the Soviet Army and most armies of the West. Less than 5 percent of Soviet NCOs are career soldiers compared with an average of about 26 percent in Western armies, particularly in the American Army whose NCO strength tends to run above 28 percent.[22] Moreover, a major Soviet effort launched in 1978 to correct this problem by introducing a warrant officer program has not succeeded.[23] Some of this failure to sustain a long-term stable career corps is directly related to the manner in which NCOs are selected. In the Soviet Army, NCOs are often selected even before they enter active military service by the local commissariat on the grounds that a conscript may have special training or show a particular aptitude during his DOSAAF training. Those not selected in this manner are often chosen after they have completed their basic training and been in active service for as little as two or three months.[24] Upon selection they are removed from their units and sent to an NCO training school which lasts about six weeks. They are then reassigned to another unit as sergeants. Not uncommonly, a conscript who has been in the military for less than two years attains the rank of a three-stripe sergeant. The predictable result of this recruitment system is a large number of minimally qualified NCOs who must occupy important positions of small unit leadership.

Along with its recruitment problems, the Soviet NCO corps is continually subjected to a tremendous amount of personnel assignment turnover. Every six months, because of the biannual conscription cycle, the army must absorb a massive influx of new conscripts. Thus, every six months approximately 25 percent of the NCO corps leaves active service to be replaced by new conscript NCOs coming directly from civilian life. In addition, the small number (less than 5 percent) of conscripts who remain on active service usually move up in rank or change assignments as well. The Soviet NCO corps is thus comprised almost totally of inexperienced amateurs subject to frequent assignment turnover.

The Soviet Army has been unable to retain qualified NCOs beyond their mandatory term of service. Although a soldier can achieve NCO rank rapidly and although rewards are offered for those who reenlist for extended service, the Soviet Army cannot convince significant numbers of conscripts to remain in service beyond their initial tour of service. Moreover, those who remain within the Soviet Army for a career in the ranks often reach top NCO rank relatively quickly. Most of the experienced NCOs are therefore positioned at the senior NCO level.[25] The lower level NCO leadership consists of squad leaders, element leaders, platoon sergeants and even company sergeants. These, the most critical leadership posts in terms of cohesion and small unit battle performance, are left in the hands of a new biannual crop of conscripts turned sergeants. These NCOs have no more dedication to the military profession or to developing unit spirit and leadership than does the average conscript.[26]

The Soviet NCO corp is probably quite large by Western standards. The Soviet NCO corps likely accounts for 30 to 33 percent of total force strength in the army.[27] Control at the NCO level is further buttressed by an officer corp that is considerably larger than that found in Western armies. Hence, many tasks which in Western armies would be left to NCOs are performed by officers.[28] Close supervision and overcontrol of NCOs is the rule in the Soviet Army, so much so that it emerges as a constant complaint in interviews with NCOs. Apparently, the level of professionalism among Soviet NCOs is further reduced by this tendency toward overcontrol which many sergeants see as rooted in a lack of trust.

In an effort to measure the quality of Soviet NCOs, soldiers were asked, "How would you rate the quality of noncommissioned officers you came in contact with while in military service?" It turns out that 20.4 percent of the soldiers in the ranks thought their NCOs were "extremely good" or "good" at their jobs. At the other extreme, 35.4 percent rated their NCOs as "fair," "poor," or "very poor:" of these, 13.2 percent described their NCOs as "poor" or "very poor." By far the largest group, 44.2 percent, rated their sergeants as only average in quality.[29] On balance, then, the men see the NCO as fair or poor.

The data clearly demonstrate the overall decline in NCO quality since World War II. Therefore, as of 1981 the objective of creating a high-quality, professional NCO corps with some stability of service to serve as a cadre around which to develop the rest of the conscript army had not been achieved. Moreover, with the failure of the warrant program, there is no reason to expect this condition to change. In the place of the professional NCO corp has arisen a cadre of short-term conscript sergeants who are not regarded very highly by their officers, their commanders, or the soldiers they lead. The army's failure to develop a professional NCO corps is one of its major institutional weaknesses.

The Soviet Officer

There are approximately 500,000 officers on active duty in the Soviet Army today; about 16 percent of total strength is comprised of officers, a somewhat larger percentage than is found in most Western armies. The large size of the Soviet officer corps can be explained by the political regime's inordinate concern for adequate political control. Large numbers of officers generally ensure this control. Moreover, in the Soviet Army a substantial number of junior officers hold positions and perform tasks that in Western armies would normally be performed by noncommissioned officers.

After assignment to active duty, the Soviet officer normally rotates through a small number of command and staff assignments. The lower degree of assignment turnover may be explained by the fact that the Soviet Army is a traditional army with a conscript base and, therefore, does not need to compete with the civilian economy for critical manpower. Consequently, there is less emphasis on staff, nor is there a great need to rotate through assignments so that every officer can maintain his upward mobility and thus decrease the chances he will leave service for employment in the civilian sector. Promotion to the next higher grade up to colonel depends upon the normal military requirements such as academic training, service experience, duty assignments, job performance, and the all-important quality of political reliability as assessed by the unit's political officer.[30]

Soviet officers may remain on active duty until they reach the statutory age of retirement, an age that varies by rank. An officer may spend as many as twenty-five years in the military never exceeding the rank of senior or even junior lieutenant. The mandatory age of retirement of a junior lieutenant, for example, is forty, which would allow an officer at least twenty years of active service at this rank, not counting his reserve obligations which remain after he retires. Thus, the Soviet Army's leadership elements are very stable. This is especially true of officers at the lower ranks, who spend their entire careers as combat unit commanders, thereby enhancing the degree of cohesion and effectiveness of small units.[31]

The quality of the Soviet officer remains open to debate. The Soviets seem to have particular difficulty in staffing their officer corps with individuals oriented toward command.[32] The emphasis placed on science and technical education and qualifications works against the development of officers oriented toward command. The tendency instead is to produce officers who are highly specialized and technically oriented; command and even personal leadership qualities are given secondary importance. The stress placed on technical qualifications minimizes reliance on judgmental qualifications, and to a totalitarian regime such practices are likely to have intrinsic merit.

Soviet training doctrine also tends to stimulate the propensity toward bureaucratic perspectives in its officers. The Soviet Army stresses conformity to existing schedules and plans.[33] This is accompanied by an exaggerated compulsion for meeting deadlines outlined in operational plans. Soviet military journals are replete with convoluted arguments which try to resolve the tension between initiative and following plans by instilling in the officer something called "correct initiative."[34] Nonetheless, initiative for the Soviet officer is still largely reduced to following operational plans. Consequently, in Soviet doctrine the duty of an officer to bring initiative and judgment to his command is subordinated to the larger requirements of observing orders and meeting operational check points and deadlines. It is difficult to escape the impression that many officers feel that the state does not truly trust the corps. The constant presence of the unit political officer, the use of KGB spies within the ranks, and the political officer's influence on one's efficiency report do little to encourage the officer to develop a sense of risk, initiative, and responsibility.[35] One consequence of these conditions is an officer corps that tends to remain aloof, if not deliberately remote, from its troops.

In order to discern how the Soviet soldier perceives his officers, soldiers were asked, "Given the general quality of officers that you served with in your military service, how would you rate their quality as officers?" The respondents provided the following assessments: 0.9 percent said their officers were "extremely good"; 9.7 percent rated them as "good"; 56.6 percent thought they were only "average"; and 14.2 percent found them only "fair." Finally, 15.0 percent thought their officers were of "poor" quality, while 1.8 percent thought them "very poor."[36] If the numbers are collapsed into ordinal categories, the number of "bad" officers exceeds the number of "good" officers by almost three times. Whatever other conclusions may be merited, it seems clear that in the general view of the soldiers themselves the Soviet officer is not perceived as a high quality leader.

Combat Ability

Soviet soldiers spend far more time learning and practicing the skills of war than their Western counterparts do. With the exception of a pass every month or two, they spend every day in the military environment. Penned in his garrison, the Soviet soldier is subject to a heavy training schedule. He spends most of his time either in the field or preparing for it by maintaining his equipment. Table 17 presents a complete schedule of an average training day in the Soviet Army.[37] The same number of hours are allotted for daily training in winter and summer, and intense instruction throughout the year leaves the soldier very little free time. At least six hours of each training day are devoted exclusively to scheduled instruction. Most of the remaining time is used for political classes, maintenance of clothing and equipment, and personal needs. The training schedule for Saturday is technically two to four hours shorter than the normal training day, but it usually runs just as long.[38]

In order to measure the quality of Soviet military training as perceived by the troops themselves, soldiers were asked, "On a scale from one to ten in which one is the worst and ten is the best how would you rate the military

Table 17
Daily Schedule of the Soviet Soldier

Activity	Hour	Time Elapsed
(1) Reveille	6:00- 6:05	5 min.
(2) Clean-up	6:10- 6:30	20 min.
(3) Personal hygiene	6:30- 6:50	20 min.
(4) Political information or inspection	6:50- 7:20	30 min.
(5) Breakfast	7:25- 7:55	30 min.
(6) Training	8:00- 14:00	6 hrs.
(7) Lunch	14:00-14:40	40 min.
(8) Afternoon rest	14:40-15:10	30 min.
(9) Care of personal equipment	15:10-15:30	20 min.
(10) a) Political Education (Monday and Thursday)	15:30-18:30	3 hrs.
b) Equipment maintenance (Tuesday and Friday)		
c) Organized sports (Wednesday and Saturday)		
(11) Self-study	18:30-19:40	70 min.
(12) Supper	19:40-20:10	30 min.
(13) Free time	20:10-21:40	90 min.
(14) Evening walk and rollcall	21:40-21:55	15 min.
(15) Taps	22:00	

Richard A. Gabriel, *The New Red Legions* (Westport, Conn.: Greenwood Press, 1980).

training you received?" The mean score for the entire sample at all ranks and positions was 5.2, which may be regarded as fairly high since it reflects training in all types of units at all rank levels.[39] The assessments of training quality varied somewhat by type of unit, but, overall, Soviet troops apparently thought that the quality of their training was good and only a few saw it as inadequate. It also seems clear that unit commanders believed that Soviet training was probably doing an adequate job in transmitting military skills.

With regard to combat-effectiveness, Soviet soldiers were asked, "In your opinion, how well do you think your unit will fight in actual combat?" Only 8.8 percent felt their units would fight "very well"; 36.6 percent thought they would fight "fairly well"; and 33.6 percent responded "moderately well." On the other side of the scale, 14.2 percent thought their units would fight "poorly," and 1.8 percent thought their units would do "very poorly."[40] If the data are combined, 45.1 percent felt their units would fight "very well" or "fairly well," while 33.6 percent said they would perform "moderately well." Only 16 percent said their units would perform either "poorly" or "very poorly."

Unit commanders also believed that their units would perform well on the battlefield. Among enlisted commanders, 43.7 percent felt that their units would perform in the top two categories, with only 6.2 percent expecting them to do "poorly." Not a single unit commander at the enlisted level expected his men to perform "very poorly." Similar patterns emerged for officers in command positions. Fully 58.4 percent believed that their units would perform "very well" or "fairly well" under fire, while not a single commanding officer assessed his men as performing either "poorly" or "very poorly."[41]

Thus, the Soviet emphasis on quality training and combat skills undoubtedly has had a positive effect. If there is a weak point in the Soviet Army, it seems to lie less in the acquisition of military technique than in the development of those human social and psychological bonds that contribute so strongly to the vital element of cohesion.

Combat Scenarios

Bloc Nation Control

One of the most likely battle scenarios for the Soviet Army is political/military intervention in the Eastern Bloc nations on the periphery of the Soviet Union. The Soviet Union has deployed a substantial number of combat-ready divisions in Poland, East Germany, Hungary, and Czechoslovakia, as well as divisions within the Soviet Union that can be redeployed quite rapidly. Such intervention occurred in 1956 when the Soviet Army invaded Hungary and in 1968 when the uprising of Czech students, intellectuals, and workers prompted invasion of Czechoslovakia. The threat of Soviet Army intervention in Poland in late 1981 and early 1982 was very plausible to the Poles who, facing increasing signs of political and military decay, initiated martial law in order to forestall a Soviet invasion. During this time, Soviet deployments of armored and infantry divisions in and around Poland increased, along with the increase in the combat-readiness of those forces. At present, more than forty Soviet Army divisions are stationed in, and external to, Poland.

How would the Soviet Army intervene in East European nations in the 1980s? If political and economic conditions collapsed, the Soviet Army would move armored and infantry forces to major ports, cities, airfields, industrial facilities (including coal and oil fields), and major communications networks. In most cases, dissident resistance would have no effect, perhaps only delaying the securing of targets by a day or so. With a stranglehold on the economic and social fabric of the nation, the Soviet Army and the military apparatus of the nation in question would then demand that all workers continue to work and that all potential as well as active resisters be punished accordingly. Any areas that resisted would be denied food and other essential material comforts as long as resistance persisted.

Since the Soviet Union itself is so close to the Eastern Bloc nations and already has well-established supply lines to this area, the Soviet Army could maintain its operations almost indefinitely. It would be ruthless in its treatment of dissidents collecting not only the agitators but all potential troublemakers as well. For instance, when the Polish Army announced the martial law restrictions in 1981, army units occupied the critical links in the Polish economy and collected a large number of Solidarity members.

Sino-Soviet Conflict

Ever since the Sino-Soviet military conflict became evident in 1969, the possibility of a major clash between the two powers has been real. From the apparent detente, indeed cooperation, between the Soviet Union and the People's Republic of China in the early 1960s, most analysts expected that the two powers would join in an anti-U.S. campaign that would extend far into the future. Such a joint effort was not long lasting, however. The first true indicator of hostility was a border dispute in 1969 that flared into a minor military operation. Ever since, the Soviet Union has stood prepared to fight the Chinese in both major and minor clashes with both conventional and nuclear weapons.

The Soviet Army is far superior to the Chinese Army because of its technologically more sophisticated weaponry. The Chinese, with their relatively primitive weapons, would easily be crushed by the Soviets. The Chinese ability to field a numerically superior force from the largest population in the world today would be of little use against the Soviets' weapons, which range from tanks, APCs, and munitions to tactical nuclear, chemical, and biological weapons.

A border clash, such as occurred in 1969, is the most likely form of conflict between the Soviets and Chinese. Accordingly, the Soviet Union stations very large military forces along the Chinese-Mongolian border. This large size is related more to the supply and logistics problem than to the anticipated war. In the unlikely event of a major war against the Chinese, the Soviets would have supply lines stretching 3,000 or more miles. Even within the Soviet Union itself with internal rail and road lines, such distances would present tremendous complications in a protracted war. If war did occur, the Soviet Army would probably contain the Chinese Army for a long period of time with a major resupply effort, using the forces presently stationed there.

In a major war between the Soviet Union and the People's Republic of China, a host of related dilemmas would become apparent. First, should the Soviet Army win a purely conventional war, would it attempt to establish a garrison force within China? With nearly 1 billion people to control, the prospects for a successful Soviet occupation of the People's Republic would be bleak at best *unless* some form of genocide were practiced *en masse*. Chinese resistance, guerrilla operations, and sabotage would present the Soviet Army with virtually insurmountble problems that would either bankrupt the Soviet Union or disrupt the operation.

The second problem associated with a major Sino-Soviet war is the threat of escalation to nuclear war. Neither the Soviet Union or China could start a conventional war without realizing that nuclear war would eventuate once one side began to lose. Thus, the third factor is the punitive expedition. However, could the Soviets fight such a limited war without risking nuclear war or facing the possibility of occupation? Clearly, the answers are "no." The Soviet Union would be cautious because of the potential for nuclear war. The Chinese would be equally constrained from any conflict in view of their tremendous vulnerability to nuclear attack. Nearly 90 percent of the Chinese population lives on 10 percent of the Chinese land mass. Thus, even a "limited" nuclear war would kill *hundreds* of millions of Chinese.

Central European War

The threat of a conventional war in Europe between the NATO and Warsaw Pact armies, while also remote, gains the most attention in any analysis of Soviet Army capabilities. With the largest deployment of ground forces in Europe and the largest number of tanks and equivalent military equipment, the Soviet Army clearly constitutes a threat. Thus, an analysis of the Soviet Army's capabilities in a conventional and nuclear war in Europe is examined here from two perspectives: first, a purely conventional war, and second a "tactical" or theater nuclear war.

Soviet Army forces deployed in Eastern Europe (namely, East Germany, Poland, Hungary, and Czechoslovakia) are organized into the Soviet Forces Germany and the First Strategic Echelon. With varying degrees of numerical superiority in men, tanks, APCs, artillery tubes, and aircraft, the Soviet Army is arrayed into three combat sectors: (1) the northern sector whose task would be to penetrate the North German Plain in an offensive tank and mobile operation; (2) the central sector, designed to hit the central industrialized area containing communications and governmental units of NATO; and (3) the southern sector, forming the southern "jaw" of the pincer in which the Soviet Army would attack U.S. Army units. At the start of the war, the Soviet Army and various units of the Warsaw Pact would attack, or counterattack as the case might be, along these three "corridors" in order to defeat NATO units. Since the Soviet Army enjoys numerical superiority over NATO, it would overwhelm substantial numbers of the enemy. Thus, the offensive would consist of armored spearheads with infantry troops in support. Soviet battle doctrine stresses the use of large forces that would continuously attack the enemy with ground and air forces, as well as artillery barrages against command, control, and communications targets, rear echelon, and frontline units.

In this conventional war, the Soviet Army would fight with combined ground and air units, and penetrate as far into NATO territory as possible. To supply this attacking force, the Soviet supply system is designed to "push" reinforcements into existing units so that the army can continue to fight even as normal rates of attrition are encountered. The Soviet supply system is organized on a "push" instead of a "pull" system, delivering material from the rear to the front on the basis of anticipated loss schedules rather than requests from fighting units. This would "push" the forward units into battle, minimizing their responsibility for repair and maintenance, and freeing local commanders of responsibility problems so that they coud continue to fight.[42] The Soviet Army is configured to maintain an offensive for sixty or more days at full intensity. The Soviet Army might well reach the Rhine River within ten days of the initial attack because NATO could not resist such massive forces attacking continuously over three battlefronts.

The second variant of a war between the Soviet and Allied Forces in Europe is the nuclear, chemical, and biological war. The Soviet Army deploys a number of nuclear delivery systems that appear designed for preemptive use. Rather than waiting for the conventional war to go badly for one side or the other, the Soviets suggest that nuclear attacks should comprise the initial attack. NATO, however, has always viewed nuclear war as a corollary to conventional war and, as such, would use nuclear weapons as a last resort. With the Soviet Army apparently planning to launch nuclear strikes at the outset of the war, NATO supplies, communications, and control might well be disrupted and the coherence of the defensive destroyed.

The significance of this doctrinal asymmetry is most striking when one considers that the Soviet Army would use nuclear weapons in addition to its massive ground forces. Even without a preemptive nuclear attack policy, the Soviet Army could well expect to defeat NATO in a European war. All this, of course, assumes that the Soviet Army would use chemical and biological weapons in much the same way as nuclear weapons, and that NATO would counterattack with these weapons. At that stage, NATO would be at a severe disadvantage with its C^3 disrupted and control over the entire operation in jeopardy.

With the Soviet Army involved in a massive conventional and nuclear war in Europe, what are the indications for victory? Since the Soviets would fight essentially an offensive war employing nuclear weapons, Soviet forces would probably defeat NATO. Such a defeat would result not only from the aggregate superiority of Soviet forces and equipment, but also from the apparent quality and training of its troops. In a very intense environment, NATO troops with their attendant drug and discipline problems would not be as competent as the Soviet soldiers who are better trained, disciplined, led, and prepared for war. Furthermore, with Soviet forces penetrating deep into NATO territory, NATO forces (which are deployed in a narrow corridor along the front in a north-south configuration) would find themselves initially outnumbered and eventually surrounded. The present generation of NATO forces, even using nuclear strikes, could not destroy the Soviet offensive once begun. The neutron warhead, however, would partially reverse this condition, but they are not yet deployed.

A nuclear war would not necessarily follow a conventional war in Europe, but NATO, without the backing of U.S. nuclear superiority, is less secure than before. In summary, the threat of a European war is quite small because both Soviet and NATO forces are aware of the costs of such a war. Whether nuclear or conventional, the probable destruction and risks associated with escalation make this scenario very unattractive except under the most extreme circumstances.

The Persian Gulf and Africa

The Persian Gulf, with 50 percent of the world's oil supply, is perhaps the most critical strategic region in the world today. Thus, this area naturally lends itself to military planning. With such a concentration of vital resources, the Soviet Army should be prepared to fight and, if possible, control the region. In view of its proximity to the Soviet Union, the Persian Gulf is vulnerable to Soviet interdiction by land, sea, and air forces.

The Persian Gulf could be attacked in several ways. The most logical method, given the Soviet Army deployment in Afghanistan, would be an invasion force across the southeastern tip of Iran with forces marshaled in Herat and Qandahar, Afghanistan. Soviet armored and infantry units would traverse Iran, a distance of approximately 400 miles, in order to reach the Strait of Hormuz and the areas contiguous to the Iranian oil fields. The primary purpose of the mission would be, not to take the Iranian oil fields, but to gain control of the Strait of Hormuz through which 50 percent of the world's oil supply flows. With coordination from Soviet naval task forces in the Indian Ocean and the Gulf of Oman, relatively few Soviet units could effectively shut down the oil flow to, say, Japan, Western Europe, and the United States. An alternative operation would be to airlift Soviet units across Iran, dropping them into the region by the Strait and the Gulf. In this way, the Soviet Army would avoid the potential vulnerability to American tactical nuclear strikes as Soviet forces moved through mountain passes in southern Iran. The Soviet airlift operation from the Turkmen District to Ethiopia in 1980 demonstrates that the Soviets have this capability.

With Soviet forces occupying the Strait of Hormuz and, thus, controlling the exit of all Persian Gulf oil on supertankers, the United States or any other military force would be hardpressed to resist. Before the United States could deploy opposing forces to the region, the Soviet Army would be well entrenched. As the Soviet Army continued to reinforce its troops, the United States could at best move two divisions into the area in thirty days. With its proximity to Afghanistan, Soviet forces could easily defeat whatever opposing forces moved into the region and ensure that the oil did not leave the Gulf region.

The Soviet Army would encounter difficulties after the initial operation was completed because it probably could not maintain a long enough supply line to sustain a large force in the Persian Gulf or any other region. But this shortcoming need not be lethal: a relatively small Soviet force could, for instance, close down the oil flow for an indefinite time simply by sinking a large supertanker by the Island of Qeshm, Iran. If it was not considered necessary to sustain several battalions for as long as political constraints deemed appropriate, Soviet forces could evacuate. Either way, the oil would be stopped. If the Soviets decided to remain, Soviet ground forces could, with air support, defeat any Allied force which would first have to establish bases in Iran or Oman. The critical concept here is not the quality of the opposing forces per se, but the *timing*: whichever force establishes a base first would have a substantial advantage. In summary, the Soviet Army could well interdict the oil supply by attacking the Strait of Hormuz, the chokepoint of the region, and hold off resistance for quite some time.

The second major area of operation for the Soviet Army is Africa, a continent containing a host of critical minerals without which the Western economies could not survive. A major military operation in Africa, however, would involve very lengthy supply lines for the Soviets, thus, the optimum operation would be a punitive political-military expedition. For instance, small Soviet units operating in concert with East German and Cuban units could harass the Shaba Province in Zaire. Stationed in friendly Angola, these forces could interrupt the flow of copper and other minerals with guerrilla actions aimed at terror and disruption.

While the Soviet Army could participate in minor operations on the African continent, it would not likely become involved in a major land war. Unless it expanded its airlift capability and developed major army bases in Africa, there is simply no realistic scenario in which it would figure as a major land force in Africa in a large-scale military operation.

Conclusions

The Soviet Army is a well-trained, well-equipped, and modern fighting force, unmatched by any army in the world today. From the turbulence of the army purges in the 1930s and the initial devastation by the Wehrmacht in 1941, the Soviet Army now presents a major opponent to all Western armies by virtue of its size and apparent combat capabilities. In addition to the acquisition of staggering numbers of tanks, APCs, and artillery tubes, the Soviet Army has undergone radical institutional changes: the adoption of the Prussian General Staff system and the tactics of the *blitzkrieg* suggests that the Soviet Army is no longer the incompetent, monolithic structure it once was. Modernization coupled with a large arsenal of conventional and nuclear munitions has made the Soviet Army a first-rate fighting force.

What does the future hold for the Soviet Army? Clearly, the Soviets possess the political will to use this military force in a variety of combat scenarios and geographic regions. The only real limitation on the Soviet Army is perhaps economic: can the Soviet Union continue the massive arms buildup which is placing an increasing burden on its domestic economy? Unlike the West, the Soviets are not constrained by consumer demands. So, with no palpable limit on their military spending plans, the Soviet Union will probably continue to spend in real economic terms *twice* what the West can on defense. Hence, the Soviet arms buildup wil continue unabated for the foreseeable future, despite the pernicious effects of such spending for the rest of the economy.

The most probable scenarios for armed conflict would be in the Eastern satellite nations and on the Sino-Soviet border. Soviet excursions into Hungary, Czechoslovakia, and Afghanistan demonstrate that the Soviet Union is quite willing to use force to quell political unrest in its allies. As the Soviet Army becomes more competent and larger, the Soviets will likely be more willing to use their force in peripheral areas. Under no circumstances can it be argued that the Soviet Union will abstain from the use of force when domestic and political control is in jeopardy.

In addition to controlling political upheavals in its satellites, the Soviet Union might be expected to engage the Chinese Army in minor border, quasi-political disputes during this decade. As the Soviet Army grows, however, the Chinese will become more reticent about any such involvement because of the Soviets' overwhelming military superiority.

In spite of the constant attention that a conventional European war receives, only a major political incident could draw either the Soviets or NATO into a large-scale land war. If such a war were to occur, the Soviet Army would probably penetrate deep into NATO territory and perhaps gain a political settlement. In summary, however, this type of war is extremely unlikely to occur.

It is unlikely that the Soviets will become entangled in a major land war in this decade. From a Western perspective, the improbability of a land war does not imply Soviet reticence but rather a recognition that any war entails great risks and uncertainty. Should war occur, the Soviet Army is well prepared to handle virtually any conceivable contingency.

Notes

1. Richard A. Gabriel, *The New Red Legions: An Attitudinal Portrait of the Soviet Soldier* (Westport, Conn.: Greenwood Press, 1980), p. 121.

2. Ibid., pp. 31-34.

3. William E. Odom, "The Militarization of Soviet Society," *Problems of Communism* (September 1976), pp. 34-51.

4. John M. Collins, *The US-Soviet Military Balance, 1960-1980* (New York: McGraw-Hill, 1980), p. 89.

5. Ibid., pp. 90-91.

6. Ibid.

7. Ibid.

8. Ibid.

9. Ibid.

10. Ibid.

11. Ibid.

12. Ibid.

13. Ibid.

14. See A. A. Sidorenko, *The Offensive: A Soviet View* (Washington, D.C.: Department of the Air Force, 1970), p. 35.

15. Harriet F. Scott and William F. Scott, *The Armed Forces of the USSR* (Boulder, Colo.: Westview Press, 1978), p. 236.

16. Richard A. Gabriel, "The Reasons for the Soviet Arms Buildup," paper presented before the National Military Intelligence Association, Fort Devens, Massachusetts, on November 8, 1980, p. 3.

17. Gabriel, *The New Red Legions*, p. 34.

18. Ibid.

19. Juri Tuomepuu, *Soldier Capability and Army Combat Effectiveness* (Washington, D.C.: U.S. Army Recruiting Command, 1981), pp. 11-12.

20. This would, of course, place the planned turbulence rate among Soviet troop units at 50 percent a year, considerably below that of the American Army which suffers at least 89 percent annual personnel turnover.

21. These figures are extrapolated from our own data. We can, however, find no serious disagreement with them as estimates from intelligence agencies.

22. Again the assessment of the failure of the Soviet warrant officer program is generally shared by most intelligence analysts, although official studies on the subject remain classified.

23. Gabriel, *The New Red Legions*, p. 120.

24. Ibid., p. 119.

25. Ibid., p. 121.

26. This is an estimate gained from conversations with army intelligence analysts.

27. Gabriel, *The New Red Legions*, p. 122.

28. Ibid., p. 123.

29. Ibid., p. 131.

30. Ibid., p. 132.

31. Ibid., p. 133.

32. Ibid., p. 146.

33. Ibid.

34. Ibid.

35. Ibid., p. 148.

36. Ibid., p. 61.

37. Ibid.

38. Ibid., p. 221.
39. Ibid.
40. Ibid., p. 216.
41. Ibid.
42. For an interesting overview of Soviet logistical operations, see Lieutenant Colonel William P. Baxter, "Logistics with a Difference," *Army* (November 1980): 30-32.

Bibliography

Babenko, John A. *Ideology, Politics, and Government in the Soviet Union.* Rev. ed. New York: Praeger, 1967.
Baranov, I. *Soviet Officers [Sovetskiye Komandiry].* Moscow: Progress Publishers, 1976.
Danchenko, A. M. and Vydrin, I. F., eds. *Military Pedagogy: A Soviet View [Voyennaya pedagogika].* Moscow: Voyenizdat, 1971.
Disciplinary Regulations of the U.S.S.R. Armed Forces [Distiplinarnyy ustav vooruzhennykh sil soyuza SSR]. Moscow: Voyenizdat, 1971.
Erickson, John. *Soviet Armed Forces: Capabilities and Changing Roles.* Edinburgh: Defense Studies, University of Edinburgh, 1971.
———. *Soviet Military Performance: Some Manpower and Managerial Constraints.* New York: U.S. Army Institute for Advanced Russian Studies, 1970.
———. *Soviet Military Power.* London: Royal United Services Institute for Defense Studies, 1971.
———. *The Soviet Military, Soviet Policy, and Soviet Politics.* Washington, D.C.: U.S. Strategic Institute, 1973.
Goldhammer, Herbert. *The Soviet Soldier: Soviet Military Management at the Troop Level.* New York: Crane, Russak, 1975.
Jones, Christopher. "The Revolution in Military Affairs and Party Military Relations 1967-70." *Survey: A Journal of East-West Studies,* Winter 1974.
Katz, Zev; Rogers, Rosemarie; and Harned, Fredric. *Handbook of Major Soviet Nationalities.* New York: Free Press, 1975.
Keefe, Eugene F., et al. *Area Handbook for Soviet Union.* Washington, D.C.: U.S. Government Printing Office, 1978.
Kolkowicz, Roman. *The Soviet Military and the Communist Party.* Princeton, N.J.: Princeton University Press, 1967.
Myagkov, Aleksei. *Inside the KGB: An Exposé by an Officer of the Third Directorate.* London: Foreign Affairs Publishing Co., 1977.
O'Ballance, Edgar. *The Red Army.* New York: Praeger, 1964.
Odom, William E. "The Militarization of Soviet Society." *Problems of Communism,* September-October 1976.
———. *The Soviet Volunteers.* Princeton, N.J.: Princeton University Press, 1973.
Record, Jeffery. *Sizing Up the Soviet Army.* Washington, D.C.: Brookings Institution, 1975.
Review of Soviet Ground Forces. RSGF1-77. August 1977.
Seaton, Albert. *The Soviet Army.* Reading, Pa.: Osprey Publishing, Inc., 1972.

Sidorenko, A. A. *The Offensive: A Soviet View.* Washington, D.C.: Department of
the Air Force, 1970.

Smith, D. "On Maneuvers with the Red Army." *Nation,* May 20, 1978.

Yerzunov, M. "An Important Factor in Enhancing Combat Readiness." *Krasnaya
Zvezda (Red Star),* July 16, 1976.

East Germany

William C. Martel

After the systemic collapse of the Nazi government in Germany in 1945 and the subsequent division of the state into eastern and western zones, the occupying powers were faced with the monumental task of rebuilding from ruins the political, industrial, and military sectors. In the case of East Germany (the German Democratic Republic, the GDR), the Soviet Union directed a transformation in the military sphere that could only be described as radical: the remnants of Nazi ideology and political authority in the Wehrmacht were replaced in the National People's Army (Der National Volksarmee, the NVA) with the tenets of international socialism, while simultaneously retaining a sense of German nationalism and the institutional and operational facets of the Prussian General Staff system. Today, the NVA is a first-rate military force modeled after the Soviet Army in terms of its organization, deployment, and strategic and tactical doctrines. This means that the NVA, as a modern force, is capable of fighting protracted, high-intensity, and complex operations on a variety of fronts.

The period between 1945 and 1970 can be considered as embryonic for the development of the NVA. With the Soviet Union serving as the model, close military supervision and daily involvement in NVA activities during this period resulted in the creation of one of the most modern and competent field armies in Europe and the world today. On the frontline where World War III may well commence, the Soviet Union apparently "trusts" the East German Army to carry out its battlefield orders with a high degree of success. There is little doubt that the main theater of action in such a war will be in East and West Germany. The outcome of that war will depend in great part on the ability of the NVA to secure its objectives.

To understand the character of the East German Army, a brief description of the Prussian military system is in order. The NVA, indeed the Soviet army, are not only products of Marxist-Leninist thinking, but are also steeped in the tradition of the Prussian Army. The Prussian military model upon which the NVA is based stresses constant drill, obedience, discipline, initiative, flexibility, and independence of commanders.[1] The ideal Prussian soldier is not the officer or conscript who practices blind obedience to his superiors, but the man who demonstrates flexible thinking in combat with a firm understanding of military technique and tactics, together with an appreciation of history and tradition.

The backbone of the Prussian model is the General Staff. The Soviet and East German general staffs in 1982 typify the Prussian staffs. It requires no great insight to recognize that the NVA is modeled after the Soviet Army which in turn is a replica, albeit hyperbatic, of the Prussian system of World War II. Given the degree of subservience to Soviet authority that the NVA appears to demonstrate, there is, as T. N. Dupuy expressed, little doubt as to whether the NVA can act with the autonomy and excellence reminiscent of the Prussian tradition.[2] It is clear that the NVA is trained for offensive warfare and that its men are prepared to remain cohesive despite the stress of modern war.

A central feature of any totalitarian system is the total control that is exercised over the military apparatus.[3] In the GDR, the SED has penetrated the NVA at both the officer and enlisted levels. It should be noted, however, that the East German Secret Service (SED), through its political officers, does not exercise control at the tactical level as was the case in the Soviet Army in World War II. In the East German government, the Ministry for National Defense is the primary axis of contact between the army and the state. The ministry is responsible for the direction and organization of the army. As Eugene K. Keefe notes, the ministry has "direct authority over the forces and their recruitment, training, logistic and other special support agencies."[4]

Recent Combat Operations

For obvious reasons, the NVA has not been a party to any hostile military actions since its inception in the early 1950s. While two East German divisions participated in the 1968 Soviet action in Czechoslovakia, it is reported that the Soviets exercised extremely tight supervision of East German actions. There are indications that NVA divisions were used to control railhead and communications points but were not actually involved in quelling the domestic unrest.[5] The NVA, however, has actively participated in all major Warsaw Pact exercises and is a regular member of the Warsaw Pact.

With respect to effective combat performance, it is essential that the NVA participate regularly in such exercises since, as the forward force in any Warsaw Pact invasion of Western Europe, it will determine to a substantial extent the outcome of the initial encounters with NATO armies. Evidence of the integral role assigned to the NVA by the Soviet Union is in the NVA arsenal: the NVA receives the most modern and, therefore, effective combat arms of any army in the Warsaw Pact. Only the Soviet Army is better equipped than the NVA.

The NVA also participates in various Third World "liberation" movements, usually in concert with Soviet and Cuban forces. The primary role of the NVA in such enterprises is the organization of intelligence, domestic security operations, and communications in the target area.[6] The area of operations is very extensive, both geographically and operationally, ranging from Africa to the Middle East.

The Officer Corps

In a modern army, multiple factors directly affect its ability to engage in sustained combat operations. One of the most important of these factors is the officer corps, its quality, training, reliability, and technical competence. Since the Soviet Union had to rebuild the NVA after its demise, it was forced to resocialize and repoliticize the GDR. More important, however, was the restructuring of the NVA and the men who would fill its ranks. Aside from the Communist party in East Germany, the officer corps is one of the more centrally and strategically located apparatuses with the state and the army. It, therefore, served as one the primary instruments of socialization and, of course, for rebuilding the army. As the elite within the NVA, the officer corps is situated to affect directly overall troop quality, expectations about military and political affairs, and to stabilize an overtly nascent system. In this regard, the Soviet Union with the support of the SED in the GDR, stressed in its selection procedures the ideological reliability of potential officers.[7] To the extent that the NVA was filled with ex–Wehrmacht officers who had demonstrated support for the socialist movement, their sole military contribution was not necessarily military expertise but political reliability.[8] Extensive purges in 1953 removed those officers from the NVA who were considered to be "undesirable" or unreliable and replaced them with men whose loyalty to the party and state were beyond reproach.

The NVA officer corps selection process stresses political reliability and social stability; namely, a commitment to socialism and evidence of a commitment to SED goals. In particular, the SED sees the NVA officer corps as a primary instrument of state control over the army and should domestic suppression prove to be necessary, as a means of establishing political legitimacy. One question that is often raised about officer corps reliability is the presence of political officers (*Politoffizieren*) in the army. Like the Soviet Army, the NVA has political officers at each level down to the company to ensure overt cooperation and to supervise ideological training.[9] Each officer in the NVA is required to participate in a part-time ideological course to refresh his understanding and memory of ideological precepts and, ostensibly, to provide a means by which any potentially disruptive attitudes can be discovered and eliminated. In view of the demonstrated competence of

Soviet techniques of mass control, the NVA officer corps is probably highly reliable and would remain so during a war. In the NVA, the military or tactical officer is not subordinated to the orders of the political officer. In this way the follies of the Soviet Army, in which military decisions are made by nonmilitary men, are not repeated in the NVA. Thus, political officers cannot override orders given by military men.

A further concern of the SED is that the NVA officer corps be truly representative of the East German population at large. The SED ensures that the officer corps finds its origins in the proletariat, that is, the working class. In 1957, the officer corps was found to have "excessive" upper-middle-class origins: 25 percent were from the upper segments of the society. By 1967, this figure had been reduced to 10 percent.[10] At present, the NVA officer corps is apparently composed of 85 percent working-class members; of the remaining 15 percent, 12 percent have white-collar backgrounds, and 3 percent upper-class or professional status.[11]

Every modern army today must depend on technical competence as well as political reliability. Accordingly, the NVA stresses the technical training and qualifications of its officers, and sees that combat-readiness is maintained at the highest possible levels. The majority of NVA officers have trained in technical schools or have learned technical skills directly applicable to the army. The NVA officer also receives extensive training in social science subjects. Such training not only prepares the officer for the emotional and intellectual rigors of war, but also teaches him to consider the psychological link between him and his men. In the NVA, aside from the emphasis on general combat-readiness, the officer is expected to be aware of the mental condition of his troops.

In terms of technical training, the officer in the NVA may choose from among thirteen different categories in officer training school. The officer is expected to master more than one field of expertise, however, so that specialization does not impair unit replacement when battle casualties displace men from their normal duties. The officer candidate's training stresses the ability to adapt to the changing conditions of modern warfare, together with the elements of a general humanistic education and combat training. In 1971, 80 percent of all officers in the NVA were graduated from three- or four-year officer training schools, and in 1973, 25 percent of these officers had received academic degrees. By comparison, only 10 percent of the officers in the Bundeswehr had such degrees.[12]

NVA officers are expected to learn Russian. The value of this skill is immediately obvious: the inability to communicate clearly in war with allied forces would lead at a minimum to less effective offensive operations, and at a maximum to a complete failure in a given military campaign. One suspects, however, that the patently offensive mission of the Warsaw Pact will preclude the high level of communication that would be required in a defensive environment, such as that of NATO.

A further measure of the quality of an officer corps is the level of political, in this case Communist, party penetration. In the NVA, the present level of SED membership in the officer corps approaches 95 percent, a figure which is the highest in the Warsaw Pact.[13] The emphasis on officer corps obedience to the orders of the state and the SED is such that "the leadership of the state controls a reliable military apparatus which cannot develop into a 'state within a state'." With the selection of officers based on class coordinates (85 percent being from the working class) and ideological coordinates (95 percent being members of the SED), it is "virtually impossible that the People's Army would ever deviate from the political direction set by the SED leadership."[14] Since all officers in the NVA are volunteers with a minimum enlistment period of ten years, and given the overt level of supervision of an officer's political and ideological reliability, the NVA officer corps would not very likely deviate from the state or party line. Even under maximum combat stress, even the most pessmistic analysis cannot fail to reject the idea of political subversion from within the army. In sum, the NVA officer corps is highly reliable, well-trained, and highly skilled in the technical arts of modern warfare.

It is always conceivable that deep systemic conflicts could develop between the party and the military in any regime; the totalitarian state, in fact, is the most susceptible system to such conflict. In East Germany, for example, the principal source of conflict tends to be the level of control exercised by the party over the military. The tension exists between the level of political control over the army and the level of independence exercised by the army in technological matters. If political factors are allowed to be dominant, then technological competence is not attainable. For this reason, "the SED leadership nevertheless took care to avoid escalating political requirements to the point where they would make technological growth impossible."[15]

The NCOs

As of 1980, the NCOs in the NVA comprised 18 percent of its total strength, or about 21,000 men. As in the Soviet Army in the 1950s and 1960s, the NCOs in the NVA enjoyed very little power, responsibility, or function. Only in the mid-1960s, with resurgence of the NCOs in the NVA, and the Soviet Army as well, was there a full-scale integration of the NCO as an essential component of the NVA. This resurgence was in effect equivalent to a complete modernization of the NCO corps with respect to the training, prestige, and power allotted to it. The NCO in the NVA is a career soldier who enlists before the age of twenty-six years for a minimum of ten years' service. The majority of NCOs, however, remain in active status until the mandatory retirement age of sixty-five. This fact alone suggests the quality of the men in the NCO corps: the soldier who makes a career of being an NCO will very likely attain greater technical competence. Furthermore the ability of NCOs to handle enlisted men will also increase as a function of length of service. It should be remembered that the NCO is the most visible force in the career of the enlisted soldier; it is the NCO who creates, or for that matter fails to create, high-quality enlisted soldiers.

The NCO in the East German Army receives general training in multiple fields: 15 percent of his training is in basic military skills; 15 to 20 percent in general military training; 40 to 50 percent in weaponry and technological training; 20 percent in social science training; and 5 percent in physical training. When the initial training phase is completed, each NCO is assigned to a unit in which he receives further technical instruction—on-the-job training as it were. He is expected to remain in that technical field for the remainder of the enlistment period. Therefore, most NCOs will spend between twenty and forty years of service in a particular field of specialization. In this way, the NVA develops well-trained and technically proficient NCOs.

To ensure the political reliability of the NCO corps, each NCO receives four hours per week of political and ideological training. Aside from the supervisory function of this session, it makes the NCOs very aware of SED goals. Such values, however politically expedient they may be, do not appear to influence combat-readiness or military capabilities. That is, socialist values are not allowed to interfere with the proper exercise of military training and operations. It should be noted that approximately 40 percent of the NCOs in the East German Army in 1956 were members of the SED; this figure was probably substantially higher in 1982. In conclusion, the NCO in the NVA demonstrates both technical competence and political reliability. The result is a group that will prepare for, and maintain the NVA in, a state of readiness for war.

The Soldier

With the strength of the NVA in 1980 at approximately 120,000 men, there are 83,500 enlisted soldiers or about 69 percent of its total manpower. This 70 or so percent of the NVA determines the army's combat-effectiveness. In order to evaluate the ability of these troops in war, it is first necessary to delineate the composition, training, and overall operational efficiency of the NVA enlisted personnel.

The most basic phase of the enlisted man's training begins with his induction into the army. The recruit's political reliability is checked through the SED in his hometown. Only after a positive result is the recruit allowed to enter the basic training phase. During this training, the NVA soldier is *"inured to soldierly discipline and order."*[16] Despite the relatively homogeneous ethnic, cultural, and religious composition of the East German population, the East German soldier, like any other soldier anywhere, must be acclimated to the rigors of military discipline and obedience. The average soldier does not learn the rudiments of military life for at least six months, and it takes him another six months to a year to absorb the discipline that will be required in combat. The East Germans initiate the training phase with a population that is, by and large, amenable to authority and has accepted the military as a necessary facet of life.

During the basic training phase, training time is distributed equally among the following skills: drill, weapons firing and instruction, the tactical "arts" of modern war, including extensive training in NBC (nuclear, biological, and chemical) warfare, as well as training for combat with protective equipment. There is also training in the rudiments of field engineering and military topography, and in physical, medical, and barracks duties. The training of the NVA is equivalent to that of NATO armies with the exceptions of the NVA's extensive training in NBC and protective warfare as well as more frequent firing practice with live rounds.

The soldiers in the NVA are trained for a variety of combat missions, or for what NVA jargon calls "interchangeability of function." The NVA soldier also spends between 30 and 50 percent of his training time in night operations, so that the NVA and Warsaw Pact nations have a high capability to conduct night-time offensive operations. As with the officer corps, the SED and the state are equally determined to see that the NVA soldier is thoroughly loyal and reliable. Each enlisted soldier is, therefore, subjected to rather constant political and ideological education. The purpose is to instill and maintain essential socialist values in the minds of the soldiers and to provide an opportunity for political officers as well as regular officers and NCOs to observe and then correct any existing behavioral or ideological pathologies.

The NVA emphasizes the value of regular live-round firing practice, night operations, and large-scale formation training; the formation training usually occurs in March and April. During large-scale Warsaw Pact field exercises and maneuvers, the NVA makes every attempt to simulate actual combat conditions that would exist in a conventional or NBC war in Europe. For example, the NVA insists that all soldiers carry a full complement of combat gear in such operations in order to test the mobility and combat-readiness of every soldier. Furthermore, all major field exercises are conducted in both summer and winter in order to maximize the effect on troops in adverse weather, and they execute such operations at night. The NVA soldier is also trained in the tactics of mobility and fluidity: hitting targets with massive firepower and concentrations of armor in order to weaken or destroy the defense, and then fading and regrouping whenever necessary.

Integration

As an example of a well-integrated and unified military command and alliance system, the Warsaw Pact and its members form a cohesive combat organization. The level of political and military control, under the aegis of the Soviet Union, suggests that in war the Warsaw Pact would operate as an effective fighting force. As the number two nation in the pact, the East German state and its army are therefore under the direct control of the Soviet Union. In particular, the NVA is operationally subordinate to the Joint Supreme Command of the Warsaw Pact and is chaired by a Soviet marshal. One factor that suggests a high level of Soviet control and guidance over the NVA, aside from the marshal in command, is the presence of ten Soviet motorized infantry divisions and 10 armored divisions in East Germany, headquartered at Wunsdorf–Zossen. Not only does this presence create an explicit instrument of control, but more importantly, it also reinforces the close coordination of the two forces in the event of war.

Both organizationally and operationally, the NVA is a product of Soviet conception, design, and control and would function accordingly in war. First, its basic organization and structure mirror those of the Soviet Army. Second, East German officers are educated in Soviet military academies. One source estimates that over 1,000 East German Army officers have been graduated from these academies.[17] Furthermore, 25 percent of the instructors in East German military academies have earned their academic degrees from Soviet schools. The requirement that "foreign" officers demonstrate loyalty to the Soviet Union has created an army that is highly attuned to Soviet military thinking.

Third, Soviet political officers and military advisers are present at all levels, tactical and operational, of the NVA. While the responsibilities of these advisers are primarily supervisory in the area of military and technical competence, their duties inevitably include political surveillance. The Soviet Union apparently understands that its performance in a European war would depend not only on actual combat capabilities but also on the level of unity in East European states, especially in the rear echelon and reserve forces.

In more general terms, the Soviet Union dominates the NVA as a result of its direct control over the tactical air squadrons that would provide air cover, the demands incumbent upon the Soviets given their large deployment of armies in East Germany, and the degree of economic dependence between the Soviet Union and Eastern Europe. The Soviet Union has assigned the NVA to the First Strategic Echelon of the Warsaw Pact.

Operational Organization and Manpower

Excluding Soviet ground forces, the NVA is divided into two army groups, each composed of three divisions. The NVA, therefore, consists of two military districts: the Northern Army Group and the Southern Army Group. Headquartered in Neubrandenburg, the Northern Army Group is under the control of the commander of Soviet forces in Germany. It is composed of two motor rifle divisions and one armored division. The deployment of individual units of the Northern group, also called the V Military District, is as follows: the 1st and 8th Motor Rifle divisions are in Potsdam and Schwerin, respectively; the 9th Armored division is in Eggesin; artillery and artillery-locating regiments, an anti-tank battalion, and an NCO training regiment are in Torgelow; an air defense regiment is at Prenzlaw; a signals regiment is at Neubrandenburg; and engineer and transport battalions and a nuclear-chemical company are at Rasewalk.

The Southern Army Group, or the III Military District, is headquartered at Leipzig. It is under the operational control of the Soviet commander of the Northern Army Group. The Southern group, like the Northern group, is composed of two motor rifle divisions and one armored division. The specific deployment of the Southern group is as follows: the 4th and 11th Motor Rifle divisions are located at Erfurt and Halle, respectively; the 7th Armored division is at Dresden; artillery, artillery-locating, air defense, and signals regiments are at Leipzig; an anti-tank battalion is at Wolfen; a transport battalion at Gottbius; an engineer battalion at Gera; an NCO training regiment at Eilenberg; and a nuclear-chemical company in Grossenburg.

In general, the deployments of the Northern and Southern army groups are symmetrical. As John Keegan observes, "this deployment produces a heavy concentration of military strength in the northern and southern districts around Berlin, but little in the central areas."[18] The reason for this deployment is obvious: Warsaw Pact armies are likely to engage in enveloping maneuvers from the north and the south in order to isolate NATO armies in the central regions; all actions are directed ultimately toward the Rhine and later the English Channel. Therefore, this deployment of the NVA, and the Soviet Army as well, is entirely consonant with established military strategy and the fundamentals of geography. Furthermore, an even deployment of NVA troops along the northern, central, and southern districts would be the optimum arrangement if the Warsaw Pact planned defensive, that is, holding, maneuvers along the East German border. Since the NVA and the Warsaw Pact appear committed to offensive rather than containment strategies, the present deployment offers the most effective means for the penetration and later disruption of NATO defenses. But more of this later.

In the NVA there are six army divisions with two tank or armored and four motor rifle or infantry divisions. Thus, the division is the basic organizational unit in the NVA; in combat actions, however, the regiment is the basic tactical unit. As a conventional army, each division is accordingly organized into regiments, battalions, companies, and platoons. If we use the 1971 figures for the personnel strength of the NVA, about 90,000, then approximately 70 percent or 60,000 would will function as combat troops, that is, would actually fight in war. In 1971, the NVA averaged 11,000 men per motor rifle division, and 9,000 men per armored division. If these same percentages are applied to the 1980 data for troop strength, about 120,000, then there are approximately 70,000 combat soldiers in the NVA's six divisions.[19] The remainder of the army, about 50,000, would function in the logistics, supply, and headquarters functions.

As a conventional field army equipped to fight modern, high-intensity warfare, the NVA stresses the motor rifle division with its increased firepower and mobility. The motor rifle division in the NVA, however, has less firepower and mobility than its Soviet counterpart.[20] In each such division, there are one tank, one artillery, and three motor rifle regiments. By comparison, an armored division is composed of three tank, one artillery, and one motor rifle regiments. In a typical tank division, for example, there are ten tank battalions with approximately 300 medium to heavy tanks. However, in an average motor rifle division there are six tank battalions with approximately 150 to 200 medium and light tanks. Each NVA division also contains anti-aircraft, rocket, engineer, communications, medical, and transport battalions, as well as reconnaisance and logistics units.

Quite dissimilar to NATO armies, each division in the East German Army is equipped with units whose primary mission is nuclear and chemical decontamination, not including the normal (like NATO) contingent of chemical and nuclear warfare troops.[21] The ability to decontaminate personnel and equipment will increase the number of troops and forces that would otherwise be put out of action. Parenthetically, the principal means for the decontamination of equipment is the use of jet engines to "blast" particulate matter containing radioactive or chemical debris off the equipment in question.

Logistics and Supply

As a modern industrialized nation with one of the largest gross national products in Eastern Europe and in the world, the GDR depends on a well-organized transportation, supply, and communications system to fuel its industrial apparatus. To support the NVA, the GDR has developed a supply system that is highly dependent on the civilian or domestic economy.[22] Since all allocation decisions are made at the top, the army does not have to compete with the other sectors of the economy for scarce resources. To the extent that the Warsaw Pact supply system is coherent with respect to distribution and planning, it may be said that a Soviet-style supply system is operating. Like the Soviet military system, the NVA has a central procurement apparatus. Its principal administrators are the deputy defense minister and the head of technology and weaponry. The deputy defense minister and the head of rear services are responsible for the procurement and distribution of general supplies, fuel, equipment, clothes, food, and sanitation facilities. Each battalion, incidentally, has its own personnel to oversee such operations.

A modern army's ability to deploy rapidly and in depth depends on two factors: first, stockpiles of essential materials in strategic areas in order to facilitate the advance once it begins, and second, a supply system that permits great tactical flexibility so that the initiative can be maintained. The NVA allows its tactical commanders to make decisions regarding consumption so as to prevent the bottlenecks that would otherwise cause delays in the resupply of troops. More important is the Soviet military doctrine of the "principle of availability" which stresses the primacy of supply to forward echelon troops.

During peacetime, the NVA's supply system is staffed with military personnel. In war, however, the NVA and the GDR are prepared to replace those troops lost through combat with civilians. Thus, the GDR has a civilian reserve that is trained to operate the military supply system. In terms of the transportation network that would distribute NVA supplies in war, the primary means are railroads, roadways, pipelines for gas and fuel, and the waterway system. As the NVA itself recognizes, its transportation system is essential to the maintenance of "operational efficiency." In the pipeline supply system, for example, there are trained pipeline construction units that will construct new pipes in order to shift supply lines to meet the needs of armored and infantry troops. In terms of its road system, the GDR has the highest road density of all Warsaw Pact nations. While the rail density in the GDR is approximately equal to that of the Federal Democratic Republic, the GDR would depend on its more extensive road net to supply advancing troops.

The NVA supply system also consists of an air transport subsidiary. There are two air transport squadrons with twenty IL-14, three TU-124, and eight TU-135 aircraft. In addition, there are six helicopter squadrons with forty-six MI-1, eighteen MI-4, and forty MI-8 helicopters. Supplemented by the Soviet Union's air transport system, the NVA air supply system is not only of superior quality but is among the best in the world. The NVA describes the air transport system as "sufficient for assault and special operations on a tactical scale, and for major supply tasks."[23] However correct this assessment may be, it is apparent that the Soviet supply system would figure dominantly in any supply effort.

The NVA stockpile system has both mobile reserves of ammunition and fuel that is carried by the NVA, and military and civilian reserves. Because of the high supply consumption rates of military goods that would occur in the next war, the NVA could realistically supply only enough materials for the initial phase of the war. The Warsaw Pact, however, could rely on a rapid reinforcement supply capability superior in all respects to that of NATO. Thus, the NVA and the Warsaw Pact would be capable of a much faster buildup of military goods in the first two to three weeks of the war. Recent improvements in the Warsaw Pact supply and logistics system suggest that whatever resupply effort was undertaken would exceed that of NATO armies, who would confront the problems of transporting materials across the Atlantic Ocean from the United States. With its interior lines of communication, and a more standardized command, control, and logistics system, the NVA and the Warsaw Pact nations would be able to sustain offensive combat operations for a considerable length of time.[24]

Weaponry

Uniforms, ammunition, and small arms are manufactured in East Germany, but virtually all heavy and medium armaments in the NVA arsenal originate in the Soviet Union. With this inordinately high level of standardization and interchangeability, the NVA can function as an integral part of the First Strategic Echelon. Over the past decade, the conventional armaments of the NVA and the Warsaw Pact as a whole have improved substantially. The NVA, which is a frontline army, now has the armored strength and infantry necessary to penetrate NATO defenses. For example, of the nearly 200,000 U.S. troops in Europe, approximately 60,000 are combat soldiers, the remainder being support, supply, and logistics personnel. Of the 120,000 personnel in the NVA, there are approximately 70,000 fighting troops. Hence, U.S. and East German ground forces are roughly equivalent.

NVA military equipment is entirely dependent on the Soviets. Of the NVA infantry arms, the Makarov pistol, Dragoonov rifle, Simonov self-loading carbine, Kalashnikov submachine gun, anti-tank launchers, and hand grenades are manufactured in the Soviet Union. The small arms that are manufactured in East Germany are produced under license agreements with the Soviets. In any case, all ammunition is compatible with Soviet and East German weapons.

With respect to the 1,500 armored personnel carriers in the NVA arsenal, one finds the following models: BRDM, BRDM-M-1966, BTR-152, BTR-50P, BTR-60P, BTR-60PA, BTR-60PB, and the BMP.[25] The most modern and effective APC in the world is the Soviet Union's BMP: with a 76mm anti-tank gun, 7.62mm machinegun, and anti-tank rockets, it is expected to be very effective against armored vehicles. The BMP is designed to allow infantry troops to fight a mobile war, without having to dismount from the APC during combat. Parenthically, the BMP will protect its crew in an NBC environment with its positive-pressure ventilation system.

The second and most important element of an armored invasion is the tank. The inventory of tanks in the NVA arsenal can be broken down as follows: T-54, T-55, T-62, and T-72 tanks for a total of 2,600.[26] The T-54 and the T-55 are the standard tanks in the motorized infantry and armored regiments. During the 1960s and early 1970s, the T-62, of Soviet manufacture, was deployed in the NVA. Defects in its armor, cannon, and battlefield performance downgraded its importance, as well as effectiveness, in the NVA. However, it became the progenitor of the newest main battle tank in the NVA and the Soviet Army, the T-72. The Soviet Union continues to deploy the T-72 in the NVA and its own army. As a result, the First Strategic Echelon in East Germany receives the most modern equipment in the Warsaw Pact. As a rule, the NVA and the Soviet Army acquire the most effective and latest arms because they would do most of the fighting, at least during the initial stages of the war. With respect to the NVA, it is essential to note that its inventory of 2,600 tanks and 1,500 APCs forms a potent and lethal fighting force that is manned by well-trained and competent soldiers.

Anti-tank weapons in the NVA arsenal include the anti-tank guided missile (PALR), the 57mm and 85mm self-propelled anti-tank guns, and the 100mm anti-tank cannon. The 100mm cannon is the standard anti-tank gun issued to artillery regiments in the motorized infantry divisions. Coupled with helicopter and fighter-bomber air strikes, as well as variable time fuse (VTF) weapons, the NVA has an effective anti-tank capability.

In a war in Europe, the NVA would have to coordinate its armored and infantry operations with an anti-aircraft capability. The anti-aircraft (AA) battalions or regiments in motor infantry and armored divisions have 14.5mm ZPUs, 23mm AA cannon, 23mm radar-guided AA guns, 57mm cannons with radar, and 100mm AA cannons. NVA ground forces also have AA guided missiles: SA-2, SA-3, SA-4, SA-6, and SA-9. These guided missiles, having a combined high- and low-altitude capability, proved to be quite lethal against the U.S. Air Force and Navy in Vietnam, and the Israeli Air Force in the 1973 Yom Kippur War.

Artillery in the NVA includes both mortars and traditional muzzle-loaded guns. NVA mortars include the 82mm, 120mm, and 160mm. With respect to the traditional artillery piece, standard equipment in the NVA artillery regiments of the motor infantry and armored divisions are the 122mm, M-1938, and D30 howitzers; the howitzers are very accurate and lethal against both troops and armored forces. The NVA also has 122mm and 152mm self-propelled howitzers. NVA military doctrine stresses the importance of artillery in war and its effective integration with armor and infantry in offensive action.

Since a Warsaw Pact offensive against NATO would utilize nuclear strikes against a broad spectrum of military targets and defensive formations, the NVA would deploy nuclear-capable guided missiles. Nuclear-capable missiles in the NVA arsenal include the FROG 4 and FROG 7 tactical rockets on self-propelled carriages for use by rocket battalions in motor infantry and armored divisions, and medium-operational range SCUD A and SCUD B missiles, which are also on self-propelled carriages. These missiles would likely be targeted against NATO command, control, and communication centers, as well as rear echelon supply and troop concentrations. According to published NVA doctrine, in order to win the war such targets would have to be destroyed during the initial phase of the war.[27]

NVA Strategy and Tactics

The military doctrine of the NVA must of necessity be a mirror image of the Soviet Union's thinking, for the NVA is a product of Soviet conception, control, and execution. The most striking aspect of NVA military writing is its notion that doctrine, not instruments, determine the outcome of war. If an attack against the NVA and the Warsaw Pact were to occur, caused by "imperialist aggression" to be sure, the NVA would respond with all possible means—nuclear, conventional, chemical, and biological—to defeat the aggressor. From the East German perspective, as far as it can be discerned from its military publications, preparations for war are inherently defensive: it will fight only in order to repulse the aggressor or in order to defend an ally from attack. Once the war commences, the response, or the offensive as the case may be, would be to penetrate NATO deployments in depth so as to disrupt the defense and perhaps cause a complete disintegration of the defender's forces. Attacking with tanks, APCs, artillery, and air support, the First Strategic Echelon of which the NVA is an integral part would form the advance guard of the Warsaw Pact.

For the NVA, the offensive is the basic type of combat action. Through the massive employment of men, equipment, and firepower, the rate of attack and depth of the penetration would increase over time. The principle is that one may create an offensive that will gain momentum in a geometric fashion. Judging from Soviet experience at the end of World War II, when the German Army was retreating, it is easy to see how this strategy dominates much of Warsaw Pact and Soviet thinking.

Thus, the NVA is preoccupied, or at least concerned, with modern *blitzkrieg* or *sturmtaktik* (storm tactics) invasions. The *sturmtaktik* is accomplished by deploying large, usually (although not necessarily) numerically superior amounts of firepower and mobile armies attacking over a large frontal area. Since the front may be superimposed over hundreds of kilometers, the defender, in this case NATO, would be contronted with hostile action from directions and in zones that he could not fully anticipate and/or cover. Even if the primary axes of attack were determined, there would be insufficient time to reposition troops and armor for counterattack. The NVA, therefore, would fight as many intense battles as possible in order to disrupt NATO. The real question, if this breakthrough fails, is whether the NVA and the Warsaw Pact are prepared to fight a war of attrition. Since the Warsaw Pact already has numerical superiority, as well as the internal morale and discipline required to maintain such operations, the answer is yes.

The NVA also stresses the amount of firepower that can be brought to bear against the enemy. The lineage to Soviet military thinking is clear: that the high density of artillery fire will prove to be critical.[28] Artillery fire, however, is not confined to conventional rounds. The Soviet and East

German Army apparently plan to use nuclear rounds, both preemptively and during intermediate stages of the war. Specifically, A. A. Sidorenko states the case for nuclear preemption in a conventional land war: "It is believed that *the side which first employs nuclear weapons with surprise can predetermine the outcome of the battle in his favor.*"[29] It is, therefore, highly probable that the Soviets and East Germany would select a wide variety of NATO targets at the earliest stage of the war, to include the possibility of nuclear strikes before the outbreak of any conventional hostilities.

In summary, NVA offensive military actions would be labeled an "integrated offensive strategy:" it would utilize conventional forces (tanks, troops, APC, and artillery) and nuclear forces in order to smash NATO with a *blitzkrieg* or *sturmtaktik* invasion. It would focus inordinately large amounts of firepower on selected enemy targets so as to preclude reinforcement, while simultaneously balancing troop concentration and dispersion to minimize its own vulnerability.

Scenarios of Employment

When we consider all the attributes of the NVA, its personnel, training, and equipment, it is evident that it is best prepared to fight a conventional land war in Central Europe against NATO forces. With six Category 1 divisions, the NVA would form approximately 30 percent of the initial attacking forces in the First Strategic Echelon; that is, when the war began, the NVA and some twenty Soviet divisions would enter the war first.

Central European War

There is overwhelming evidence that the NVA would participate in a *blitzkrieg*-type of war against the full range of NATO signatories. Some definable aspects of NVA deployments suggest that an offensive war would be the only logical course of action.

First, the main battle tank in the NVA inventory, the Soviet T-72, is deployed in greater numbers per unit area and in aggregate terms than the deployment of NATO tanks. With an average of sixty to eighty more tanks per NVA motorized infantry and armored divisions than a NATO counterpart, the NVA would have a 3:1 aggregate tank advantage over NATO (assuming that Soviet forces were committed as well) at the earliest stage in the war. This calculation obviously neglects the greater concentrations that would perforce occur randomly. More specifically, on the first day of the war, $D+1$, the Warsaw Pact advantage at the forward edge of battle, that is, localized advantage, would approach 7:1. Numerical superiority of this magnitude is characterisitc of an offensive tactic, one that seeks to penetrate NATO fronts and thereby envelop NATO as the pincers from the north and south close on the NATO forces. The NVA would engage in a maneuver reminiscent of the Schlieffen Plan of World War I. While army groups attacking from the northern and southern sectors in East Germany would form the pincers that would surround NATO forces, a smaller army group would attack directly into the heart of West Germany. Located right in the middle of that central sector is Frankfurt, which is the nerve center of the West German communication, supply, and organizational infrastructure; to sever the lines running north and south out of Frankfurt would severely hamper, if not terminate, effective West German/NATO resistance. Even the scale of this potential Warsaw Pact invasion would be analogous to World War I: approximately twenty divisions each in the northern and southern groups would converge, sequentially, on the Rhine and on the English Channel, first in Belgium and then in France.

Second, the NVA offensive *blitzkrieg* would see the deployment of substantial numbers of armored personnel carriers. The APC has become the workhorse after the tank for infantry maneuver in war because it permits high mobility while providing maximum available protection. Over the last few years, the NVA has increased the number of Soviet-built APCs, most notably the BMP-60 mechanized infantry combat vehicle (MICV). This weapons system affords the NVA soldier greater ability to fight continuous, high-intensity warfare with superior mobility on the battlefield so that it can rapidly shift the axis of attack as required and simultaneously offer protection to its crews. Thus, troops can fight while riding in the MICV because of the firepower on the MICV; the BMP-60 carries both light and medium guns and is armored. With the mobility of the BMP-60 and other APCs in the NVA arsenal, the NVA would be able to cover between 80 and 120 kilometers per day. The anti-tank gun on the BMP would also allow for the destruction of opposing defensive tanks.

Third, the NVA has shifted its deployment from towed to self-propelled artillery. According to NVA military doctrine, artillery would assume a critical role in war because the amount of artillery fire directed against the enemy would weaken his resistance. The NVA has mated self-propelled artillery tubes with its armored and infantry units in order to increase the firepower per unit area. With a 50-percent increase in the number of artillery tubes in the NVA arsenal since 1970, the NVA can concentrate superior firepower.

Fourth, the tactical air defense system of the Warsaw Pact would figure prominently in the *blitzkrieg* equation. with a 200-percent increase in the number of Soviet fighter-bombers in the Warsaw Pact arsenal over the last decade, NATO would find its fighters outnumbered by a factor of 2:1. With twice the number of aircraft, as well as evidence that smaller and less capable aircraft can beat the more expensive and sophisticated models in large-scale operations, there are indications that the Warsaw Pact air defense system would not be defeated very easily.

The fifth, and final, factor is the NATO anti-tank capability. Although the NVA would attack as a force with superior numbers of tanks, NATO often asserts that its anti-tank (AT) capability would destroy sufficient numbers of tanks to defeat the offensive and thereby deter attack. With more than 40,000 AT weapons, NATO appears to threaten the offensive might of the Warsaw Pact and the NVA. Against even superior forces, an AT system would destroy large numbers of attacking vehicles. The NVA, however, is not defenseless against this threat: helicopter and aircraft strikes, as well as variable-time fuse weapons, could reduce the number of AT "stations," however mobile they might be. If a NATO TOW AT missile launcher were mobile, it would be the quality and training of the troops that would determine their ability to stay put and withstand very intense action. With the present disarray in NATO, there are doubts whether its troops could withstand the Warsaw Pact onslaught.

Study of the military doctrine and operational deployments of the NVA leads inexorably to the conclusion that it would engage in a brief, yet intense, offensive war. Moreover, with the aid of the Soviet Army, the NVA would defeat NATO in a conventional land battle. The presence of nuclear weapons at the forward edge of battle introduces greater complexity and uncertainty into calculations about the outcome. But there is no reason to assume that nonnuclear superiority would melt in the face of NATO tactical nuclear attacks, for the Warsaw Pact and the NVA, too, would launch nuclear strikes in order to disrupt the defense.

If both the Warsaw Pact nations and the NVA rejected the assumption that nuclear war was mutually undesirable and equally irrational *under all conditions*, then it might well use such weapons before NATO. Given the deployment of SCUD and FROG nuclear missiles in East Germany, the optimum strategy would be to destroy the NATO nuclear option: NATO nuclear weapon storage sites, as well as the command posts, both being relatively few in number, are highly visible and vulnerable to destruction. Furthermore, since NATO never intended to match the conventional deployments of the Warsaw Pact, the assumed irrationality of nuclear war, combined with overwhelming U.S. tactical and strategic superiority, always mitigated against escalation to nuclear war in Europe. Now, however, NATO finds that its deterrent strategy of nuclear war is opposed in particular by East German and Soviet preemptive nuclear systems and conventional superiority, as well as Soviet nuclear superiority at the strategic level.

With respect to the conventional war scenarios in Europe, the unavoidable conclusion is that the NVA and the Warsaw Pact forces would win. It is a superior force quantitatively, and perhaps qualitatively as well, and it could defeat the NATO forces in a nuclear and/or conventional environment. First, it is trained extensively in NBC warfare, night-fighting, and frequent live-fire simulations. Second, it is not apparently plagued with drug and authority-related problems. Third, in a tactical nuclear war, the NVA would probably perform quite well in comparison with NATO. All indicators point to excellence in the NVA: its soldiers, officers, equipment, supply and logistics, and training are first rate both relatively and absolutely.

Third World Scenarios

Although the Cuban Army is frequently cited as the primary agent of the Soviet Union's foreign military policy, the role of the NVA may well equal that of the Cubans. Beginning with reports of East German pilots fighting in the Biafra War of 1966, the East German military presence in Africa and the Persian Gulf/Middle East has been quite pronounced.[30] According to the International Institute for Strategic Studies in London, the East German Army is presently deployed in Algeria, Angola, Ethiopia, Mozambique, South Yemen, and Syria.[31] There are further indications that NVA personnel are atationed in Guinea, Nigeria, Congo-Brazzaville, and Libya. The scope and intensity of NVA activity in Africa and the Third World are extensive, and include both military training and direct combat intervention.

Perhaps the most blatant example of NVA participation in African "liberation" movements is in Angola, where NVA advisers train Marxist revolutionaries. Dr. David Owen, the British foreign secretary, affirms that the NVA has been involved in Angola for years in these and similar Angolan affairs, together with a network of military training centers.[32] The Angolan invasion into the Shaba Province in Zaire, a region rich in copper, was directed and planned by Heinz Hoffmann who is the Soviet-trained minister of defense in East Germany and the commander of the Red Africa Corps. Given the relative sophistication of the raid, NATO experts concluded that NVA participation was virtually certain; there are indications that similar raids were executed under the supervision of approximately 100 NVA staff officers.[33] To support the assertion that the NVA does indeed participate in these events, Zaire, for example, claims to have NVA prisoners of war and "large quantities of East German weapons and ammunition."[34] The pertinent data show that the Red Africa Korps, a term reminiscent of General Rommel's World War II Africa Korps, is a brigade-strength force of officers and NCOs that freely participates in equivalent events all over the Continent. Moreover, it trains guerrilla forces for military and terrorist raids.

In Ethiopia, for instance, the NVA has been involved in several military raids. Mengistu Haile Mariam, the Ethiopian leader who deposed Haile Selassie in 1974, said, "Progressive comrades from the Soviet Union, Cuba, South Yemen, and *East Germany* are living, *fighting*, and *dying* side by side with us."[35] On an equally overt level, the NVA maintains active relations with various liberation movements in Namibia (SWAPO), Zimbabwe (the Patriotic Front), and South Africa (the ANC). In southern Africa and Ethiopia, there are approximately 3,000 advisers training guerrilla forces for military raids into surrounding nations.

In order to support terrorism in Third World as well as industrialized nations of the West, the NVA supplies highly sophisticated automatic weapons to various organizations. For example, the NVA supplies the Palestine Liberation Organization (PLO) with rocket launchers, automatic weapons, and small arms.[36] Perhaps the most common function of the NVA, aside from the activities listed above, is its training and support apparatus for the development of internal security organizations in developing nations. The East German secret police (the SSD or "Stasi") is reportedly operating in numerous African, Middle Eastern, and Central American nations where it trains clients in modern methods of political control: domestic surveillance and torture. With the political and military situation in El Salvador reaching crisis proportions, the infrastructure of the guerrilla forces, according to the director of the CIA, is composed of 6,000 Cubans with 1,800 to 2,000 in military and security work and perhaps 50 to 100 East Germans involved in the security system.[37]

According to Western intelligence reports, the NVA has several thousand "specialists" training Marxist forces in twenty-five African, Arab, and Central American nations.[38] The NVA has demonstrated a high level of competence to engage in Third World wars and scenarios of guerrilla support, counterinsurgency, and terrorism. It is a first-rate guerrilla warfare force and, therefore, seems well adapted for modern insurgency warfare. Furthermore, it actively supports a host of terrorist organizations whose sole objective is the physical destruction or disruption, and the psychological dislocation, of Western industrialized nations.

Conclusions

In a very short period, the East Germans, with the aid of the Soviet Union, developed a very competent army from the ruins of the Wehrmacht of World War II. Following the revolution in East German political and military affairs, the army emerged as a thoroughly socialist organization committed to the preservation of international socialism, as interpreted by the Soviet Union.

In the earliest stages, the East Germans were concerned with developing reliable political and ideological cadres within the army. Only later did they focus on true military excellence, as best illustrated by the German General Staff system between 1807 and 1945. Only after the East Germans could be certain that their army would not fade on the battlefield against their "compatriots" in the West did they begin to socialize large numbers of youth into the military system. In 1980, approximately 120,000 Germans were enlisted in the land forces alone, to exclude those in the air force, navy, and frontier troops. The present evidence suggests that the East Germans in the army are totally reliable, seeing the state as the duly constituted authority. Analysts generally agree that, with more than 95 percent of army officers in the SED, the army would remain loyal to the state even under the most extreme battlefield conditions.

The East German Army, and all the other Warsaw Pact forces, especially the Soviets, are better prepared to fight a conventional or NBC war in Europe than NATO. The East German Army is experienced in the use of modern methods of warfare and is also conditioned to accept the hazards of such. As a modern military force destined for offensive action, it appears that the East Germans with the Soviet Union would defeat the NATO armies. Victory is, after all, a product neither of a genetic predisposition to fight well nor of an inherent right to win, but only of proper training and preparation, a notion for which the Germans have sufficient historical and sociological evidence.

Notes

1. T. N. Dupuy, *A Genius for War: The German Army and General Staff, 1807-1945* (Englewood Cliffs, N.J.: Prentice-Hall, Inc., 1977). The central thesis of Dupuy's first-rate work is that the key to the institutionalization of military excellence is the General Staff system rather than biological, ideological, or largely accidental factors.

2. Dupuy, *A Genius for War*, p. 310: "...the East German armed forces, although largely modelled on those of Moscow, have incorporated many features—including military doctrine and control mechanisms—from past German history."

3. Kurt Sontheimer and Wilhelm Bleek, *The Government and Politics of East Germany* (New York: St. Martin's Press, 1976), p. 181. "In this way the leadership of the state controls a reliable military apparatus which cannot develop into a 'state within a state'."

4. Eugene K. Keefe, Donald W. Bernier, Lyle E. Brenneman, Wayne A. Culp, William Giloane, and James M. Moore, Jr., *East Germany: A Country Study* (Department of Army, Washington, D.C.: U.S. Government Printing Office, 1980), p. 284.

5. See Thomas M. Forster, *The East German Army: The Second Power in the Warsaw Pact* (London: George Allen & Unwin, Ltd., 1980), pp. 89-93; John Keegan, *World Armies* (New York: Facts on File, 1979), p. 235, in defense of the thesis that East Germany is a loyal ally in the Warsaw Pact, argues, "It is an index of its reliability that the East German government apparently insisted, and the Soviet government agreed, that part of it should be used in the invasion of Czechoslovakia in 1968."

6. *National Review*, "For the Record," September 18, 1981, p. 1056.

7. Forster, *The East German Army*, p. 266. "The SED realizes that the army's officer cadres are *one of the most important links in the all-embracing command-and-control chain* of a communist state."

8. Forster, *The East German Army*, p. 60.

9. Dale R. Herspring, "Technology and Political Reliability in the East German Military," *Journal of Political and Military Sociology* 3 (Fall 1975): 155.

10. M. Donald Hancock, "The Bundeswehr and the National People's Army," *Comparative Defense Policy* (Baltimore: Johns Hopkins University Press, 1974), p. 68.

11. Keefe, et al., *East Germany*, p. 293.

12. Dale R. Herspring, "Detente and the Military," in Lyman H. Leytes, ed., *The German Democratic Republic* (Boulder, Colo.: Westview Press, 1978), p. 204.

224   WILLIAM C. MARTEL

13. Hancock, "The Bundeswehr," p. 69, lists the figure of 95 percent of membership of officers in the SED. Herspring, "Detente and the Military," p. 230, suggests that membership approaches, or even exceeds, 99 percent.
14. Sontheimer, and Bleek, *The Government and Politics of East Germany*, p. 181.
15. Herspring, "Technology and Political Reliability," p. 154.
16. Forster, *The East German Army*, p. 256. Italics in original.
17. Ibid., p. 81.
18. Keegan, *World Armies*, p. 237.
19. Keefe, et al., *East Germany*, p. 285; Forster, *The East German Army*, p. 119.
20. Keefe, et al., *East Germany*, p. 285.
21. Forster, *The East German Army*, pp. 256, 264, 269.
22. *The Military Balance, 1979-1980* (London: International Institute for Strategic Studies, 1979), p. 113. See also Forster, *The East German Army*, pp. 173-75.
23. Forster, *The East German Army*, p. 180.
24. See *The Military Balance, 1979-1980*, pp. 113-15 for an analysis of this issue.
25. Ibid., p. 16; Forster, *The East German Army*, pp. 191-228.
26. *The Military Balance, 1979-1980*, p. 16.
27. Forster, *The East German Army*, p. 28. The NVA "is ready and able to do combat under any conditions of conventional or nuclear warfare."
28. Richard A. Gabriel, *The New Red Legions: An Attitudinal Portrait of the Soviet Soldier* (Westport, Conn.: Greenwood Press, 1980), p. 162.
29. A. A. Sidorenko, *The Offensive: A Soviet View* (Washington, D.C.: U.S. Air Force, Government Printing Office, 1979), pp. 19-20.
30. *The Military Balance, 1979-1980*, p. 16.
31. Ibid.
32. "Did 'Red Africa Korps' Help Plan Shaba Raid?", *German International* 22 (June 1978): 13.
33. Ibid.
34. Ibid., p. 15.
35. Ibid.
36. Ibid.
37. "The Real Soviet Threat in El Salvador—and Beyond: Interview with CIA Director William L. Casey," *U.S. News and World Report* 92 (March 8, 1982): 23.
38. "Did 'Red Africa Korps' Help?", p. 15.

Bibliography

Almanac of World Military Power. New York: R. R. Bowker Company, 1972.
Canby, Steven L. "Territorial Defense in Central Europe." *Armed Forces and Society* 7 (Fall 1980): 51-67.
Collins, John M. *U.S.-Soviet Military Balance: 1960-1980*. New York: McGraw-Hill, 1980.
Department of the Army. *FM 100-5, Operations*. Washington, D.C.: U.S. Government Printing Office, July 1, 1975.
———. *Soviet Army Operations*. Washington, D.C.: U.S. Government Printing Office, April 1978.
Dupuy, T.N. *A Genius for War: The German Army and General Staff, 1807-1945*. Englewood Cliffs, N.J.: Prentice-Hall, Inc., 1977.

Forster, Thomas M. *The East German Army: The Second Power in the Warsaw Pact.* London: George Allen & Unwin, Ltd., 1980.

Gabriel, Richard A. *The New Red Legions: An Attitudinal Portrait of the Soviet Soldier.* Westport, Connecticut: Greenwood Press, 1980.

——— and Savage, Paul L. *Crisis in Command: Mismanagement in the Army.* New York: Hill and Wang, 1978.

German International. "Did "Red Africa Korps" Help Plan Shaba Raid?" June, 1978, pp. 13-15.

Hancock, M. Donald. "The Bundeswehr and the National People's Army," *Comparative Defense Policy.* Baltimore, Maryland: The Johns Hopkins University Press, 1974, pp. 65-72.

Herspring, Dale R. "Civil-Military Relations in Poland and East Germany: The External Factor." *Studies in Comparative Communism* 3 (Autumn 1978): 225-36.

———. "Detente and the Military." Leytes, Lyman H., ed. *The German Democratic Republic.* Boulder, Colorado: Westview Press, 1978, pp. 199-216.

———. "Technology and Political Reliability in the East German Military." *Journal of Political and Military Sociology* 3 (Fall 1975): 153-63.

Jones, Christopher. "The Warsaw Pact: Military Exercises and Military Interventions." *Armed Forces and Society* 7 (Fall 1980): 5-30.

Keefe, Eugene K., Bernier, Donald W., Brenneman, Lyle E., Culp, Wayne A., Giloane, William, and Moore, James M. *East Germany: A Country Study.* Washington, D.C.: Department of the Army, U.S. Government Printing Office, 1980.

Keegan, John. "The Human Face of Deterrence." *International Security* 6 (Summer 1981): 136-51.

———. *World Armies.* New York: Facts on File, 1979.

Kuhne, Winrich and vonPlate, Bernard. "Two Germanys in Africa." *Africa Report* 25 (July/August 1980): 11-15.

Lodge, Milton C. *Soviet Elite Attitudes Since Stalin.* Columbus, Ohio: Charles E. Merrill Publishing Company, 1969.

Military Balance, 1978-1979. London: The International Institute for Strategic Studies, 1978.

Military Balance, 1979-1980. London: The International Institute for Strategic Studies, 1979.

Military Balance, 1980-1981. London: The International Instutute for Strategic Studies, 1980.

National Review. "For the Record." September 18, 1981, p. 1056.

Ownes, M.J. "Artillery is the Real Threat in the Soviet Weapons Arsenal." *Marine Corps Gazette* (July 1977), p. 37.

Perlmutter, Amos. *The Military and Politics in Modern Times.* New Haven, Connecticut: The Yale University Press, 1977.

Sidorenko, A.A. *The Offensive: A Soviet View.* Washington, D.C.: The U.S. Air Force, U.S. Government Printing Office, 1979.

Sodaro, Michael J. "Ulbricht's Grand Design: Economics, Ideology, and the GDR's Response to Detente—1967-1971." *World Affairs* 142 (Winter 1980): 147-68.

Sontheimer, Kurt and Bleek, Wilhelm. *The Government and Politics of East Germany.* New York: St. Martin's Press, 1976.

Starrels, John M. and Malinckrodt, Anita M. *Politics in the German Democratic Republic.* New York: Praeger Publishers, Inc., 1975.

U.S. News and World Report. "The Real Soviet Threat in El Salvador—and Beyond: Interview with CIA Director William J. Casey." March 8, 1982, pp. 23-26.

1979 WeiBbuch zur Sicherheit der Bundesrepublik Deutschlands und zur Entwicklung der Bundeswehr. Bonn, Germany: Ministry of Defense, September 4, 1979.

Poland

Leszek K. Stachow

The Polish People's Republic represents the largest and most populous (35.7 million) member of the non-Soviet Warsaw Pact states. Since the beginnings of the Communist takeover at the end of World War II, Poland has played a pivotal role linking the USSR with Soviet combat forces in Central Europe. Possessing no boundaries with a non-Warsaw Pact nation, Poland presently has two Soviet tank divisions stationed within her borders. However, Soviet strategists and planners regard with crucial concern the integrity of Poland's communication and transportation links which provide a key role in reinforcing and supplying the nineteen Soviet divisions stationed in East Germany.

Consequently, a system of roads, railways, shipping, and telecommunications facilities established in the interwar period has been extensively reorganized. Today, as the fifth largest freight carrier in the world, Poland possesses over 16,500 miles of railway track, providing four major East-West links across Poland. A fifth is already under construction.[1] A total of 190,000 miles of roads cover Poland at a density of 1.5 miles per square mile, providing four main highway crossings into East Germany. Four major Baltic ports have been built: Gdynia, Gdansk, Swinoujscie, and Szczecin. Szczecin can handle over 5,000 ships per year. A major pipeline has been constructed under the guidance of the CMEA, transporting oil 420 miles across Poland from the USSR to East Germany; and an extensive telecommunications system has been established which at present handles both civilian and military traffic.[2] The reliability and uninterrupted functioning of these facilities are of utmost importance to the Soviet military.

Following Poland's defeat by Germany, the Ribbentrop-Molotov Treaty facilitated the occupation of eastern Poland by the Red Army on September 17, 1939. As a consequence, over 180,000 Polish officers and men were led into Soviet captivity.

After the Nazi attack on the USSR in 1941, the Polish government in exile, based in London, made its peace with Moscow, largely at Britain's insistence. Prisoners of war and others deported to labor camps were permitted to establish a Polish Army on Soviet territory commanded by Polish General Władyslaw Anders. Following Soviet demands that the Polish forces be deployed as separate units rather than as a national force on the Russian front, Polish military leaders objected. The army subsequently left the USSR under General Anders to fight with distinction in North Africa, Italy, and Western Europe.

Relations between the Soviet Union and the London government in exile became increasingly strained and were ultimately broken off after the Germans discovered the mass graves of thousands of Polish officers at Katyń in April 1943. There was overwhelming evidence that the mass killings of Polish officers, captured by the Red Army in September 1939, had been the work of the NKVD. The Soviets in turn accused the Germans and used this opportunity to break off diplomatic relations with the London exiles. Thereafter, two Polish political groups emerged: the London government in exile, a coalition of prewar party leaders, directing the Home Army (a force of almost 400,000 on Polish territory); and the Polish Communist party, guided by Moscow, and with a relatively insignificant People's Army comprised of Communist partisans.

A communique on May 8, 1943, invited the Union of Polish Patriots to establish a division on Soviet soil to fight alongside the Red Army. There followed a new Communist-sponsored army formally created in June 1943 under the command of General Zygmunt Berling. By the summer of 1944, the first Polish Army was serving in Marshal Constantine Rokossovsky's First Bielorrussian Front.

In August 1944, General Tadeusz Bór-Komorowski of the Home Army led the Warsaw uprising, but the Russians failed to press forward to assist Komorowski and the uprising was brutally suppressed.

The Poles' inevitable hostility towards the Soviets resulted in early efforts to make Berling's army as Polish and as apolitical as possible. Traditional Polish uniforms, ranks, and distinctions were utilized. The scarcity of Communists (the Stalinist purges had taken a heavy toll of prewar Polish Communists) and the shortage of native Polish officers resulted in an army dominated by Soviet men. By the end of the war, over one-third of the officers were Soviets.[3] Berling's army subsequently participated in the final Soviet offensive of World War II, that is, the battles along the Baltic coast and across the Oder and the Elbe.

Throughout the period of the Communist takeover of Poland from 1945 to 1948, the army representing the largest military force in Eastern Europe was largely neglected. To consolidate their power, the Polish Communists had to eliminate the existing opposition. At that time, various army groups roamed around Poland, including remnants of the Home Army still faithful to the former London government in exile (AK), units of the anti-Communist nationalist underground (NSZ), and detachments of the Ukrainian Insurgent Army (UPA) as well as various others. To achieve their objective, the party developed strong and reliable internal security forces, especially the internal security corps (KBW) whose units were used to successfully suppress anti-Communist partisans rather than having to rely on the regular army.

Following the consolidation of power in 1948, the party turned its attention to strengthening the armed forces. However, these actions coincided with the Sovietization of the Polish military, a process simultaneously imposed on other East European countries of the region. At Stalin's insistence, party leader Wladyslaw Gomułka was purged from his post, as were many members of the officer corps previously recruited from the various Polish armies, both East and West. Rising tensions between Eastern and Western Europe caused the Soviets to embark on a major buildup of their own military forces as well as those of the other Soviet Bloc countries.

In Poland's case, Soviet equipment began arriving to replace obsolete World War II armaments. After conscription was reintroduced, Poland's armed forces were increased to 400,000 men. Simultaneously, organizational changes took place with training patterns, doctrine, tactics, and even uniforms modeled on those of the Soviet Army. To assure that the Polish Army would be responsive to Soviet needs, Soviet Marshal Constantine Rokossovsky was appointed minister of defense and commander-in-chief of the Polish armed forces in November 1949. Other Soviet officers assumed the posts of chief of the General Staff, commander of ground forces, heads of all service branches, and commanders of all military districts. Within the lower echelons, many Soviet advisers were brought in.[4] Rokossovsky, although a member of the Polish Politbureau, took his orders from Moscow, thereby directly subordinating the Polish Army to the Soviet high command.

Throughout the period 1949-1955, the Polish Army suffered internally from poor organization, inadequate weaponry, and limited combat capability; it became alienated from the remainder of Polish society which regarded it as an instrument of Soviet control. Not until 1956 was the Polish Army able to recover a measure of its independence, standing, and prestige in the eyes of the people. The rioting by workers in Poznan in June 1956 was a prelude to the Polish October crisis. The unwillingness of regular army units to fire on striking workers when called upon by the government led to the deployment of elite KBW units from Warsaw who fired on the workers with devastating results. The spontaneous national revulsion towards the party and the KBW for the brutal use of force led to the August reappointment of General Komar (purged with Gomułka in 1948) as head of the KBW. Gomułka's success in his confrontation with Nikita Khrushchev in October 1956 can certainly in part be attributed to the support he received from units of the Polish Army which, although nominally under Rokossovsky's control, combined with a spontaneous committee established for the defense of Warsaw. These units then took up defensive positions around the city in preparation for resistance against advancing Soviet divisions.

The 1956 crisis found the Polish Army weakened by internal divisions between generals under Rokossovsky on the one hand and junior Polish officers sympathetic to Gomułka on the other. However, an effective threat of armed resistance was posed by General Komar's KBW and a number of regular unit commanders, including Admiral Jan Wisniewski (commander of coastal defense units) and General Jay Frey-Bielecki (an air force unit commander). Khrushchev's decision to give way and accept Gomułka as party leader is often attributed to the willingness of the Polish military to support the process of liberalization.

After the changeover, Gomułka insisted that Rokossovsky and other Soviet officers and technical advisers return to the USSR. Efforts were made to de-Sovietize the armed forces and to place a renewed emphasis on national characteristics. National military uniforms and songs were reintroduced, and the former Soviet organizational model was largely discarded. Soviet officers were replaced by national Communists, many of whom had been in prison. In December 1956, a "state of force" agreement was concluded with the USSR, which gave the Polish government some control over Soviet forces still in Poland.

Liberalization led to the weakening of the political apparatus which had been introduced within the military during the Stalinist era. The loss of party influence within the military coincided with the professional military leadership's increased assertiveness. Thus, the Polish military once more came under the direct control of the Communist leadership but with severely weakened instruments of party control. Citing the speed of involvement of the Polish armed forces in the "Soviet revolution in military science" at the end of the 1950s, some observers believe that a legacy of the period of Soviet domination of the Polish Army was the "creation of a cadre of Polish officers trained by and in many ways attuned to the thinking of the Soviet military and unwilling or unable to divorce Polish national security considerations from Soviet military imperatives."[5]

Indeed, by the end of the 1950s, the Polish military elite was formally linked to the Soviet military establishment via the institution of the Warsaw Pact and numerous bilateral Soviet-Polish military agreements. It was, therefore, not surprising that fundamental changes in Soviet military and organizational policy also influenced Polish military strategists. Thus, they subsequently established a new doctrine of "coalition warfare" which anticipated rapid offensive operations into NATO territory by the Warsaw Pact. Associated with it was the concept of "defense of national territory." In recognition that Poland's geopolitical position had made it a likely target for nuclear strikes, a proportion of Poland's armed forces was earmarked for internal defensive actions. The doctrinal changes outlined above were to provide the impetus for a process of intensive modernization of Poland's armed forces into the most modern of the non-Soviet Warsaw Pact military establishments.

The final intervention of the military in internal Polish events took place on December 13, 1981, when the collapse of the political authority of the Communist party resulted in the political vacuum that was filled by the Polish Army. The takeover, following a declaration of a state of emergency, was aimed at severely limiting the actions of Solidarity, an organization that had effectively challenged the party's monopoly of political power. Despite its prior involvement in political events, the Polish military throughout the 1970s had emerged as a pressure group anxious to stress its purely professional identity and purpose.

Weaponry and Manpower

Modernization has been pursued in line with Polish military doctrine, with ground force divisions restructured since 1960 on the Soviet model. Today the operational army possesses fifteen divisions organized in three military districts: the first is based in Warsaw, the second covering Pomerania has its headquarters in Bydgoszcz, and the third in Silesia is commanded from Wroclaw.

Apart from five tank divisions and eight motor rifle divisions, Poland has two special purpose divisions unique in the non-Soviet Warsaw Pact countries: an amphibious assault division and an airborne assault division. Ground forces include approximately 3,800 man battle tanks (T 54/55, T 62s) and a few elderly T34/85s which are presumably confined to training. In addition, approximately 300 PT-76 light tanks are in service, together with a variety of APCs, including Soviet BTR-152s and Polish Czech OT 62 and OT 64s. The naval strength includes four W-class submarines as well as a naval aviation regiment with fifty-two combat aircraft. The air force has some 700 combat aircraft, mostly MIG 21s and 17s, but also thirty-five SU-20 modern fighter-bombers. Approximately ninety FROG 3/7 and SCUD tactical missiles are in Polish hands as well as a variety of Swatter, Snapper, and Sagger anti-tank missiles (see Table 18).

Despite the modernization process, two constraints have led to considerable dissatisfaction within the Polish officer corps: the first concerns the pace of Soviet assistance, and the second, limitations imposed by an already strained Polish economy. In the first case, the Polish military is aware that the pace of modernization in Poland lags far behind that of the Soviet Army, while Soviet client states are being placed at the top of the list for deliveries of new weapons systems. Dissatisfaction with the latter Soviet policy surfaced during the Israeli Six-Day War when the Polish military openly admired Israeli tactics and equipment and criticized Soviet equipment and efforts.

The second issue concerns the problem of the Polish economy. Some observers[6] maintain that the modernizing efforts of the 1960s may have placed additional strain on the Polish economy, thus contributing to the worker riots in 1970 and a change in party leadership.

Table 18
Polish Army Equipment

Item	Number
Total manpower	210,000 (154,000 conscripts)
Tank divisions	5
Motor rifle divisions	8
AB division	1
Amphibious assault division	1
Artillery brigades	3
AA artillery regiments,	5
Artillery,	1
ATK regiments	3
SSM brigades with SCUD	4

3,400 T-54/55,100 T-72 med, 100 PT-76 1t tks; 2,000 OT-65 and BRDM-1/-2 scout cars; 5,500 BMP, OT-62/-64 APC; 400 76mm, 85mm, 100mm, 122mm, 250 152mm guns/how; 122 mm SP guns; 600 82mm, 120mm mor; 250 BM-21 122mm, 140mm MRL; 54 FROG 3/7, 36 SCUD SSM; 680 76mm, 85mm towed, ASU-85 SP ATK guns; 73mm, 82mm, 107mm, RCL; Snapper, Sagger, ATGW; 400 23mm, 57mm, 85mm and 100mm towed, 100 ZSU-23-4 SP AA guns; SA-6/7/9 SAM
Deployment: Syria (UNDOF) 129

Statistics that rely on official Polish data on defense spending involve a substantial underestimate of the real cost of military spending when expressed as a percentage of GNP at market prices in domestic currencies.[7] Nevertheless, the data indicate a peak in military spending as a percentage of GNP in 1970, followed by an almost continual relative decline until 1978. After gaining power in 1970, the Edouard Gierek regime fundamentally redirected the Polish economy, providing concessions to consumerism and utilizing foreign credits to accelerate the process of technological modernization. The consequent redirection of the economy inevitably led to post-1970 constraints on military spending.

If Dale R. Herspring[8] is correct when he suggests that the Polish military lobbies for greater defense spending and more weapons systems, principally through the Soviet military in Moscow, and if we assume that in the early 1970s the Soviets steadily built up Warsaw Pact forces in Eastern Europe, then it is indeed surprising that the Kremlin has apparently accepted considerable constraints on Poland's defense contributions. As the price of internal stability in Poland, the Soviet leadership appears to have accepted developments which it would not have tolerated either within the USSR or in any other East European country; "This is additional testimony as to just how much Soviet preferences have become hostage to domestic problems and the ever present prospect of severe internal instability in Poland."[9]

Scenarios of Employment

Gomułka's commitment to maintain Poland as a faithful ally of the USSR, her incorporation within the Soviet Bloc, and the frequent formal and informal interaction between the Soviet and Polish military establishment made it inevitable that changes in Soviet military strategy in the late 1950s would find their expression in Polish military doctrine.

Leaning heavily on Soviet strategic thinking, Polish military specialists drew up a doctrine of coalition warfare[10] which assumed that national defense for a small Communist state would be illusory and that, therefore, security could only be achieved through a Soviet military coalition—the Warsaw Pact. Prior to 1970, although postulated threats to Poland's national security were represented by NATO, fears were raised concerning the significantly expanded West German Bundeswehr. In this sense, military doctrine echoed the apparent fears of the Polish Communist party which stressed that only a close alliance with the USSR would ensure Poland's territorial integrity in the face of a perceived German threat. Denying the role of limited national defense, the party claimed that Poland's security needs could be met only by fulfilling internationalist alliance obligations.

The assumption that Polish forces must fight in the interest of the Warsaw Pact and regard the borders of the socialist camp as their defensive line has led to significant practical and organizational complications.[11] Coalition doctrine postulates a European conflict on an "external" front which would be nuclear in nature. Thus, Polish military writings have stressed the conditions and requirements of nuclear warfare.[12] Although some analysts concede the possibility of a "short conventional phase," it is widely believed that conventional warfare would be most likely to escalate. The implications of nuclear warfare have led to a focus within Poland on the consequences of sudden attack and an analysis of the initial phase of contact.

As a result, the former mobile defense doctrine has been replaced by an emphasis on rapid offensive operations. By utilizing surprise, deception, and maneuverability, superior conventional Warsaw Pact forces will ensure that the war would be fought on NATO territory.

The operational army would be employed entirely on the "external front," along with the Warsaw Pact allies. The expressed aim would be to limit a potential opponent's aggression and transfer military operations into his territory. The deployment of Polish forces has led to a number of alternative scenarios. In the event of a European war, the Polish forces would be divided into three armies which would embark on offensive operations together with their Soviet and Warsaw Pact counterparts. However, General Zygmunt Duszynski, former chief of the Inspectorate of Training and deputy defense minister, has attempted to ensure direct command over Polish forces in wartime by proposing a combined Polish Front. According to his proposal, the Polish Army would be organized under an independent Polish Front, with a Polish commander in turn responsible to Moscow.

Presumably, the Soviets have their doubts about the efficiency and the reliability of autonomous Polish units. The stated objectives of the Polish Front would be to advance across the northern German plain towards the Low Countries, occupying Denmark on the way.

A unique component of Polish military doctrine concerns the concept of defense of national territory (OTK). Formulated principally at the end of the 1950s by General Boleslaw Chocha,[13] the concept recognized Poland's vulnerability in the event of a nuclear air strike. Thus, OTK strategy anticipated the need to prepare the country against nuclear air strikes by establishing a strong air defense force and a sophisticated civil defense system capable of evacuating major target areas. Specially organized territorial internal security units would be assigned a dual role: resisting enemy penetration and limiting internal unrest, thereby facilitating the Soviet logistical effort across Poland.

The OTK doctrine began to be implemented in the early 1960s. It was finally established in 1965 following the formal separation of OTK forces from the regular army and subordinated to a newly established Chief Inspectorate for the defense of national territory, a body parallel to the General Staff and led by a deputy defense minister. As part of the reorganization process, air defense forces (WOPK) were subordinated to the OTK as well as the KBW, now renamed the Internal Defense Forces (WOW). Similarly, Border Security Forces (WOP) and Territorial Units (TO) came under the jurisdiction of the OTK Inspectorate.

Despite a new defense statute passed in 1967 in order to stress mass involvement in defense issues, OTK strategy proceeded slowly. Only since the passage of a new government regulation in 1973 have civil defense efforts received a major boost. Polish Communist party skeptics doubt that the Polish people could be mobilized for a massive defensive effort against a Western threat.

Since Poland's armed forces have not seen combat since World War II, estimates of combat ability and political reliability must be confined to an examination of the military's involvement in internal crises and their role in the 1968 invasion of Czechoslovakia.

As Dale Herspring and Ivan Volgyes suggest, political reliability may be measured on the basis not only of the military's willingness to comply with instructions issued by the ruling party, but also whether the party's directives are carried out from a normative commitment to the system or out of self-interest. Herspring and Volgyes list four categories of political reliability: internal offensive, internal defensive, external defensive, and external offensive. These categories provide a useful starting point for our analysis.[14]

The category of internal offensive reliability attempts to assess whether various segments of the officer corps would be willing to challenge the party's leading role and either impose their interests upon the party or attempt a coup d'etat. The Polish military elite was seriously divided by factionalism until Jaruzelski's consolidation of power in 1971, and only since the early 1970s has the military elite become aware of its power as an effective interest group.

Rioting in the coastal cities of Gdansk and Gdynia in December 1970 led to the use of military force to put down social unrest. This represented the first use of the military in an internally repressive role since World War II. The military's response to internal unrest and factional in-fighting within the party had been to refuse to take sides in the struggle between Gomułka and Gierek. Jaruzelski presumably wished to distance the military from involvement in internal political disputes, thereby avoiding the demoralizing effects of carrying out repressive acts against fellow countrymen.

In addition, the armed forces had recognized that their best interests would not be served by carrying out acts of mass repression against fellow-citizens. Not only had the Polish officers' self-image become severely tarnished, but also public opinion had turned against the military, and recruitment into the officer corps had declined sharply.

The second category of political reliability, internal defensive reliability, concerns the willingness of the armed forces to support the regime against an internal threat. In the event of civil unrest, units of the police and security forces are normally called upon to defend the regime. Their privileged position within society (for example, they have access to special stores and housing) enhances their party loyalty. Only when they have failed to contain the unrest is the miitary called upon. However, the party recognizes that, quite apart from officer loyalty, the conscript himself may hesitate before firing on relatives and friends. Clearly then, the conscripts' evaluation of the political situation will play a critical part in how civil unrest is handled.

Prior to 1981, the armed forces had consistently refused to support the regime when confronted with internal disturbances. During the Poznan crisis, regular army troops had declined to disperse rioters and in many instances identified with the protesters themselves. Only the rapid deployment of special security units from Warsaw eventually put down the unrest, with the regime emerging as the major casualty. In Gdansk in 1970, the army procrastinated, unwilling to carry out the commands to use "overwhelming force." In June 1976, after renewed civil unrest, Jaruzelski allegedly advised Gierek that Polish soldiers would not fire on Polish workers. Gierek quickly gave way, rescinding a previously announced price increase, and thereby defused the crisis. Many observers[15] have concluded that, before 1981, the utility of the Polish military in suppressing internal dissent was highly questionable. Indeed, where repressive measures had been employed, the police and special security forces had played the primary role.

With regard to the third category, external defensive reliability, the major concern is to evaluate the probability that Polish forces would defend the state against external threats. To provide an effective defense against an external threat, the regime would have to rely on the loyalty of the officer corps and on recognition by the conscripts that the defensive action initiated by the regime would be in Poland's national interest. The army's willingness to support government actions would, therefore, be significantly influenced by the nature of the enemy.

Considering threats from non-Soviet Warsaw Pact forces first, Poland's immediate neighbors—Germany and Czechoslovakia—have traditionally threatened her national sovereignty and have, therefore, generated widespread public animosity. Therefore, the public's willingness to offer military resistance to threats posed by these neighbors would tend to be high. In addition, one need only recall that the Poles have already shown ample evidence of their willingness to resist threats against their national sovereignty.

Threats of invasion or intervention by the USSR have also led to a willingness to use force in defense of Poland's national interests. In 1956, units of the Polish Army demonstrated their support for the party leadership's struggle with Moscow by taking defensive measures against an anticipated Soviet intervention. Again in 1970, there was evidence that the Polish Army once more took action to ensure the nonintervention of Soviet troops.

The withdrawal of Soviet advisers after 1956, the increasing homogeneity of the officer corps, rising professionalism, and greater political integrity have all contributed to the senior staff's more effective control of the internal military organization. There is every likelihood that in the event of a Soviet invasion military resistance in Poland would be significant and protracted, for the Poles have shown a willingness to offer resistance, and they would be facing the USSR, a traitional foe.

The final category of political reliability considers the external offensive case, that is, the willingness of the military to support the regime in offensive campaigns against other countries. Once more the conscripts' evaluation of the circumstances is critical. Perceiving that he was being called upon to fight an offensive war primarily to serve Soviet interests, and not those of his homeland, the conscript's commitment and initiative might be severely strained. Indeed, the only offensive action within this category in which Poland has played a part was the April 1968 invasion of Czechoslovakia. The Warsaw Pact invasion of Czechoslovakia clearly demonstrated the Soviet Union's ability to mobilize Pact allies to intervene in a member's internal affairs, but not to conduct an effective joint military operation. In Poland's case, despite traditional animosity towards the Czechs, the invasion was unpopular, and subsequent investigations into the role of the Polish military demonstrated a considerable lack of commitment to the invasion's goals. Since 1968, official military histories have completely omitted any mention of Poland's role in the invasion.

In examining the Polish military's reliability in carrying out external defensive actions against NATO, the increasing interaction between Soviet and Polish military staffs has inevitably led to a gradual identification of Poland's national security considerations with Soviet military interests. An expression of this phenomenon has been the growing interrelationship between Soviet and Polish military doctrine. The reform of the Warsaw Pact command structure in 1969 provided greater symbolic roles for the East European states in decision-making and has further reinforced the tendency to closer cooperation with the USSR.

On the other hand, Moscow's failure to supply up-to-date weapons to the Polish armed forces has resulted in considerable resentment within the officer corps. Although coalition doctrine anticipates a major role for Poland's forces in the event of a Warsaw Pact attack on NATO, their reliability would be conditioned by the degree of initial success and the nature of the immediate enemy. Given her traditional ties of friendship with many of the major NATO allies, Poland's reliability would be questionable, except in the event of a rapid and highly successful engagement.[16] Only in the case of offensive actions against her traditional foe, Germany, could Polish soldiers be expected to fight with conviction. However, since the 1970 Ratification Treaty, the German threat has begun to fade. Inevitably, awareness of the repercussions of nonparticipation in a Soviet-inspired Warsaw Pact invasion of Western Europe would be likely to ensure Polish compliance, at least in the initial stages of conflict.

The most recent example of Polish military action was the intervention by the armed forces on December 13, 1981, following the collapse of the Communist party's political authority. The imposition of a military takeover established a new precedent in the history of the Communist states. Formerly, when Communist regimes chose to exert force against their own people, they did so at the behest, or under the control, of the ruling party. In this case, General Jaruzelski, the head of Poland's armed forces and defense minister, had also been appointed prime minister and leader of the Polish United Workers party (PUWP). However, his proclamation of a state of emergency and the introduction of martial law occurred when the party and the government failed to perform the task of governing the country. His action not only introduced a new variable into the nature of civil-military relations within the Communist Bloc, but it also removed any illusions that some Western observers may have possessed concerning the Polish military's willingness to act as an arbiter between the party and the independent trade unions.[17]

Party Control of the Military

In order to understand the significance of party control over the military in Poland, we must review how the Communist government came to power and sought to convince a largely hostile population that the imposition of the system was in their interest. Clearly, the party objective was to develop a stable, viable system with a military force that would be reliable and combat-ready, and would display a normative commitment to the status quo. From the party standpoint, the military with its traditions and monopoly over complex forms of violence, represented potentially the most dangerous institution in the system. Thus, the party established a series of institutions based on the Soviet model, which it hoped would ensure its hegemony over the military.

Ross Johnson, et al.,[18] have identified eight forms of control that the party may exercise in the Polish context: (1) selection of the commander-in-chief has inevitably involved a search for a politically reliable candidate, that is, a military leader who is also part of the party leadership. The only exception to the rule has been General Jaruzelski who was appointed defense minister in 1968 but was not admitted to the Politbureau until 1971. (2) The PUWP is able to maintain supervision over military affairs via a Central Committee secretary and Central Committee Administrative Department, both offices serving as liaison between the Ministry of Defense and the Politbureau. (3) As in other Warsaw Pact armies, political matters within the Polish military are the responsibility of the Main Political Administration (MPA) a body with the power of a Central Committee Department and responsibility to the Secretariat and the Politbureau of the PUWP. (4) The Polish officer, subordinate to the MPA and representing the party's major control mechanism, has a number of responsibilities, namely, to carry out party propaganda and indoctrination work and to exercise public control over the authority of regular officers. In addition, the political officer may assume the duties of a chaplain or personnel counselor, assisting individuals in solving their personal problems and being readily accessible to lower level officers and men. (5) A series of party organizations is established at all levels of the military hierarchy to facilitate opportunities for indoctrination and political discussion, as well as creating additional levels of control for the higher levels of the military. (6) Party membership is encouraged for the socialist military officer. In return, the officer may expect greater opportunities for professional advancements. (7) Communist military youth organizations are established to recruit young conscripts, indoctrinate them, and prepare them for future party membership. (8) Finally, the party maintains control over the professional soldier through the military security service, a body that also fulfills counterintelligence and disciplinary functions.

The new cadre of political officers which emerged in the 1960s much more closely resembled their professional counterparts, for they had considerably less political training and a great deal more military expertise. Questioning the utility of the new political officer in effecting party control of the military, the party reorganized the training program in the 1970s. Specific programs were established for prospective political officers at regular military schools which emphasized social science and political training. The graduates were to immediately assume the function of political officer, acting as informal deputy commanders for political affairs at the company level. Today, the political officer at the battalion level continues to be concerned with personnel issues as well as party indoctrination, while also devoting considerable time to assessing the sociopsychological state of members of his unit, advising his commander in this regard.

Notwithstanding the degree of stability of the present scheme, as modernization continues, the desire for increased professionalism will inevitably increase the gap between the political officer and his professional counterparts. For the party, the increasing professionalization of the officer corps with its emphasis on military affairs may lead to neglect of political issues and ideological commitment.

The spectre of a professionally autonomous military has no doubt encouraged further efforts on behalf of the party to retain existing controls over the armed forces. Yet, the events of 1970, 1976, and 1980 suggest that the party may have been less than successful in its efforts.

Professionalism

The nature of the Polish military officer changed considerably both immediately following the war and in more recent times. As a result of the political transformations created by World War II, the recruitment base of the Polish officer changed abruptly. Although exact figures for the composition of the prewar officer corps are not available, the proportion of workers and peasants was relatively low. In fact, efforts were made to preserve the elite nature of the officer corps. J. J. Wiatr[19] has suggested that changes in political and economic relations, rapid economic growth, and the losses experienced by the Polish intelligentsia following the war made the social advancement of the lower classes imperative. Thus, a postwar policy of proletarianism was promoted. The party felt that workers and peasants represented a more appropriate class background, one that would identify more closely with its interests. Furthermore, many officers who had served in the prewar army were deemed unreliable and were phased out. Thus, in 1950, 19.2 percent of officers had served in the prewar Polish Army; by 1955, that figure was down to 2.9 percent. Moreover, the percentage of workers and peasants in the Polish officer corps rose from 64 percent in 1950 to 88 percent by 1958.

Bengt Abrahamsson[20] has drawn attention to the problems of personal adjustment which faced the new recruits. Those from farm or factory backgrounds who advanced rapidly into the officer corps achieved a lower level of satisfaction with the profession than either those who possessed a wartime military background or those who had already graduated from the military academies. Apparently, the lowered entry requirements had contributed to the officer corps' loss in prestige.

This picture has been changing. A study of the social origins of army officers shows that, while the Polish Army is still dominated by the working class, that dominance appears to be declining.[21] In 1964, 71 percent of Polish officer candidates were workers, farmers, and craftsmen, a 17-percent decline from the 1958 sample of officers. On the other hand, the percentage of officer candidates with professional and related backgrounds has risen: 29 percent in 1964 against 10 percent in 1958 for existing officers with professional backgrounds.

The growing educational demands of increasingly sophisticated military technology have also led to significant changes in the educational level of the Polish officer since World War II. In 1958, 17 percent of officers held academic degrees, while 43 percent had secondary school diplomas. In addition, only 13 percent possessed technical and engineering skills. By 1975, over 50 percent had acquired academic degrees, with that figure expected to reach 70 percent by the end of 1980. All officers had acquired secondary school diplomas by 1975, and over 50 percent had advanced technical and engineering skills.[22]

One consequence of the emphasis on military skills, and the institutionalization of a formal officer promotion scheme, has been the downplaying of political qualifications required of the professional officer. However, an examination of party membership within the officer corps demonstrated that, by 1974, 85 percent held party cards, including all senior officers. The general dissatisfaction and resentment directed towards the party during the 1980-1981 unrest may well have significantly altered the percentage of officers currently holding party cards. Given the Church's authority and influence among the Polish people, chaplains are allowed within the Polish Army—a unique phenomenon in Eastern Europe. Thus, the Church also exerts a marginal influence on military attitudes.

Finally, with the almost complete withdrawal of Soviet advisers and the departure of Poles of Jewish origin, today the Polish Army is probably more ethnically homogeneous than at any other time since the last war.

As some observers have concluded,[23] the process of modernization has engendered a professional attitude among Polish officers. Andrzej Korbonski concludes that the military has become aware of its distinct professional identity and its capacity to articulate its own interests.[24]

Conclusions

Today, Poland's armed forces are the most modern within the Warsaw Pact. An integral part of Soviet military planning, Polish forces are primarily geared for a massive offensive strike role into NATO territory under conditions of nuclear war. In recognition that Poland's vulnerability arises from her geopolitical situation, a key part of her military doctrine envisages the establishment of a sophisticated system of national defense.

As a result of modernization within her armed forces, Poland has a higher level of education and expertise than any other Warsaw Pact force. However, these gains have occurred at the expense of ideological indoctrination. Despite the party's attempts to maintain control over the military by strengthening the role of the political officer, party authority has declined.

Meanwhile, from 1971 to 1981, the Polish military elite has avoided involvement in intraparty factional disputes. Attempting to maintain neutrality, the armed forces have stressed the importance of professionalism and institutional detachment. This emphasis has reinforced the emergence of an autonomous elite. The military perceives its primary objective to be the defense of Communism and protection of Poland's national interests. Growing professionalism has led to grievances directed against the USSR over the pace of delivery of sophisticated military technology. Trends towards professionalism and modernization have also encourged the reemergence of nationalism.

The reliability of the Polish Army in a given situation is conditioned by the attitudes and prejudices of its conscripts. In any encounter against NATO forces, the Polish Army would be more than capable of completing its assigned task, assuming a short, sharp offensive action. In the event of a more prolonged conflict, the conscripts' unreliability and traditional animosity towards the USSR would weaken the military's effectiveness. At home, the armed forces are relatively unsuitable as an instrument of repression. That function is more reliably performed by the internal security forces.

The failure to implement effective economic reforms in Poland has led to an inability to satisfy rising consumer expectations. This inability has in turn generated a challenge to the party's leading role as representative of the working class.

With the party weakened, only the military can fill the political vacuum. Modernization has created an autonomous military elite, unaffected by party factionalism. The armed forces are not only cohesive, disciplined, and able, but they also have the power to act in a crisis.

Abandoning the principle that military power must remain subordinate to a civilian force, the Polish military elite, when it declared a state of emergency, established a precedent for the military takeover of a party organization within the Soviet Bloc. This action understated both the outmoded ideological legitimacy of the Communist party and the willingness of the armed forces to replace it with authoritarian pragmatism, thereby ensuring state control over civil society. With the failure of the party, the armed forces emerged as the most efficient, rational, and potentially the most modernizing influence within Poland. One consequence of the present developments has been the total loss of prestige suffered by the armed forces in the eyes of the public. The military's claim to uphold the traditional value of nationalism has been completely denied by events; no doubt, as a result the ranks have suffered a severe loss of morale.

In the event of a prolonged military administration, one may assume that, excluding internal security units, the Polish Army would encounter serious problems of reliability. The consequent defections from the military might well increase the likelihood of an eventual Soviet intervention. Furthermore, having gained control of the party organization, the military would find it difficult to withdraw and reestablish an autonomous party apparatus.

The events in Poland may be viewed as a potential model for other Soviet Bloc states, where similar inability to satisfy growing economic demands could result in the party's loss of political power and the possibility of a military intervention. The application of a military solution to the social and political crises facing the Soviet Bloc would tend to support Richard Falk's premise concerning the growing global trend towards authoritarian regimes,[25] and the concurrent inability of states either to be receptive to proposals for innovation or to achieve humane governing structures.

Notes

1. There are four routes across Poland: The northern route via the shipbuilding port regions of Gdansk and Gdynia, then crossing into East Germany at Szczecin; the southern route via Krakow and Katowice; and the two central routes, both passing via Warsaw. A fifth route, now under construction, is to pass from Hrubieszow via Kielce and Czestochowa to Silesia.

2. The Soviet Union has been building an independent telecommunications network since the labor unrest, utilizing microwave relay towers, at present under construction near Jaroslav and Rozwienica.

3. *Voenno-istoncheskii zhurnal* (Moscow: July 1974), p. 63, quoted in Ross Johnson, Robert W. Dean, and Alexander Alexiev, *Eastern European Establishments: The Warsaw Pact Northern Tier*, The Rand Corporation R-2417/1-AF/FF, December 1980.

4. Johnson, et al., *Eastern European Establishments*, p. 22.

5. Ibid., p. 26.

6. Ibid., p. 38.

7. Joint Economic Committee, East European Economic Assessment, Part 2, Regular Assessments, 97th Cong., 1st Sess. (July 1981).

8. Dale R. Herspring and Ivan Volgyes, "Political Reliability in the Eastern European Warsaw Pact Armies," *Armed Forces and Society* 6, No. 2 (Winter 1980): 276.

9. Johnson, et al., *Eastern European Establishments*, p. 40.

10. Ibid., p. 31.

11. Marian Dowada and Maciej Janislawski, *Obrona kraju obowiazek kazdego obywatela* (Warsaw: MON 1970), p. 37, cited by Johnson, et al., *Eastern European Establishments*, p. 29.

12. Johnson, et al., *Eastern European Establishments*, p. 30.

13. Boleslaw Chocha, *Obrona terytorium kraju* (Warsaw: MON. 1974), p. 52.

14. Herspring and Volgyes, "Political Reliability," p. 271.

15. Ibid., p. 279.

16. Ibid., p. 289.

17. Andrzej Korbonski, "The Dilemmas of Civil-Military Relations in Contemporary Poland: 1945-81," *Armed Forces and Society* 8, No. 1 (Fall 1981): 18.

18. Johnson, et al., *Eastern European Establishments*, p. 41.

19. J. J. Wiatr, "Military Professionalism and Transformations of Class Structure in Poland," in J. A. van Doorn, ed., *Armed Forces and Society* (The Hague: 1968), p. 234.

20. Bengt Abrahamsson, *Military Professionalization and Political Power* (Los Angeles, Calif.: Sage, 1972), p. 53.

21. Ibid., p. 54.

22. Dale R. Herspring, "Technology and the Changing Political Officer in the Armed Forces: The Polish and East German Cases," *Studies in Comparative Communism* 10, No.4 (Winter: 1977): 376.

23. Johnson et al., *Eastern European Establishments*, p. 46.

24. Korbonski, "The Dilemmas of Civil-Military Relations," p. 12.

25. Richard Falk, *A World Order Perspective on Authoritarian Tendencies* (New York: Institute for World Order, Inc., 1980).

Bibliography

Herspring, Dale R. "Civil-Military Relations in Poland and East Germany: The External Factor." *Studies in Comparative Communism* 11, No. 3 (Autumn 1978).

———. "Technology and the Changing Political Officer in the Armed Forces: The Polish and East German Cases." *Studies in Comparative Communism* 10, No. 4 (Winter 1977).

———, and Volgyes, Ivan. "The Military as an Agent of Political Socialization in Eastern Europe: A Comparative Framework." *Armed Forces and Society* 3, No. 2, (Winter 1977).

———. "Political Reliability in the Eastern European Warsaw Pact Armies." *Armed Forces and Society* 6, No. 2 (Winter 1980).

Johnson, A. Ross, Dean, Robert W., and Alexiev, Alexander. *East European Military Establishments: The Warsaw Pact Northern Tier.* The Rand Corporation R-2417/1-AF/FF, December 1980.

Korbonski, Andrzej, "The Dilemmas of Civil-Military Relations in Contemporary Poland: 1945-81." *Armed Forces and Society* 8, No. 1 (Fall 1981).

Weydenthal, Jan B. "State of Emergency Declared in Poland." *Radio Free Europe Research*, January 8, 1982.

Wiatr, J. J. "Military Professionalism and Transformations of Class Structure in Poland." In J. A. van Doorn, ed. *Armed Forces and Society* The Hague: 1968.

Index

About the Contributors

CHARLES COTTON is a lieutenant colonel in the Canadian Army and is chief of the Military Leadership Department at the Royal Military College of Canada in Kingston, Ontario. He is the author of a number of definitive articles and books on military subjects.

JAMES M. DUNN received his doctorate from the University of Michigan and entered active service as a U.S. Army Intelligence officer. He taught at the U.S. Military Academy until 1973 and at Princeton University until 1978. He currently works in the Washington, D.C., area as a defense analyst.

RICHARD A. GABRIEL is a professor of politics at St. Anselm's College in Manchester, New Hampshire. He is the author of many books and articles on military subjects, including the first major treatise on military ethics written by an American. He is a major in the Army Reserve attached to the Directorate of Foreign Intelligence at the Pentagon.

DOMINICK GRAHAM is professor of military history at the University of New Brunswick in Fredericton. A former British officer, he saw action in Europe and North Africa during World War II. He is the author of a number of books on British military history and is the founder of the Center for Conflict Studies.

WILLIAM C. MARTEL holds a Ph.D. from the University of Massachusetts at Amherst and is the author of a number of articles on nuclear strategy and tactics. He is currently doing research on computer-based war gaming.

WILLIAM C. RENNAGEL is the director of the Bureau of Politico-Military Affairs in the U.S. State Department. He is a much-decorated former army officer who last served as assistant executive officer to the Supreme Allied Commander in Europe.

STEVEN T. ROSS is a professor in the Department of Strategy at the U.S. Naval War College in Newport, Rhode Island. He is the author of a number of articles on military history as well as several basic source books in the field of French military history.

PAUL L. SAVAGE is a professor of politics at St. Anselm's College in Manchester, New Hampshire. He is the author of several books, including the first major critique of American miitary performance in Vietnam. He is a retired army officer.

LESZEK K. STACHOW is a professor of economics at St. Anselm's College in Manchester, New Hampshire. He is a graduate of Keele and Sussex College in England and is the author of a number of articles on politics and economics.